ON OPERATIONS

ON OPERATIONS

OPERATIONAL ART AND MILITARY DISCIPLINES

B. A. FRIEDMAN

NAVAL INSTITUTE PRESS
Annapolis, Maryland

Naval Institute Press
291 Wood Road
Annapolis, MD 21402

© 2021 by Brett Friedman

All rights reserved. No part of this book may be reproduced or utilized in any form or by any means, electronic or mechanical, including photocopying and recording, or by any information storage and retrieval system, without permission in writing from the publisher.

First Naval Institute Press paperback edition published in 2024.
ISBN: 978-1-68247-945-2 (paperback)

Library of Congress Cataloging-in-Publication Data

Names: Friedman, B. A. (Brett A.), author.
Title: On operations : operational art and military disciplines / B. A. Friedman.
Description: Annapolis, Maryland : Naval Institute Press, [2021] | Includes bibliographical references and index.
Identifiers: LCCN 2021024742 (print) | LCCN 2021024743 (ebook) | ISBN 9781682477069 (hardback) | ISBN 9781682477076 (ebook) | ISBN 9781682477076 (pdf)
Subjects: LCSH: Operational art (Military science) | Operational art (Military science)—Case studies.
Classification: LCC U162 .F8 2021 (print) | LCC U162 (ebook) | DDC 355.409—dc23
LC record available at https://lccn.loc.gov/2021024742
LC ebook record available at https://lccn.loc.gov/2021024743

♾ Print editions meet the requirements of ANSI/NISO z39.48-1992 (Permanence of Paper). Printed in the United States of America.

9 8 7 6 5 4 3 2 1

This one goes out to the adjutants. I see you.

CONTENTS

Preface ix

Introduction 1

1. Operations and the Napoleonic Revolution 11
2. German Operational Thought 20
3. Soviet Operational Thought 30
4. American Operational Thought 39
5. The Operational Level and the Civil-Military Relationship . . . 46
6. A Theory of Operational Art 52
7. Administration 60
8. Information 69
9. Operations 83
10. Fire Support 94
11. Logistics 100
12. Command and Control 108
13. Campaigns, Battles, and Decision 113
14. Campaign Taxonomy I 118
15. Campaign Taxonomy II 122
16. Operational Art Actualized through a Modern Staff System . . 130
17. A Note on Force Protection 138

Conclusion 139

CASE STUDY 1. The Austerlitz Campaign, 1805 143

CASE STUDY 2. The Königgrätz Campaign, 1866 154

CASE STUDY 3. The Atlantic Campaign, 1914–18 165

CASE STUDY 4. The Battle of Britain, 1940 174

CASE STUDY 5. Operation Watchtower, 1942 185

Notes 203

Bibliography 223

Index 231

PREFACE

This book, like my previous book, is Clausewitzian. By that, I mean that it falls within a framework of what war, warfare, strategy, and tactics are as a phenomenon as described by Carl von Clausewitz (1780–1831). Olivia Garard, rhyming with Alfred North Whitehead, has said that all strategic theory is a series of footnotes to Clausewitz. I would instead say that all *good* strategic theory is a series of footnotes to Clausewitz. Good footnotes to Clausewitz is all I hope these books to be. If you are looking for something non-Clausewitzian, this is not it. There are certainly publications that can provide that, but I do not recommend any of them.

This volume would still be a formless jumble of notes were it not for my wife, Ashton, whose comment triggered the chapter that really ties the whole book together.

During one conversation, Col. Doug King, USMC (Ret.), said one sentence that clarified all of my thinking about the command-and-control chapter, "Control is what the staff does." I have a lot to thank Doug King for, but this is the one most relevant for this book.

Capt. Wayne Hughes, USN (Ret.), greatly influenced my previous book, *On Tactics: A Theory of Victory in Battle* (2017), and generously shared his experience and knowledge with me as I worked through the manuscript for that volume. He was also instrumental in its acceptance for publication. In December 2019 he passed away. His influence will live on in the naval and strategic theory communities, and I remain grateful for his guidance. Fair winds and following seas.

Conversations with colleagues have sharpened the ideas contained herein on a number of occasions, especially those with Lt. Col. Gregory Wardman, USMC (Ret.), and Capt. Olivia Garard, USMC. Olivia especially helped me think through the campaign taxonomy, while Greg considerably shaped my thoughts on the information discipline. I owe them both a debt of gratitude.

David Alman pointed me in the direction of motivator-hygiene theory, which strengthened the chapter on administration.

There are two weaknesses in this book, I believe. One is an unfortunate focus on so-called Western history and thought. This is a function both of the paucity of sources readily available to an independent writer such as myself and the fact that the operational level of war is a fundamentally Western concept. So, while the operational art of the People's Liberation Army (PLA) of modern China is an interesting subject, its discussion is excluded from the following chapters. Briefly, however, current PLA thought has what might be described as four levels: military thought (*junshi sixiang*), military strategy (*zhanlüe*), campaigns (*zhanyi*), and tactics (*zhanshu*). Nonetheless, these concepts do not exactly map to Western conceptions of the operational level or operational art, which is the focus of this book. Western writers sometimes conflate campaigns, joint warfare, and the operational level when describing PLA ideas, but this is a misunderstanding of U.S. doctrine and an assumption about Chinese thought. For example, the Western operational level of war is sometimes depicted as the "ways" part of an ends-ways-means formulation of strategy. But the "ways" of this construct is more similar to the Chinese idea of strategic means (*zhanlüe shouduan*) than to the operational level. Works in English that connect Western, especially American, doctrinal concepts with PLA doctrinal concepts as direct equivalents should be viewed with extreme skepticism. The Chinese do not have a military doctrine as it is understood in Western militaries, but rather a unique style of military regulation that precludes easy comparison. Those interested in the PLA especially should see M. Taylor Fravel, *Active Defense: China's Military Strategy since 1949* (2019).

The other weakness herein is an excessive focus on land warfare. This is a function entirely of my own shortcomings and background when it comes to aviation and naval operations. I have made an attempt to include more on those subjects than I did in my previous book, but the attention is still far less than they deserve.

This book, like the last, is not a work of history but one of theory. It uses history extensively, for evidence and explanation to support the theory, but is not intended to be a work of history. It therefore relies mostly on secondary sources. Primary sources in the form of doctrinal manuals and, in one case, a discussion between myself and an author of doctrinal manuals were used, but secondary sources necessarily underpin the development of the theory itself.

If there is any one takeaway from this book and *On Tactics*, it is that there is no one route to victory in war. There are too many factors that come into play, and theory is at its best when it helps one think about those factors without trying to prescribe solutions. Where I prescribe solutions, they address organizational issues. Hopefully, that is what this book is: a tool for greater clarity. I hesitate to say that I am following in Clausewitz's footsteps except in one respect: that he railed against the purveyors of shallow prescriptions, salesmen promising success if only the proper rules and guides are followed. There are no new rules of war, just as there were no old ones. There are no guarantees and no certainties. There are definitely no simple answers. Anyone saying otherwise is selling snake oil.

Unfortunately, there is far too much of that in the defense world today, growing and accumulating on the U.S. military, especially, like plaque. Some of it comes from academia, some of it from the political punditry rackets on the right and left. Some of it, like the operational level of war, grows from misunderstandings within the U.S. military itself. But all war is subject to probabilities, so there is no way to know whether or not my attack on this particular misunderstanding will be as successful as Clausewitz's was. The only way to know is to launch it.

INTRODUCTION

A revolution is an idea that has found its bayonets.
— **NAPOLEON BONAPARTE**

Regarding the general-staff system that first sprang up in Prussia and then spread throughout Europe and the world, Sir Michael Howard writes, "This General Staff was perhaps the great military innovation of the nineteenth century."[1] *On Operations* argues that Howard was correct and that general staffs were developed to cope with the expanding complexity and scale of modern warfare since the Napoleonic Wars (1803–15). At the same time, another coping mechanism was the invention of the operational level of war, a concept that is, this book argues, problematic at best and ruinous at worst. In contrast, operational art, a sister concept, is useful as a descriptor of what military staffs do to support and sustain tactics in the pursuit of strategy. The operational art performed by staffs is best described in theory as a set of disciplines, commonly known as warfighting functions. The military success usually attributed (wrongly) to the "discovery" of an operational level of war should instead be credited to the rise of general staffs. This adoption of the operational level by Western militaries especially has amputated tactics from strategy, with tragic effect, and blinded those militaries from effectively instituting military staffs.

My previous book, *On Tactics*, focused on the commanders of military units who are responsible for employing force against an opposing military force. Commanders are, necessarily, tacticians. *On Operations* focuses on staff officers who support those commanders by performing the functions of operational art.[2] While tactical acumen is certainly desirable and useful to any staff officer, these people do not perform tactics. This also applies to major subordinate commands of a unit, whose own staffs perform operational art at their level.

THE OPERATIONAL LEVEL OF WAR

Although the invention of the operational level of war is usually credited to the Red Army of the Soviet Union, this is a myth. The Soviets began using the terms "operations" and "operational art" to refer to the increasing complexity of planning military operations and perhaps also as a way of discussing strategy without the risk of voicing ideas contrary to those of founder Vladimir Lenin, who fancied himself a strategist. Lenin's view of strategy was permeated with politics. In a speech in 1917, he claimed, "It seems to me that the most important thing that is usually overlooked in the question of the war . . . is the question of the class character of the war: what caused that war, what classes are waging it, and what historical and historico-economic conditions gave rise to it." He went on to quote Clausewitz, of whom he was a devotee, but twists the meaning of the Clausewitzian view of war as a political contest to one of class struggle: "War is a continuation of policy by other means. All wars are inseparable from the political systems that engender them. The policy which a given state, a given class within that state, pursued for a long time before the war is inevitably continued by that same class during the war, the form of action alone being changed."[3] Strategy was spoken for in the Soviet system. Josef Stalin assumed the mantle of master strategist from Lenin, and operational art became the safe space in which Soviet officers could discuss their trade. Sometime thereafter, when these ideas and terms spread to other military forces, the concept morphed into the idea of an operational level.

Be that as it may, warfare was indeed becoming more complex as a result of the Industrial Revolution, and the idea of an operational level of war was a possible way to cope with that expanding intricacy. While warfare has always been complex, after the Industrial Revolution the sustainable size of armies increased, as did their rates of fire, effective range, and movement. The complexity of weapon systems increased, causing a concomitant expansion in all manner of sustainment: spare parts, fuel, oil, and the level of training and expertise required by servicemembers. The Russian Army was directly presented with this complexity, not just due to the fact that they were defeated by Germany in World War I (1914–18) and then immediately fought a civil war, but also, during the latter, they had to build a new military from scratch, and along Marxist-Leninist ideological lines as well.

These two aspects of the concept— that it was a response to Marxist-Leninist requirements and the complexity of industrial warfare—remain its most solid distinguishing characteristics even today. Proponents of the operational level of war view it as "a politics-free zone where commanders could demonstrate their mastery of managing large forces over wide areas in a series of complex engagements."[4] Its relationship to strategy and tactics is hierarchical; strategy passes down objectives or goals to the operational level, which further passes them down to the tactical level. At times, it has been viewed as "grand tactics"; at other times, as closer to strategy.

Its apolitical and complex nature, however, has remained constant, even though the concept quickly devolved into a competing set of definitions. Some have defined it as a level of command, such as the corps level and above. Others have simply used scale, as in the numbers of men and amount of material involved, as well as the distance over which military forces could travel. Still others have focused on its function. For example, Jim Storr has described it thus: "Operational art is the link: it concerns the planning, sequencing, resourcing, and conducting a series of battles [or tactics] within a theatre, in order to achieve the strategic objectives of the campaign."[5] Yet he also refers to it as a level of command above the division.[6] Still elsewhere in the same book, the operational level is defined by large units and "very large distances."[7]

Almost all proponents peg the emergence of the operational level to changes in warfare sometime during the decades between the Napoleonic Wars and World War II (1939–45). There were indeed many changes during this period (and chapter 2 argues that modern war began with the Napoleonic Wars). But the idea of an operational level poorly captures the changes and dynamics that led modernity.

Robert M. Epstein, professor at the U.S. Army School of Advanced Military Studies and one of the originators of the concept, sees the emergence of an operational level during the Napoleonic Wars.[8] He describes "operational campaigns" as "characterized by symmetrical conscript armies organized into corps, maneuvered in a distributed fashion so that tactical engagements are sequenced and often simultaneous, command is decentralized, yet the commanders have a common understanding of operations methods. Victory is achieved by the cumulative effects of tactical engagements and operational campaigns."[9] This is as solid a description of the operational level as can be found since, it accounts for all of the aspects generally attributed to the concept: scale (maneuvered in distributed fashion); command level (the use of corps and decentralized command); doctrine (common operational methods); and the linking of tactics across time (sequenced into cumulative effects).

The problem is that none of the aspects in this description was new to the Napoleonic Wars. Every one of them occurred well before, sometimes centuries before the time when Epstein claims they emerged, and were not even new in European history. The identified attributes are also aspects of, to highlight only major conflicts in Europe, the Peloponnesian Wars (431–405 BC), the Second Punic War (218–202 BC), the Gallic Wars (58–50 BC), the Roman Civil War (49–45 BC), the Arab Conquests (AD 622–750), the Mongol Conquests (AD 1237–91), the Seven Years' War/French and Indian War (AD 1756–63), and the American War for Independence (AD 1775–83). The only exception is the use of the word "corps" to describe units of that size, but corps-sized organizations were certainly used prior to that point, as was the articulation inherent in the corps system. The emergence of a "new" level based on the presence of ancient characteristics is patently absurd.[10]

As we shall see, this conceptual inconsistency is common across the literature on the operational level of war, even among its supposed inventors, the Red Army. This is not solely a problem of definition; it is a problem with the concept itself. The operational level of war cannot find solid purchase as an idea because there is simply no logical space for it. The parameters described above are frequently cited interchangeably, but never is the logic of the operational level of war addressed. The classic definitions of tactics and strategy—those descended from Clausewitz's *On War*—focus on their logic. What distinguishes them is not level of command, scale, size, or even complexity. Rather, it is their logic that made the difference for Clausewitz: the logic of tactics is to gain battlefield victory; the logic of strategy is to use those victories for the purpose of the war. The first is linear; the second is nonlinear. These definitions leave no logical space for an operational level of war: no matter how big the operation, they have a linear logic (defeat the opponent) and therefore have the same logic as tactics. As soon as the operational level moves closer to strategy, politics and strategic effect become involved, and the nonlinear logic of strategy takes over.[11] Nor are strategy and tactics strictly hierarchical, as proponents of the operational level of war claim. Rather, they exist in a dialectic relationship—a relationship broken by the insertion of the operational level of war. The result is an orphan concept shoehorned into a theory of war that neither requires it nor has room for it.

Harold R. Winton, a professor at the U.S. Air Force School of Advanced Air and Space Studies, has written that military theory's first task is to "define the field of study," and its second task is to categorize.[12] The conflicting, confusing, and capricious conceptions of an operational level of war fail this test, neither producing a solid definition of the field of study nor assisting in the categorization within that larger field. Indeed, they simply complicate categorization already accomplished.

THE OPERATIONAL ART OF WAR

A related but distinct concept to the operational level of war is operational art, which Soviet military thinkers did pioneer. Despite their distinction, the terms are frequently used interchangeably. Milan Vego describes operational art as "a component of military art concerned with the theory and practice of planning, preparing, conducting, and sustaining campaigns and major operations aimed at accomplishing strategic or operational objectives in a given theater."[13] This is a bit of a circular definition, and Vego also uses operational art as synonymous with the operational level of war. Yet the focus on planning, preparation, conducting, and sustaining military actions is compelling, and these activities are distinct from both tactics and strategy. Vego is not alone in this view. Shimon Naveh, an influential proponent of the operational level of war, has written, "the essence of this level . . . is the preparation, planning, and conduct of military operations."[14] Operational art has more in common with what Clausewitz referred to as "preparations for War," which is distinct from the conduct thereof, which is the realm of tactics and strategy.[15]

We can better ascertain the place of operational art if it is disconnected with the operational level. Removing operational art from the requirements of its own level, which would require their own logic, allows us to ground it in something besides the vague "linking" of tactics and strategy and retain it as a descriptor of "planning, preparing, conducting, and sustaining" military operations. It still requires a foundation in tactics and still requires a connection to strategy, but it no longer encroaches on or interposes itself between them.

Operational art, then, is the planning, preparation, synchronization, and sustainment of tactics over a sustained period of time, a large geographic expanse, or both. The linear logic of tactics remains the same (victory in combat) as does the nonlinear logic of strategy (using combat results to secure an advantageous peace). Operational art comprises the disciplines required to place military forces in an advantageous position to employ tactics to achieve strategic effect. Because it remains tied by tactical tenets to achieve that advantage, yet beholden to strategy to give it direction, it exhibits no logic of its own. Operational art is a supporting effort to both.

PUSHBACK AGAINST THE OPERATIONAL LEVEL

Of course, the widespread acceptance of the operational level of war is not total. The concept and its proponents have their opponents. In 2009

Justin Kelly and Mike Brennan wrote a report for the U.S. Army's Strategic Studies Institute titled *Alien: How Operational Art Devoured Strategy*. It was an inauspicious time for American strategy. The previous presidential administration had mired the country in two strategically aimless quagmires. A new administration would involve it in yet more of the same. The operational level of war as a doctrinal concept was in constant practice, and it was uniformly failing. The U.S. military, far from exhibiting the mastery of a link between tactics and strategy, was instead clearly and painfully adrift.

Kelly and Brennan conclude that when the Soviet concept of an operational level of war was copied into U.S. Army doctrine without the historical or doctrinal context, it severed campaign planning from the concept of strategy. This produced an American conception of war that magnified the importance of campaigns and tactics while minimizing the importance of strategy.[16] Decades of intellectual effort to ascertain the connection between tactics and strategy, from Clausewitz on, were simply jettisoned.

Another commentator, William F. Owen, also strongly disagrees with the concept of the operational level of war. He makes a similar argument, agreeing that the operational level not only undermines strategy but also, in so doing, marginalizes tactics.[17] The idea of the operational level as a "link" between the two also falls flat. Tactics and strategy are inextricably linked already, having been understood as such for centuries.[18] Owen goes on to argue, convincingly, that the adoption of the operational level of war has led to a poor understanding of tactics in Western militaries, reflected, in turn, in the practice of bad tactics on the battlefield.

Still another critique is the inconsistent definition of the operational level of war. This is found in U.S. Army doctrine itself (as will be seen). Sir Hew Strachan, a British military historian, has also found this problematic, describing how the operational level has described strategy at some times and tactics at others, never finding its own purchase.[19] He writes, "Operational art has been stretched hither and yon because it is not contained by a sure grasp of the relationship between war and policy, and by proper structures to debate and guide strategy." To be fair, he goes on to write that, "once they exist, operational art and the operational level of war will rediscover both their true purpose and their proper place."[20] An equally likely outcome, however, is that the operational level of war will discover that it has no place. A sure grasp of war and policy, and the tactics that underpin them, has no need for it. Nor is this limited to American doctrine. Major

Will Viggers of the Australian Defence Force has also written about how his country's doctrine "struggles to explain coherently the rationale for these levels," as their conceptions are "confused" and "blurred."[21] This confusion is worldwide.

Strategic theorist Colin S. Gray has also written about the operational level. He defines operations as "combinations of purposefully linked military engagements, generally though not necessarily on a large scale. Operations are strategy as action."[22] Gray also warns that the interpolation of an operational level of war between strategy and tactics, far from being a link, may more often than not be a barrier between the two or, worse, an excuse to ignore one or the other.[23] For him, operations are about the "orchestration of military action (tactics)."[24] Orchestration is less of a level than an independent act of arranging. A symphony also requires orchestration of various groups of instruments, but the principles of musical theory—rhythm, melody, chords, and harmony among others—do not change in the act. Gray's vision of operations, then, is closer to operational art than to the operational level.

The concept of an operational level of war is failing also in practice, not just in theory. Jonathan Schroden has written about how U.S. policymakers are increasingly turning to special-operations forces to "bypass the operational level of war and connect tactical actions by small groups of military individuals directly to strategic aims."[25] This is a recognition by national leadership that tactical action and strategic effects must be linked and that conventional forces have lost the know-how required for this. Both the concept of an operational level and the bureaucracy that has accreted around it have disabled American strategy to the point where a large portion of U.S. military forces—those that are thought to work on the operational level—are viewed as ineffective, placing more and more of the burden on a small number of special operators.

These critics, theorists, analysts, and others have warned about the deleterious effects of the concept of the operational level of war. This is not, however, just an exercise in academic debate. War is a human phenomenon, executed by real people. Conducting it on the basis of erroneous assumptions and concepts is just as much a threat to their lives as the actions of the enemy force they encounter. Understanding the operational level of war and operational art, therefore, is not pure pedantry and sophistry. It has real implications in real-world engagements, both for policymakers and for military personnel.

CONCLUSION

The conventional wisdom regarding the operational level of war is that it was created by either the Germans or the Soviets in response to the increasing complexity, scope, and scale of war during and after the Industrial Revolution, with the United States and others adopting it in response. As we shall see, this has never been true, no matter how many times it has been or will be asserted. Nor is the creation of operational or theater commands equivalent to an operational level of war. We will see many different ideas on which command level is "operational" and which are not, but the sources examined will indicate such chaotic confusion about this concept that it ultimately has no purchase. Tactics and strategy were not and are not conceived as a command level. Attempts to do so for the operational level of war have only failed.

Clausewitz has a test for theory: "The first business of every theory is to clear up conceptions and ideas which have been jumbled together, and, we may say, entangled and confused."[26] The operational level of war fails this test. It has introduced confusion and misconceptions to both tactical theory and strategic theory, entangling and confusing them. Operational art, however, rightly understood, passes Clausewitz's test by clarifying the role of staffs, the military disciplines they bring to war and warfare, and how they contribute to tactics and strategy. These two concepts must be disentangled, and the latter cut away from the whole.

The operational level of war is intimately connected with World War I. It was military organizations, especially the Red Army, trying to look for an answer to the problems of industrial war that divined the concept that eventually became the operational level. Since then, however, its nebulous nature has made it flexible enough to be anything to anyone, doing little but introducing confusion as to the nature of war and strategy, amputating strategy from tactics, and undermining the efficacy of both.

Nor was World War I examined holistically. The Soviets especially focused on conditions in Europe during that war and the Russian Civil War (1918–21), which closely followed it. Ignored were other theaters of the Great War, such as the Middle East and Africa. There, military operations did not resemble whatsoever the stasis that pertained on the western front in Europe. Naval operations were also disregarded. Other military conflicts throughout South America and in North America were similarly dismissed. A concept claiming to apply to all warfare was predicated solely on a very restrictive and unique data set. Of course, this was not clear to the Soviets at the time. From the perspective of the 1920s and 1930s, the European western front certainly seemed to be typical. We know now that it was not.

Clausewitz's definition of strategy and tactics based on the logic of each is sound. Not only has it pertained since his time, but no proponent of the operational level of war nor any institutional doctrine seriously disagrees that the two should be characterized by their function. Certainly, there are definitional differences, disagreements about where one ends and the other begins, and even disputes about what the functions of each are. But there is wide agreement that their logic is determinant. Such agreement breaks down, however, upon considering the operational level. Some define it as scale, some define it as a level of command, while others define it as practice. Some do not bother to define it at all, and others use multiple conflicting definitions with abandon. Aspects of operational art and the Soviet system—not to mention its origins in Marxist orthodoxy—were stitched together to fit neatly in between preexisting conceptions of tactics and strategy in the West. The resultant Frankenstein's monster has proven remarkably difficult to kill.

Yet even if its origin were sound, based on a thorough understanding of Soviet doctrine, and transferred faithfully and accurately to American strategic thought, the operational level would still be problematic; it has destroyed the understanding of the relationship between strategy and tactics and damaged the effectiveness of the U.S. military in real and practical ways. Its confused and shallow origins only lend weight to the necessity of striking it from strategic theory.

The concept of the operational level of war remains unconvincing and, to echo Colin Gray and others, dangerous. But the debate has raged for so long and at such an intensity because the idea of operational art is convincing. Vego's view of operational art as support to campaigns (which are composed of tactics and guided by strategy) makes sense. Ascribing a supporting role to operational art, however, does not require the operational level of war, and we should be wary not to throw the operational-art baby out with the operational-level bathwater. What is left is a view of operational art as a parallel discipline that performs its supporting but not unimportant role—planning, preparing, conducting, and sustaining—for tacticians and strategists without the erroneous interpolation of a new and specious level of war. Clausewitz refers to these activities as those required for "the maintenance of the military force" and "preparations for fighting," differentiating them from combat itself (and therefore tactics).[27] This bears out, most conspicuously, in campaigns. Although the operational level of war is sometimes also referred to as a campaign level, a campaign is just a grouping of connected tactical actions. The principles of tactics do not change in the grouping.

While operational art is defined by its role and not as a level, it can be tied to physical forces. Not to corps, front, army, or division level, for such units are tactical and employ tactics, albeit at larger scale than smaller units. Not to the nexus of political and military objectives, for this remains the province of strategy. Rather, operational art is the realm of the staff: the organizations that act to support and arrange tactics to achieve strategic effect.[28]

Operational art is what military staffs do to manage the complexity of modern warfare as a parallel supporting function to strategy and tactics without there being an interposing operational level of war. The following study seeks to make an admittedly small contribution to rescuing both strategy and tactics from the problems identified by Kelly, Brennan, and Owen.

1 OPERATIONS AND THE NAPOLEONIC REVOLUTION

In historic events the so-called great men are labels giving names to events, and like labels they have but the smallest connection with the event itself.

—LEO TOLSTOY

The Napoleonic Revolution occurred when a number of developments, military and nonmilitary, all made progress and matured simultaneously, drastically changing the character of warfare. Napoleon Bonaparte (1769–1821) himself was responsible for almost none of these developments. Yet they did coincide with his career, and he first understood their import.

Despite the fact that he was a user rather than an originator of many of these developments, Napoleon was probably—and definitely mathematically—the best general of all time.[1] He was lucky enough to be born so as to enter the French military at the tail end of what Professor Christy Pichichero has identified as the Military Enlightenment.[2] A component of the wider intellectual movement known as the Enlightenment, it was a period of increased rationality and scientific examination of military events and organizations. This was the beginning of modern war. Chris Hables Gray attributes the development of modern war to three trends that began during the sixteenth century: a growing preference for rationality over tradition, the creation of military administration, and the application of science and technology.[3] Napoleon's brilliance was his ability to combine the disparate military advancements of his age on the battlefield itself. These trends were tinder and the French Revolutionary armies, with Napoleon at their head, were the spark.

Still, the idea of military revolution is a tricky subject. Historians and theorists usually pinpoint the introduction of new technologies as revolutionary, but this rarely—if ever—displaces everything else already there. The introduction of gunpowder cannon displaced the catapult and trebuchet, for example, but not infantry or cavalry. Additionally, artillery assumed the same role as earlier siege weapons, at least initially. Nor did the introduction of personal firearms among the infantry and cavalry immediately invalidate earlier weapons—even today infantry still carry bayonets. Across history, technological progress breeds evolutionary, not revolutionary, changes in warfare.

The Napoleonic Revolution, however, was not strictly about technology. Rather, it was about the rational integration of technology with systematic planning and professionalized armies. These were political changes in the makeup of European states that subsequently enabled changes in warfare: larger armies, better trained and supplied, operating farther from their own territory. This did not produce a change in war itself; war was and is a complex sociological phenomenon produced by the dynamic interaction of rational, irrational, and nonrational forces in and between populations. It did, however, make *warfare* more complex. No longer could armies consist of hastily assembled and trained groups of illiterate peasants without the wherewithal to avoid the press gang, or even hired mercenaries. Weapons became weapon systems manned by crews of technicians. Armies became bureaucracies and begat ministries to administer and support them. The miles that military units could travel multiplied as fast as the number of mouths it was necessary to feed and the feet it was necessary to keep in shoes. The complexity of warfare outpaced the intellect of conscripts, mercenaries, and the pampered nobility. Only the career professional could gain the expertise necessary to manage the application of organized violence. Western military officers and politicians did not miss these changes, but Napoleon was the first to unite them all in practice. This combination ushered in modern warfare and, with it, operational art as the domain of the staff officer.[4]

THE ENLIGHTENMENT

Philosophers thought about everything, war included. Both philosophers, like John Jacques Rosseau and Immanuel Kant, and military thinkers rejected the idea of war as a normal, even noble, outlet for the aristocracy and monarchs to achieve glory.[5] War came to be viewed as a necessary evil, a critical component in its professionalization. Prior to the Enlightenment, military officers were seen as noble and professional, while enlisted soldiers and sailors were treated with contempt and as servants by their own officers as well as society.[6] After the reign of Louis XIV, this began to change, with reformers decrying the poor effect on morale—and the consequent poor performance of soldiers—and proposing instead a "military society" that included all those who served in uniform as brothers-in-arms.[7]

The nonmilitary aspects of Enlightenment thought are beyond the scope of this work, but those ideas still affected the military environment at the turn of the nineteenth century. After the French Revolution, the Girondins, upon seizing power, launched no less than a war of worldwide liberation.[8] It was not just this bellicosity that changed warfare, however. Rationality led to more effective institutions and, thus, better exploitation of a country's potential. Michael Howard states, "The growing capacity of European governments to control, or at least to tap, the wealth of the community, and from it to create mechanisms—bureaucracies, fiscal systems, armed forces—which enabled them yet further to extend their control over the community, is one of the central developments in the historical era which, opening in the latter part of the seventeenth century, has continued to our own time."[9]

In economic terms, a global economy began to emerge as travel and international communication became more reliable. This led many thinkers to believe that war would become extinct since it would disrupt commerce and trade.[10] Instead, economic policies quickly became a servant of war, most notably for Napoleon himself, whose Continental System was an attempt to weaken and thus defeat Great Britain through the imposition of a Continent-wide economic blockade.

The Scientific Revolution also affected warfare. Improvements in agriculture meant that more food could be produced for armies, while improvements in storage meant that food could be transported to wherever those armies might be. Improved road surfaces throughout Europe, following the scientific examination of road construction by French engineer Pierre Trésaguet, meant that not only could armies move faster but so too could the food and supplies necessary to sustain them.[11] It was also during this period that detailed and (comparatively) accurate maps became increasingly available.[12] A rational and scientific approach to medicine also found use in the military sphere. French military doctors sent reports on experiments and observations back to the war ministry from various posts throughout the colonies. These were collected into a journal, printed, and distributed to medical professionals by the army free of charge.[13]

ENLIGHTENMENT MILITARIES

The most important effect of the Enlightenment for the armed forces, however, was how it changed militaries themselves. Again, Michael Howard comments on the change in military affairs: "By the eighteenth century European wars were being conducted by professional armed forces of a kind with which we would be familiar today. Their officers were not primarily members of a warrior caste fighting from a concept of honour or of feudal obligation; nor were they contractors doing a job for anyone who would pay them. They were servants of the state who were guaranteed regular employment, regular wages, and career prospects and who dedicated themselves to the service of the state, or rather of their 'country' come peace, come war."[14] Even prior to the French Revolution, the Military Enlightenment caused drastic changes. Frederick the Great invented the division, which was adopted by France in 1759.[15] Corps, brigades, and battalions were standardized. Other reforms in the French Royal Army included better soldier pay and barracks, the establishment of military schools, and equipment modernization. Larger armies were now also possible.[16] This, combined with the expulsion of officers who had gained rank solely on the basis of their family lineage and wealth, allowed young, talented officers to rise very quickly—Napoleon, for example, was made a general at twenty-four. These modernized forces began to fight more for their nation than for a paycheck, although group solidarity was another strong motivation, especially among veteran troops.[17]

On the battlefield, light infantry performing screening and skirmishing functions was another innovation, enabled by rifled weapons that allowed these troops to disrupt opposing formations prior to the charge of heavy infantry or cavalry.[18] Around 1808 the distinction between light and heavy infantry disappeared.[19] Artillery also matured, organized into siege artillery, field artillery to support infantry, and horse artillery to support cavalry. Cannons were sometimes centralized into a reserve and held to fire at a decisive point or dispersed and used in direct support of individual infantry units.[20] By necessity, artillery officers attained a higher level of professionalization than other arms, leading Frederick the Great to criticize their "jargon" and "pretensions."[21]

Even before Napoleon, the French army was at the cutting edge of military innovation, although few improvements were not yet fully institutionalized. The use of divisions was proposed by Pierre-Joseph Bourcet, a French officer, in 1775.[22] Most infantry forces attacked in a column formation instead of the line of battle, emphasizing shock action.[23] The line formation was sometimes used for offense but more often for defense to maximize firepower. A British innovation, the two-rank line was brutally effective and one of the few new methods tried but not adopted by Napoleon. This formation depended on expertise in marksmanship, a British specialty. French troops, whose leaders preferred massed firepower and shock, could not match them.[24]

Howard has also pointed to the importance of civil bureaucracies in manning, training, and equipping national armies.[25] The increasing size and complexity of military organizations necessitated the creation of bureaucracies to create and administer military policy, and they began rationalizing and systematizing military affairs. The civil bureaucracy under Lazare Carnot steered the French army through the years of the revolution, modernizing much of it even before Napoleon's time.[26]

THE NAPOLEONIC REVOLUTION

Napoleon Bonaparte was perhaps the first to see the practical potential of the Military Enlightenment and the Scientific Revolution for warfare.[27] Here the word "revolution" is used as Albert Camus defined it: Revolution "is the injection of ideas into historical experience. . . . [A] revolution is an attempt to shape actions to ends, to fit the world into a theoretic frame."[28] Napoleon literally did this, executing the theoretical ideas of French Enlightenment military sophists such as the comte de Guibert, Bourcet, and Maurice, comte de Saxe. In the words of historian Robert S. Quimby, "Napoleon alone clearly took advantage of all that was thus made available. Drawing from these varied sources, he welded them into a consistent practice far superior to any previously employed."[29]

Of course, "revolution" is a bit of a rhetorical flourish. Historian Clifford J. Rogers has described how warfare evolves as akin to the biological evolution in a process of punctuated equilibrium. In a punctuated equilibrium, there are periods of slow, nearly static changes punctuated by periods of rapid change usually in response to the previous period of rapid change.[30] This process certainly occurred over centuries in Europe before Napoleon. What was different about the Napoleonic "punctuation" is that it was revolutionary in the sense of Camus. Napoleon unlocked the potential of that long process of punctuated equilibrium in both military and political senses. Warfare's long evolution and the Enlightenment seeded the wind, but it was Napoleon's mastery of every aspect of these changes that led to the whirlwind.

That revolution was expressed in the next few decades of war. Revolutionary France aimed not at occupying foreign territory in order to extract concessions from established government, but rather to uproot those governments entirely and replace them with ones similar to its own.[31] Napoleon would do the same, redrawing the map of Europe, creating and destroying nations, and imposing the Civil Code of France, or the Napoleonic Code.[32]

There was a clear inflection point in warfare centered on Napoleon's career and specifically around the year 1800. Historian Anders Engberg-Pederson calls this point an epistemological revolution, in which warfare became a "problem of knowledge."[33] The Enlightenment and other intellectual movements, like Romanticism, reexamined military affairs. The knowledge necessary to understand warfare and employ military forces in combat became far too expansive for one human brain to comprehend, heralding the end of singular generalship. One eventual response, as we shall see, was the extension of the human brain by forming a collective of brains—a staff, with each "brain" responsible for a certain discipline.

From a young age, Napoleon was enamored with military subjects (although he read many subjects and even tried his hand as a novelist). He first gained fame when he took over command of French forces at the Siege of Toulon (1793), where he personally led troops to seize enemy redoubts and then operated cannon after crewmen were killed to deal Britain's Royal Navy a rare defeat, being wounded himself in the process.[34] He was beyond comparison as a tactical commander, but his greatest strength was perhaps his Enlightenment-inspired egalitarian leadership. In an age when most European generals viewed their soldiers as little more than beasts of burden, Napoleon fawned on his enlisted troops, remembered their names, and was genuinely concerned for their well-being and equipment. The soldiers returned his attention in kind, fighting and drilling at a higher level than their opponents.

The Grande Armée was the most direct reflection of Napoleon's vision. Initially formed in 1803 as the Army of England for a cross-channel invasion, it was wholly designed by Napoleon, down to individual weapons and uniforms. When he abandoned plans to invade Britain, Napoleon instead turned this force eastward and rechristened it the Grande Armée. For almost two years previously, these troops were incessantly trained and drilled to ready them for the invasion. By the time the army was put to use elsewhere, it consisted of about 350,000 of the best-trained and best-organized professional troops on the planet.[35]

The key innovation of the Grande Armée, however, was the corps system. Napoleon's corps, self-contained combined-arms units with infantry, artillery, and cavalry under a single commander, were unique at this time.[36] They could combine to fight together as a single army or maneuver and fight independently. That flexibility enabled better and more responsive tactical dispositions, such as the *manoeuvre de derrière* and fighting from a central position. At times, Napoleon would place his army between two enemy armies, risking a two-front fight but depending on the speed and responsiveness of his corps to first attack and defeat one, then the other.

Napoleon attempted to reform the entirety of the three combat arms—infantry, artillery, and cavalry—and institutionalized the use of a tactical reserve. Not all of his reforms took root, but the major change was the ability to use them together. Artillery would blast away at a chosen point on the enemy line, infantry or heavy cavalry then would attack that point, and light cavalry stood by to exploit any breach, running down fleeing soldiers or outflanking other units. He was the first modern combined-arms commander.[37]

The French army's logistics system was another of Napoleon's reforms. Supplies were traditionally gathered and carried by extremely corrupt civilian contractors until Napoleon militarized the process by forming transport battalions and a network of depots.[38] Despite his efforts, a logistic system dependent on horse-power could never supply his massive armies sufficiently, and they continued to subsist through looting and pillage. Napoleon has also been called the world's first "media general."[39] The use of the Chappe telegraph system, a recent invention, was significantly accelerated by Napoleon, who adopted it to campaign in Italy and Germany. His command of what today is referred to as information warfare extended across the whole of Europe, enabling him to confound and deceive opponents (as discussed in later chapters).

Most important, Napoleon was the first to use a modern military staff system that is still in use today. As a young general (before his rise to power), he was posted to the French Historical and Topographical Bureau, which then planned military operations.[40] It was there that he learned the importance of staff work, especially cartography and intelligence. This permanent staff was itself a new system. Prior to the Seven Years' War, what aides there were disbanded after hostilities.[41] France was the first to set up a permanent staff, but adjutant generals were only assigned at the field-army level in 1792.[42] The invention of permanent staffs with professional officers is usually attributed to Bourcet, who, because he was a low-ranking noble and thus could not command, became a key advisor in many wars prior to the French Revolution.[43]

In command, however, Napoleon would develop his own system. Prior to the advent of military staffs, armies and navies made military decisions via councils of war, in which the commander would assemble his major subordinates, solicit and pitch courses of action, and seek a consensus on which one to pursue. Napoleon eschewed such meetings once he had enough rank to forego them, calling them "a cowardly proceeding" intended more to shift blame than to determine an effective plan.[44] Instead, he built a staff that included members who were not military per se, but rather from the civilian government, such as the Secretariat, the Statistics Bureau, and the Topographical Bureau.[45] Napoleon was the first military commander to employ a chief of staff in the modern sense, but the practice was not immediately institutionalized. He only ever had one chief of staff all the way to 1814, Alexandre Berthier.[46] The chief of staff and his subordinates generally worked out the details of operational plans (provided by Napoleon himself) and handled written communications between the commander and his units; they also engaged in interunit communication and some intelligence-dissemination duties.[47] A separate administrative and economic staff, this one entirely composed of civilians, also handled logistics, pay, and medical functions.[48] While this was a leap ahead in organization as compared to earlier staffs, it was not formalized or institutionalized. Functions and processes were highly dependent on the personalities of the staff officers and clerks, and not the least upon Napoleon himself. It was designed by and for "one of the most unrelenting micromanagers in history."[49] He even insisted on analyzing raw intelligence personally, rather than allowing his staff to do so.[50]

While Napoleon's system also depended on staffs at lower levels of command, it fell victim to the Achilles' heel of all command-and-control systems: overcentralization.[51] Napoleon tried to do everything himself, running the French Empire and fighting battles simultaneously. He never delegated enough authority and responsibility to make it work. Also important to note is that Napoleon cherry-picked ideas from the Enlightenment and ignored them and others when it suited him. He reinstated vicious, race-based slavery in the French colonies, even though it had been banned, to fuel his imperial ambitions, and snuffed out nascent French democracy in his pursuit of personal power.

The French army would retain this staff system through the twentieth century. The U.S. Army adopted it from the French during World War I. Britain and the Commonwealth countries used a slightly different system, the major difference being that operations and intelligence staffs were combined.[52] German staffs were inspired by Napoleon's example (and will be covered extensively in chapter 3).

CONCLUSION

The intellectual developments of the eighteenth century—both civil and military—mixed in such a way as to transform warfare. The Enlightenment and the Military Enlightenment occurred just before an immense series of changes in warfare driven by technology.[53] Napoleon Bonaparte's career also began just before this inflection point. For centuries, war in Europe was the personal interest of sovereign rulers and aristocrats, which placed a strange form of cultural limitation on it.[54] If wars became too destructive, they became unprofitable. Nationalism—the identification of individuals with the state—and the destruction of the aristocratic system in much of Europe itself broke this chain. Ironically, Enlightenment thinkers never intended for their ideas to enhance the application of armed violence. Most believed that in the light of rationality, war would disappear from human affairs. They were wrong.

To be clear, the phrase "Napoleonic Revolution" is used here as shorthand to describe the numerous changes in the character of warfare just prior to and during Napoleon's career. He was simply the man who translated the Military Enlightenment into a revolution in tactics and strategy, war and warfare, all subsequently elucidated by Clausewitz. Importantly, all of these trends made the nation-state more robust; a single military defeat could rarely convince political leaders to capitulate as they could now draw on greater resources, especially on a population bound tighter to a national identity. In essence, once larger armies could be maintained, the loss of one battle did not mean the loss of a war.

Nor was the Napoleonic Revolution limited to the French army. By 1812 many of Napoleon's methods were being adopted by other militaries. His victories triggered major reform efforts in the Prussian, Austrian, and Russian militaries to name a few, and every major military adopted his corps system before his career was over. Napoleon defeated each major European military at least once. But by doing so, he also taught them how to win.

In short, Napoleon came to power at a time when military disciplines were becoming professionalized. These disciplines included administration, information and intelligence, the coordination of military forces, the arrangement of fire support, logistics, and command and control. Each was becoming professionalized through necessity as the size and potential of military organizations continued to increase. Napoleon's method to master these trends was the development of his staff.

The ideas of the Enlightenment, along with those of de Saxe, Guibert, and their like, were made flesh, given uniforms, placed under the command of a man who had risen by merit rather than birth, and called the Grande Armée. These soldiers injected those ideas into the historical experience of the world at the point of a bayonet, and the world broke first. But then it was transformed. The military staff, its worth proven by Napoleon, would be the vehicle that would integrate all subsequent changes in the character of war.

2 GERMAN OPERATIONAL THOUGHT

> *I am becoming more convinced every day that without a well-organized general staff no army can be well led. A poorly organized and slightly trained army with a good general staff will accomplish more than a good army with a poor general staff.*
>
> — **Gerhard Johann von Scharnhorst**

The rise of operational art is intimately connected with the rise of general-staff systems. The Prussians first noticed its import and subsequently institutionalized staffs, marrying them to a human-resource system to ensure that staff officers were professional and competent. They did so after the October 1806 disaster of Jena-Auerstedt, the shock of which spurred major reforms in the Royal Prussian Army. Shocked though those in the high command were to see the forces of Frederick the Great routed and dissipated, the rot was evident even before the battle to no less a military mind than Clausewitz himself.[1] The Prussian army had ceased to evolve, entranced by the past glories of Frederick the Great, and was unable to cope with the complexity of modern warfare. The Prussian (later German) general-staff system was designed to ensure that the rot never occurred again.

Whereas as the Soviets (and subsequently Western countries) attempted to deal with the scale of modern warfare in terms of men and matériel through the development of the concept of the operational level, the Royal Prussian and then the Imperial German Army instead turned to an institutional solution: the creation of a general-staff system.

The term "system" is used here because it was not just the creation of a general staff and subordinate staffs among field units. Many other militaries took that step as well. What made the Prussian General Staff work was its marriage with a personnel system that ensured the selection, education, and assignment of high-caliber officers to populate it. The general staff was effective so long as very junior officers were selected as fit for its various duties, sent to rigorous educational facilities, and then were alternately assigned to key posts in field commands and in the central general staff itself. In modern terms, this is not unlike the U.S. Special Operations Command and its associated subordinate units. Talented soldiers, sailors, airmen, and Marines are selected through rigorous testing and qualification courses, providing Special Operations Command with high-quality personnel capable of the most dangerous and complex tactical missions. Where the U.S. military does this for talented operators, the Prussian and German armies did so for officers with the intellectual ability necessary to analyze and coordinate complex operations. The system functioned so well that it provided Prussia and then Germany with armies quantitatively superior to every opponent they faced on the battlefield until the system began to be dismantled before World War I and subsequently neutered by Adolf Hitler during World War II.

ORIGINS

Before Napoleon's reforms, military staffs slowly developed over centuries as the size and complexity of military organizations grew. The earliest staffs were composed of advisors and technical clerks, who most likely only copied written orders and carried messages.[2] The advisory function of staffs came in the form of a council of war. Alexander the Great employed surveyors, who scouted and mapped routes.[3] Surviving Roman staff reports focus on personnel and duty assignments—how many men were present and when they were on duty.[4] Intelligence was mostly gained from local sources and deserters.[5]

Medieval staffs usually consisted of the nobility's retainers who functioned in peace and war, such as seneschals and constables.[6] Early military staffs revolved mostly around logistics. The term "quartermaster" is derived from this period.[7] Quartermasters combined the functions of a combat engineer and a logistician and also conducted reconnaissance. Frederick the Great recommended a staff of seven quartermasters.[8] Napoleon, as we have seen, expanded the functions of staffs beyond logistics, but this was very much designed to meet his own personal, rather than any institutional, needs.

THE SCHARNHORST MODEL

After the Prussian army was virtually annihilated by Napoleon at the twin battles of Jena-Auerstedt and Prussia was forced to sign humiliating peace terms in 1807, Major General Gerard Johann von Scharnhorst was appointed to head the Military Reorganization Commission.[9] Scharnhorst stacked the committee with likeminded reformers, including his former student Captain Carl von Clausewitz as its secretary.[10] Scharnhorst set out to explicitly design a military based on the lessons demonstrated by Napoleon and to institutionalize their application. Where Napoleon created a military revolution for his immediate needs, Scharnhorst designed a system to survive him. He had far less time than he thought.[11]

The commission believed that military genius, such as Napoleon's, could not be counted on to appear when needed. It was inevitable that unsatisfactory leaders would be appointed, especially in the armies of the time, when birth often counted more than merit. Moreover, generals were usually conservative and ill equipped to keep up with the rapidly changing character of warfare. Scharnhorst himself described the solution: "Normally it is not possible for an army simply to dismiss incompetent generals. The very authority which their office bestows upon generals is the first reason for this. Moreover, the generals form a clique, tenaciously supporting each other, all convinced that they are the best possible representatives of the army. But we can at least give them capable assistants. Thus the General Staff officers are those who support incompetent generals, providing the talents that might otherwise be wanting among leaders and commanders."[12] Finally, the commission had to account for the changes in warfare wrought by the French Revolution and its resultant Napoleonic Revolution. The development of the general staff was a major component of that response.[13]

Scharnhorst himself died before the work of the commission was complete, when a wound he received at the Battle of Grossgörchen in 1813 became infected, but the commission continued and established the Prussian General Staff along with a raft of other reforms.[14] The general staff took shape in 1816 comprising five departments, three of which took a regional focus on potential theaters of war and potential enemies: Eastern (Russia), Southern (Austria), and Western (France or a coalition of western European states). Another department studied military history, while the other housed and trained staff officers ready to rotate between the general staff and the staffs of corps and divisions. Even when these officers were serving with those units, they remained part of the greater general-staff system.[15] Staffs at the corps and division levels comprised four sections: tactics and strategy, administration, logistics, and fire support.[16]

General staff officer candidates were chosen from the regular army's officer corps to take a rigorous examination. If they passed, they were then sent to the academy system for years of educational studies. If they passed that, they were then full general-staff officers and assigned and administered not by the regular army, but by the general staff itself. These men served not only as advisors to unit leaders but also as links between units and the planners of the general staff. Their capabilities were fostered through a robust educational system and frequent rotation between the line units and the general staff, cognitively equipping them for both tactics and strategy.[17]

The lifeblood of the Prussian (and later German) general-staff system was the *Ia*. The Ia was a lieutenant colonel or a major member of the Prussian General Staff who worked on the staff of an operational unit of division size or larger. He ran the unit's staff, taking that requirement off the commander himself; communicated directly with general-staff headquarters; and was the primary advisor to the unit commander. This last relationship was so close that a commander and an Ia would sometimes progress up the ranks as a pair, always assigned to the same unit together. The presence of the Ia, who could also be rotated back to the general staff, performed two functions. First, he was at once a subject-matter expert and mentor-teacher on operational art to the commander and other staff officers who were not selected and trained members of the general staff. Second, he linked the Prussian General Staff with operational units, ensuring they did not lack for up-to-date information on movements and tactics. Such a simple and effective system to ensure connectivity between the highest and lowest levels of a military organization simply no longer exists.[18]

THE RESULT

The Scharnhorst Model extended the professional practice of operational art below the level of high command down through frontline units like a military nervous system. Historian Robert Citino describes the result as a structure that "combined the man of action with the man of intellect in a highly potent mix."[19] Trevor Dupuy describes it as "institutionalized military excellence."[20] He has identified ten distinguishing traits of the Scharnhorst Model: selection, examination, specialized training, emphasis on historical study, inculcation of the initiative, responsibility, goal of technical-tactical proficiency, objectivity in analysis, regeneration, and a leavening process.[21] Spenser Wilkinson, a British academic who studied German General Staff documents, including Moltke the Elder's papers from the late nineteenth century, coined the phrase "the brain of an army" to describe the Scharnhorst Model, writing, "The metaphor is peculiarly apt, for the staff, like the human brain, is not independent but a part of an organic whole. It can perform its functions only in connection with a body adapted to its control, and united with it by the ramifications of a nervous system."[22] This explains why, when other armies created a general staff but not the personnel policies that provided its regeneration and communication, results were never as good as they were in Prussia and Germany.

This system was not just a good idea, nor was it merely a response to the defeat at Jena-Auerstedt, although it was both of those. The development of the Prussian General Staff was a direct response to the increasing size of armies; the subsequent increase in difficulty when it came to sustaining, moving, and commanding those armies; and the increasing complexity of weapons systems.[23] In short, the staff system was created to address the very issues that the concept of the operational level of war claims to address, but it does so in a tangible way instead of just foisting a theoretical concept into the mix.

What made the Scharnhorst Model so effective was that it was a complex adaptive system. Such a system "evolves and changes over time through the interaction of its components with each other and with the external environment."[24] The interaction of the general staff, the academies, the operational staffs, and the individual staff officers who moved among them with the experience gained through combat operations allowed the Prussian and then the German military to identify, test, integrate, and disseminate new concepts and methods faster from the bottom up than other militaries could impose new ideas from the top down. From railroad deployments to artillery-fire coordination, infiltration tactics, and the integration of tanks and aircraft with maneuver forces, the general-staff system kept German military forces in the lead when it came to innovation.

MOLTKE THE ELDER

Helmuth Karl Bernhard von Moltke, known as Moltke the Elder, was the quintessential general-staff officer, and his leadership of the Prussian and then German armed forces indicates the potential of such a system. Military genius of the kind Clausewitz described is rare throughout history, and its appearance is random. Moltke's appearance as such a leader was not random, he was created.

He was first appointed as chief of the general staff, on a provisional basis, in 1857.[25] Moltke had served in the Topographical Bureau for years before officially joining the general staff itself in 1833.[26] He was an unlikely candidate to one day become the most talented product of the Scharnhorst Model.

When he was made chief of staff, Moltke had never held a command higher than the company level, and the general staff itself had little power and less influence in Prussia. Both, however, soon proved their worth. His performance in the Second Schleswig War (1864) earned him the attention of the king of Prussia.[27] Earlier, in 1862, domestic political competition between the Crown and the Diet over the control of the Prussian army ended with a decisive victory for the king.[28] This had two effects. First, the general staff received more and more authority over the Prussian military and society. Second, it severed the army from any kind of civilian oversight whatsoever. Moltke's tenure, therefore, marks both the apex of the Scharnhorst Model in action and the beginning of its slide into militarism.

Moltke's first real test was against Austria. During the Austro-Prussian War of 1866, Prussian armies proved able to rapidly deploy to the designated theater and outmaneuver Austrian and Saxon forces, culminating in the Battle of Königgrätz (July 1866), where the Prussians decimated a larger enemy army. Prussian forces made some mistakes, but Moltke's detailed preplanning, coupled with a loose, decentralized command-and-control style, allowed them the flexibility needed to salvage the campaign. Historian Robert Citino calls it "the most impressive battlefield achievement from the Napoleonic era to World War II."[29]

In the later Franco-Prussian War (1870–71), Prussian forces repeatedly outmaneuvered French forces, finding and attacking flanks and threatening encirclement. Two attempted encirclements were successful, one at Sedan and one at Metz, inducing entire armies to surrender.[30] Paris itself was also besieged, and a surrender secured. It was during this time that the word "operations" (*Operationen*) came into fashion among Prussian staff officers. It was explicitly used in reference to strategy, however, as that term had fallen out of fashion, but not as an additional level of war.[31]

After the tenure of Moltke the Elder, the German General Staff became a sword without a scabbard. His successor moved the general staff, and thus the army, even further from the legislative oversight and control of which Scharnhorst was a proponent. It was this factor, not any inherent militarism caused by the general staff itself, that led to defeat and tragedy in World War I and eventually the last resurgence of German aggression under Hitler.

THE WORLD AT WAR

The German General Staff developed the opening gambit of a European war for years before it happened. The resulting plan was a reflection of their country's strategic environment, sandwiched between France to the west and Russia to the east, both of which could generate larger armies and economically sustain wars for longer than Germany could. The result was the Schlieffen Plan, which consisted of a massive enveloping attack to knock France out of the war quickly. When finally executed in 1914, it failed. The French and British managed to halt the German offensive and stayed in the war. Germany had greater success against Russia, but it did not occur soon enough. The general staff designed the Schlieffen Plan on the assumption that Germany could not win a long war, which proved correct.

The German General Staff could still tap the expertise of its members when it came to tactics, however. It achieved a rare thing in war; the systemic development, dissemination, testing, and coordination of new tactics while simultaneously fighting. Built on the tactical tenets of maneuver and surprise, infiltration tactics as a whole unlocked the static trench defense on the western front—for a time. Large portions of the German army were essentially retrained on new doctrine while waging war, akin to building to an airplane while in flight. Not only did this happen, the tactics divined by general-staff research and analysis were the right ones for the situation and worked. British and French lines, static for years, crumpled and shattered. To be sure, by the time the new tactics were executed, it was too late, and even if the Germans had the logistics in place to support them, the nation as a whole no longer could.[32]

But World War I is also where the fatal flaw of the German General Staff began to tell. The failure of Scharnhorst to permanently attach the army to the legislature and the success of Moltke and others at severing legislative oversight entirely created a German army committed more to the war and the win than to the people and the government they ostensibly served. The general staff was only ever designed to achieve tactical success, but without a strong and strategic hand like Otto von Bismarck's to guide those tactics—and a tug on the leash when necessary—it simply engineered a more efficient suicide.

After the war, the general staff was banned. Additionally, the German army, headed by Hans von Seeckt, a general-staff officer who had seen action on every front during World War I, was severely limited. Seeckt selected the four thousand officers the country was authorized to keep, favoring former general-staff officers over frontline commanders. It was these experienced staff officers who honestly evaluated the lessons of World War I and, in turn, created the doctrine the Wehrmacht (the reconstituted German military) would later use during World War II—a doctrine focused on envelopment, combined arms, rapid decision making through decentralized command and control, and asymmetric concentration.[33] The general-staff system was rebuilt in secret, with the Wehrmacht reaping the tactical benefits when war broke out. But the fatal disconnect from strategy remained.

Even so, the German General Staff frequently pushed back against Hitler's aggressive moves and warned him against such actions early in the war. This led to the führer neutering the staff entirely. In 1937, after the general staff disagreed with his timetable for launching offensive action, Hitler had his political apparatus run a counterplanning process designed to give him the results he wanted.[34] Thereafter, the general staff became ever more politically isolated. In 1938, Hitler created the Oberkommando der Wehrmacht (OKW), a staff that replaced the War Ministry entirely and was placed above the general staff, by then known as the Oberkommando des Heeres (OKH).[35] The OKW was staffed by Hitler loyalists, eclipsing the OKH entirely.

THE GERMANS AND THE OPERATIONAL LEVEL OF WAR

Citino attributes German success during this period to the "discovery" of the operational level of war between the emergence of Prussia as a state in 1525 and the end of World War II in 1945. The first problem with this thesis is that the terms "operational art" or the "operational level of war"—or anything equivalent to it—do not exist anywhere in Prussian or German military thought at any point during this time period. Even the term "operation" was not formally defined in German doctrine until 1977, and then it was defined as "an action of a force connected in time and space that is always directed at a particular objective and may include maneuver, combat, and other actions of any type and any extent."[36] This is a good definition of an operation and captures how it was used by German military writers and others. What it is not is a level of war.

The second problem is inconsistency. Citino begins his thesis with a definition of the operational level of war that is little more than a copy of the Soviet version, problems and all. In the preface to his study *The German Way of War*, Citino defines it as "movement and command of large units: armies, corps and divisions."[37] Later, he defines it temporally as "prebattle maneuvers." What is operational and what is not varies depending on the events being described.[38] At points, even the very same maneuver (Frederick the Great's flanking march at Rossbach in 1757) is alternately referred to as tactical and operational.[39] Citino also pins the operational level of war on the

German term *Bewegungskrieg* (war of movement), which is counterposed in German documents against the term *Stellungskrieg* (war of position), usually used to describe the trench warfare of World War I's western front. Nowhere is a case made for doing this or is there a reason given why *Stellungskrieg*, which involved just as many corps, armies, and troops on just as great a scale as *Bewegungskrieg*, is somehow not the operational level of war but *Bewegungskrieg* is.

This sounds like criticism, but Citino is a military historian (and one of the finest at that). What he is not is a military theorist. Here, he is deploying a theoretical concept, not a historical one. Citino is not inconsistent and confused—it is the concept of the operational level of war itself that is inherently inconsistent and confused.

Shimon Naveh, a military theorist, points to the development of "operational cognition"—a proto-operational level of war—in the German army during the interwar years. Specifically, he points to the German military manual *Truppenführung* (HD-300). But this is a leadership manual—the title translates as "troop guide"—and covers topics as detailed as the use of passwords for sentries. It is hardly an operational vision.[40] While Naveh is right that it is one of the most important German doctrinal publications of the time, it does not contain anything close to a vision of an operational level of war.

The Wehrmacht was—initially—a better fighting organization than any of its opponents, so much so that it looked like the Germans had discovered something new, something beyond what other militaries understood. But neither blitzkrieg nor the operational level of war were codified by the Wehrmacht. Rather than trying to pin its success to things that were not real, that success can be explained by what was real: professional staff officers, steeped in the study of war, and experienced, skilled commanders produced by the general-staff system regenerated by Seeckt. The Germans were able to master the tactics of the 1930s and 1940s first, but they were by no means the only ones to do so.

In the end, though, this tactical mastery availed them little. The inheritors of the Scharnhorst Model never fully integrated logistics into their system. Indeed, the inspector general who oversaw logistics fell under the Ministry of War and not the general staff at all.[41] The Prussians and then the Germans struggled with sustainment, especially in 1848 and 1849, 1866 during the Austro-Prussian War, 1870 during the Franco-Prussian War, and during both World Wars. German staff officers and logisticians, from Moltke the

Elder down, focused far more on the logistics of moving combat forces and never enough on sustaining them, leading to decisive defeats in the 1918 spring offensives of World War I, the African and Mediterranean operations of World War II, and the invasion of the Soviet Union. The Schlieffen Plan, for example, was repeatedly analyzed, tested, and wargamed to ensure that troops could be moved from one place to another. Yet the general staff did not put the same rigor into the question of whether they could be fed or supplied.[42] One could make the case that this tendency explains a great deal of both their successes and their failures.

CONCLUSION

As the Napoleonic Revolution faded and the Industrial Revolution began, the Scharnhorst Model of a general staff enabled the Prussian, then the German, military to better understand the changes in the character of war, the implications of new technologies, and how to exploit them on the battlefield. It was so successful that, by 1871, most major military forces had copied the staff itself, although not the manpower system that was its foundation.

The German General Staff is frequently seen and evaluated as an institution in and of itself. Yet it actually should be seen and evaluated as a human-resource system. Staffs are only good as the personnel that comprise them. The marriage of formalized staffs with a human-resource pipeline designed to identify and produce the right people for those positions was the key to the system's effectiveness. The Scharnhorst Model has yet to be replicated.

Writers who detect the invention of an operational level of war in the pre-1945 German way of war are instead detecting the advantage the German military gained through institutionalizing and professionalizing military staffs and staff work. The Scharnhorst Model produced measurable superiority at the tactics. It was strategic failure that, fortunately, made these advantages irrelevant.

3 SOVIET OPERATIONAL THOUGHT

> *It is natural for strategy to try to gain emancipation from bad politics, but strategy cannot exist in a vacuum without politics and is condemned to pay for all the sins of politics.*
>
> — **ALEKSANDR A. SVECHIN**

Ideas about operations and operational art were first codified by the Red Army. Like the German development of the general-staff system, the development of these ideas in the Soviet army was fundamentally an attempt to come to grips with the changing character of warfare in the late nineteenth and early twentieth centuries. A military tradition that glorified battles like Borodino was confronted with the end of major, formal engagements as decisive affairs at a time of necessary reinvention and transition between the Imperial Russian Army of the tsars into the Red Army of the Soviet Union. An intellectual environment flush with a sense of newness mistook the evolving character of war for a new nature of war. The need to cumulatively wear down an opposing force at grand scale and length was pinpointed as that change. One would think that the Russian experience during the Napoleonic Wars, when battle after battle failed and only the erosion of the Grande Armée as a cohesive organization granted victory, would have warned against this sense of newness. The chaos of the Russian Revolution, the Russian Civil War, and their aftermath, however, cleared a path for a confusion that took hold, outlasting even the Marxist-Leninist creed that spawned it.

The concepts arose during an intense period of innovation in the Red Army, from the 1917 Bolshevik revolution until political officers began to clamp down on such innovation around 1930.[1] They are usually attributed to two officers, Alexandr Andreyivich Svechin and Mikhail Nikolayevich Tukhachevsky, and occasionally a third, Vladimir Kiriakovich Triandafillov. Lenin and Stalin's insistence on a "break from the past" in all things, including military doctrine, virtually forced the Soviets to develop new theories, operational art included.[2] This effort produced a flowering of innovative thought, but those flowers grew in the ashes of older lessons sound and unsound; only new ideas in line with Marxist-Leninist socialism were safe. Because strategy is inherently political, discussing the topic openly risked violating Marxist-Leninist beliefs, a fatal error. Further, Marxist theory held that there were scientific rules to war and combat that, if followed, would automatically lead to victory. These political precepts on war and strategy were subsequently captured in the official book *Marxism-Leninism on War and Army,* used to teach Soviet officers attending military school.[3] The volume is full of demands to display "sustained, strictly consistent devotion to the Party" and "adherence to a class point of view," further stating, "An essential condition for the creative use of Marxist-Leninist philosophy in military affairs is its deep mastery, a knowledge of its essence, [and] the observance of all its demands and principles."[4] It was a result of a long-running debate on Soviet military science that occurred in the 1920s, which historian James J. Schneider has termed the "Bolshevization of the Red Army."[5] Such a constricting intellectual environment could only have been stifling and deadening for those seeking to improve the ability of the army to do its job. Soviet officers may have leaned into the idea of operations to shield themselves from accusations of betrayal even if they disagreed with the strategic orthodoxy. If so, it did them no good.

The concept's problematic origins were compounded as Soviet officers may have been influenced by National Socialist ideas when the Wehrmacht and the Red Army worked together to develop mechanized ground forces before World War II. These are curious origins for what would later become a centerpiece of U.S. Army doctrine, but they cannot be ignored when assessing even modern views on the operational level of war.

SOVIET OPERATIONAL THEORISTS

Three Red Army officers influenced the creation of operational art: Svechin, Triandafillov, and Tukhachevsky. All served in command and high-staff billets and were incisive writers on military history and contemporary warfare. Svechin was a brilliant theorist; his book *Strategy* remains in print. His ideas were extremely influential prior to Stalin's purge of the Red Army high command and were revived in later years. A veteran of the Russo-Japanese War (1904–5) and World War I, Svechin was head of the All-Russian General Staff in 1918 and thereafter appointed to various staff positions, including as a professor at the Academy of General Staff. *Strategy* was required reading at this and other schools.

Throughout his book, strategy and operations are used almost interchangeably. Svechin defines no operational level of war, nor mentions one at all. He does define, however, what an operation is: "We call an operation an act of war if the efforts of troops are directed toward the achievement of a certain intermediate goal in a certain theater of military operations without any interruptions."[6] In short, an operation is a campaign.

Svechin makes no clear differentiation between levels, and he frequently uses the dichotomy of strategy and tactics, ignoring operations entirely. "While tactics live by decisions required by the moment, and all tactical work is extremely urgent," he writes, "strategy begins when we see a series of successive goals, or stages, toward the achievement of the ultimate goal of the war."[7] While strategy being connected with "a series of successive goals" sounds more like some modern definitions of the operational level of war, here it is subsumed within strategy. Svechin's ideas are closer to those of Clausewitz—he even wrote a biography of the Prussian theorist—than usually thought, although the implications of economic and social influence on war implicit in Clausewitz is explicit in Svechin's work.

Where Svechin does define a clear term, it is operational art, which he says should "place the troops in the best possible *tactical* position."[8] Operational art involves "tactical missions" and "logistical requirements." Furthermore, "operational art also dictates the basic line of conduct of an operation, depending on the material available, the time which may be allotted to the handling of different tactical missions, the forces which may be deployed for battle on a certain front, and finally on the nature of the operation itself."[9] Svechin is clearly concerned here with the planning and sustaining of military actions. While there is no operational level in his work—nor any real levels at all—he was clearly influential in creating a strategic and tactical vision for the Red Army.

V. K. Triandafillov is sometimes overshadowed by Svechin and Tukhachevsky but is no less important. Where Svechin focused more on strategy, Triandafillov took his operational art and imagined it in practice. For him, an enemy army could no longer be defeated in a single day or in a single action lasting a few days à la Napoleon. Because of the greater size of twentieth-century armies, it would take many days, even weeks, to defeat one. The solution revolved around two principles: combining penetration of the enemy army with a deep envelopment to attack its rear and lines of communication, and the logistical sustainment of friendly forces.[10] The tactics of large-scale penetrations and envelopments required improvements in sustainment, planning, and command and control. These consumed the bulk of Triandafillov's attention. The term "operation" came to mean a portion of a campaign that must be planned, sustained, and controlled in detail. His vision of an operation is not at all a level of war, but rather equivalent to a "phase" in modern military-planning doctrine.[11] The idea of deep-envelopment tactics would be taken up by Tukhachevsky after Triandafillov's death.

Sally W. Stoecker views Tukhachevsky as "the chief catalyst" of Red Army innovation from the Russian Revolution to World War II, the period in which the operational level of war was developed.[12] He was greatly influenced by the use of "large cavalry forces employed over very large distances" during the Russian Civil War.[13] He also "challenged the importance of one climactic battle and instead emphasized the importance of successive military operations" in the years afterward.[14] Later, Tukhachevsky still identified only a difference in scale between tactics and operations:

> Modern tactics are characterized primarily by organization of battle, presuming coordination of various branches of troops. Modern strategy embraces its former meaning; that is the "tactics of a theater of military operations." However, this definition is complicated by the fact that strategy prepares for battle, but it also participates in and influences the course of battle. Modern operations involve the concentration of forces necessary to strike a blow, and the infliction of continual and uninterrupted blows of these forces against the enemy throughout an extremely deep area. The nature of modern weapons and modern battle is such that it is an impossible matter to destroy the enemy's manpower by one blow in a one-day battle. Battle in a modern operation stretches out into a series of battles not only along the front but also in depth until that time when either the enemy has been struck by a final annihilating blow or when the offensive forces are exhausted. In that regard, modern tactics of a theater of military operations are tremendously more complex than those of Napoleon, and they are made even more complex by the inescapable condition mentioned above that the strategic commander cannot personally organize combat.[15]

Tukhachevsky clearly elucidates that the warfare of his time occurred at a greater scale and complexity—both in terms of time and space—than previously but continues to refer to them as tactics ("modern tactics of a theater of military operations"). Any kind of independent operational level is absent.

Another of his concepts, that of *udar* (hit), is usually described as "shock" but is more akin to paralyzing the opponent rather than destroying enemy forces outright.[16] *Udar* is accomplished through "slashing strikes which pierce the outer defence and penetrate into the depth" of an opponent.[17] It is little more than a rebranding of German infiltration tactics.

The development of Soviet concepts was also extremely politicized; military ideas could only survive and propagate within the Soviet system if they were in accordance with Lenin's and Stalin's mercurial views on strategy.[18] By the 1930s, Svechin and Tukhachevsky were rivals. Tukhachevsky's ideas won out in part because he denounced Svechin as a traitor to the Marxist-Leninist cause, whereupon Svechin was arrested.[19] As adept as he was at playing Stalin's games, Tukhachevsky was not adept enough. Neither he nor Svechin would live to see either the outbreak of the war they were preparing for or the Red Army's eventual victory, as Stalin had both men executed.

SOVIET OPERATIONAL DOCTRINE

The leadership of the Soviet army had to wrap their heads around contradictory evidence in their military's recent past: the industrial warfare of World War I and the maneuver warfare of the Russian Civil War.[20] Operations in those two conflicts shared a common overarching characteristic: scale. The Soviet development of operational art was directly and explicitly in response to this, specifically, the large scale of armies and theaters of operation in both. Still, the Soviets did not conceive of an operational level of war with a logic or purpose distinct from strategy or tactics.[21] The difference they observed was strictly one of size and command level. From the start, the focus of operations and tactics are identical, even in Soviet theory: "The aim of each operation and battle is the destruction of enemy forces and his technical means of combat."[22] They did, however, also ascribe scale to strategy and tactics.

Operations and operational levels are presented in Soviet doctrine as connected to the levels of strategy and tactics, though not always independently. The terms "strategic-operation" and "operational-tactical" are common.[23] Where operations (*operatsiia*) are defined independently, they are "actions conducted by large operational units"—again, tied to scale.[24] Yet the operational level is not present in all Soviet doctrine of the period. It is totally absent from the Red Army's Provisional Field Service Regulations of 1936, for example. These regulations were signed by Marshal of the Soviet Union Kliment Voroshilov, whose assistant was Tukhachevsky, and later cited as extremely influential by Georgy Zhukov.[25] The creation of the operational level of war is frequently credited to Tukhachevsky and sometimes to Zhukov. That it is absent from their personal and professional work is telling.

Operational art, however, was ascribed unique functions. Whereas the functions of strategy involved politics and tactics focused on combat, operational art focused on methods to organize and support combat forces, equip them, and command and control them. This required intensive study.[26] But even these were not distinct; many of the same functions were ascribed to tactics.[27]

The operational level is also connected to Soviet deep operations (*glubokaia operatsiia*). Even here, however, scale and not purpose or function is the prime characteristic.[28] Deep operations were simply envelopment actions conducted at large scale and through a great distance by Soviet fronts and armies (two unit designators), combined with deep strikes behind the enemy's forward line of troops. It was uniquely suited to the flat plains and great expanses of western Russia, not intended to be a one-size-fits-all concept. This idea was first proposed by Triandafillov; Tukhachevsky later developed the concept and units, such as paratroopers, intended to carry it out.[29] Deep operations is also not a level but equivalent to a modern concept of operations.

By 1936 deep operations developed into an envelopment intended for a complete encirclement, another age-old tactic presented as new.[30] Further development of Soviet theory was arrested in 1937–38 by Stalin's purge of the military.

WORLD WAR II AND ITS AFTERMATH

Deep-operations thinking was preserved by Zhukov, who would apply it at the Battle of Khalkhin Gol (1939) against Imperial Japan and later on the eastern front against the Germans. After the German invasion of the Soviet Union in the summer of 1941, the Stavka—the Russian General Staff headed by Stalin himself—hastily regenerated operational concepts. Again, an aspect of scale is present. Stavka directives addressed the use of fronts and field armies in combat, including bringing "maximum force to bear on German defenses," the coordination of combined arms.[31] Field regulations of 1942 and 1944 directed "tactical penetrations" and exploitation thereof.[32] These themes fall squarely into the realm of tactics, albeit those of fronts and armies. Again, scale is the only difference.

Any distinction between the operational level and strategy also washed out with the torrent of blood spilled on the eastern front. By 1945 the Russian front was viewed as simultaneously operational and strategic.[33] Soviet ideas on operations, confronted with the reality of warfare, reverted to a dichotomy between tactics and strategy. After the war, the advent of nuclear weapons diminished Soviet interest and focus on an operational level and operational art.[34]

RESURGENCE

Soviet operational thought enjoyed a resurgence in the late 1960s and 1970s, becoming commonplace as a term but no more clear and consistent as a concept. One influential Soviet work seemed to imply that "military operations" are everything below the level of nuclear war.[35] Operations were also connected with "operational directions," which, in Soviet doctrine, were territorial sectors of the battlespace, giving it another scale component, this time connected with geography.[36] At this point, the definition of an operation is self-referential, being simply everything that takes place within an operational direction. This circular reasoning—an operation occurs within an operational direction for an operational mission that is the goal of an operation—occurs throughout Soviet doctrine.

Deep-operation theory also evolved during this time. Previously, its intent was to fix an opposing force in place, penetrate its defensive line at one point, then exploit that penetration by flowing armored forces through the breach to the opponent's rear area. In the early 1980s, Marshal Nikolai Ogarkov developed operational-maneuver-group (*operativnaia maneuverennaia gruppa*) units. These were purpose-designed forces whereby a breach and exploitation would be executed before the opponent's development of a defensive line could be completed.[37] These concepts are, quite simply, infiltration tactics on a large scale and not altogether different from previous German methods.

In the 1965 *Dictionary of Basic Military Terms*, the Soviet army's equivalent of the U.S. JP 1-02, *Department of Defense Dictionary of Military and Associated Terms*, the depiction of tactics, operations, and strategy are intertangled, contradictory, and confused, which may have led to the later mistranslation of the concepts into American military thought. At some points, "operational" and "tactical" are used interchangeably; at other points, they are not. Actions deemed "operational" are sometimes ascribed to certain levels of command, but other times are not. For example, the word "operational" is sometimes used to describe the actions of "subunits" regardless of the size of the subunit and its parent unit. Operational art is defined as "a component of military art, dealing with the theory and practice of preparing for and conducting major formations of the Services."[38] An operation is defined as "the aggregate of nuclear strikes and combat operations by troops (a fleet), coordinated with regard to target, time, and place, and conducted in accordance with a unified plan by a major field force or strategic formation, in order to attain an assigned goal."[39] There is no definition of an operational level of war. The omission is important because this is the time when the U.S. Army began looking for a coherent vision of the operational level in Soviet doctrine, and one did not exist.

The clearest Soviet conception of operational art comes not in a work on operational art, but rather in the 1984 Red Army textbook *Tactics*. It describes operational art as "the theoretical and practical aspects of *preparation* for the conduct of operations (combat actions) by large formations of the Armed Forces."[40] Even this late in Soviet history, it was not depicted as a level but rather as the necessary planning and preparation necessary to undertake large-scale tactics. Strategy, operational art, and tactics are depicted as interrelated components of military art. Tactics is defined as encompassing all actions of military forces, not just certain command levels or certain scales. It is subdivided into two components, tactics that focus on the actions of military units within a certain service branch and "general tactics" that focus on the combination of cross-service military units, or combined arms.[41] This highest plane of tactics in Soviet doctrine at this time was more equivalent to Western views on joint operations or combined arms than to an independent operational level of war.

CONCLUSION

Critics of the operational level of war frequently point to its consequences for ensuring that strategy is rooted in politics, specifically that it amputates the use of organized violence from its political effects. For its creators, this was far from a concern. In fact, that was the point. Politics could not be safely discussed or questioned; Marxist-Leninist ideas could only be parroted. Both Svechin and Tukhachevsky, among many others, died in political purges. They first walled off military thought from politics. Excised from the Soviet context, the operational level of war retained this feature. In the American context, however, it became a bug, a virus that still infects doctrine and hobbles U.S. strategy today.

In Soviet doctrine, the words "strategic," "operational," and "tactical" do not always mean the same things as they do in the West or in strategic theory.

Whereas Clausewitz defined "tactics" as the winning of engagements and "strategy" as the use of the results of those engagements, defining them by purpose and logic, Soviet doctrine used, or rather abused, them to simply denote size of unit, from army front (strategic) down to regiments and battalions (tactical). This is another Soviet habit that has unfortunately been transmitted to the American military. Justin Kelly and Mike Brennan argue that the Soviet conception of operations was not a level at all, but rather a phrase meant to convey the idea of "a sequence of tactical actions."[42] Foreign observers of the Red Army confused the deep-operations concept, a well-designed and important concept though it is, with the invention of a new level of war.

While there can be doubt about whether there was an operational level of war in Soviet doctrine, an examination of Soviet theory leaves no doubt about the concept of operational art. First, it was not a level but a practice or discipline. It involved the planning, coordinating, and sustaining of military forces and actions based on critical examination and study of military history and contemporary trends. Second, it was conducted by staffs and multiple levels in the chain of command, primarily by the Stavka. Operational art is what military staffs do to support tactics and strategy. It was only when Soviet ideas were transmitted to American doctrine that operational art and the operational level were erroneously conflated.

These errors in translation, along with the influence of Marxist-Leninist reasoning, produced the uniquely opaque and slippery concept of the operational level of war. During the interwar years, older, more solid ideas were purged from Soviet doctrine along with the Red Army's best minds. American observers viewed what they thought was the Soviet development of the operational level of war as progress when, in reality, it was anything but. The circular reasoning that characterized the later resurgence of that concept was a function of earlier confusion, its hasty reintroduction during the crisis years of World War II, and the break in the Soviet intellectual tradition caused by Stalin's purge of the high command.

Tukhachevsky was executed on 12 June 1937. Svechin was executed on 29 August 1938. Triandafillov was spared from the purge only by having died in 1931 in a plane crash. These men were dedicated professionals, trying to do right by their country and their people. Their focus on operational concepts was necessary in order to survive as the Soviet Union turned toward totalitarian. In the end, it failed. They were only the first of its victims.

4 AMERICAN OPERATIONAL THOUGHT

> *Whatever argument can be drawn from particular examples, superficially viewed, a thorough examination of the subject will evince, that the Art of War, is at once comprehensive and complicated; that it demands much previous study; and that the possession of it, in its most improved and perfect state, is always of great moment in the security of a Nation.*
>
> — GEORGE WASHINGTON

So far, this book has examined the origins of modern military thought in the Napoleonic Wars. It has also reviewed Prussian/German and Soviet thought about how to respond to the challenges of modern war, specifically the Prussian/German institutionalization of a general-staff system and the Red Army's development of operational art as ways to perform the planning, preparing, conducting, and sustaining of tactical actions in modern combat. The focus now turns to a third response: the adoption of the operational level of war by the U.S. Army. The Army was the first to embrace this idea, and the concept was subsequently adopted by the other branches of service.

After World War II, plans to keep the Soviets at bay centered on the extensive use of nuclear weapons in Germany should the Red Army invade. America's new German allies, understandably, were less than enthusiastic about these plans. After middling success in Korea and outright defeat in Vietnam, the U.S. Army had a desire for conceptual change and rebirth. It needed an organizing concept and began looking for one.

It found one in an unlikely place. Although Army doctrine is criticized for being overly influenced by German (and even by Israeli) methods, in fact, American concepts of the operational level of war and operational art were pulled from Soviet doctrine.[1]

ADOPTION

In 1973 the U.S. Army established Training and Doctrine Command (TRADOC) to centralize concept development.[2] Previously, Army post–World

War II tactics and doctrine focused on structure: specifically, how to organize ground forces given the threat of nuclear war. Efforts prior to the existence of TRADOC included the Pentomic Army and the Reorganization Objective Army Division. TRADOC was also established to recalibrate as the Army left Vietnam, although a lack of battlefield success was hardly the problem in that conflict. The command oriented on a specific military problem: how to defend Western Europe against the Red Army while outnumbered and outgunned.

TRADOC's first commander, General William E. Dupuy, focused on adopting German tactics for the defense of Western Europe along with lessons learned from the Yom Kippur War (1973).[3] Like the Soviets, the staff of TRADOC dealt with a limited mission and employed a limited data set, armored warfare in Europe. This was not necessarily a bad thing: the primary mission of the Army during this time was the defense of the Fulda Gap in West Germany against a Soviet invasion. It was incumbent upon TRADOC to examine it, but it was poor fodder for the creation of a new and allegedly universal level of war.

The first major conceptual development was "Active Defense," explained in the 1976 FM 100-5, *Operations*, which focused on battalions and brigades. The concept aimed to "win the first battle of the next war" through an elastic defense in depth.[4] Its theory of victory was to destroy enough Soviet forces to enable a counteroffensive after a defensive battle had been won.[5] It was mostly sound as a concept, built as it was on the fact that defense is the stronger form of warfare and on the need for an exploitation phase. Yet critics attacked it because of this elevation of the defensive over the offensive and its sole focus on the initial echelon of Red Army troops, ignoring follow-on forces.[6]

Another event in 1976 accelerated the adoption of the operational level of war: the publication of a new translation of Clausewitz's *On War* by Peter Paret and Michael Howard. The translation, which has become to date the standard edition among academics and military officers alike, included the insertion of the words "operational" and "operations" in numerous places, although Clausewitz did not use either word even once.[7] This undoubtedly gave the text some added clarity for modern readers, but it imparted on the operational level a kind of classic legitimacy and pedigree that was artificial.

By 1979 the critics had won out, and TRADOC got a new commander, General Donn A. Starry. FM 100-5 was revised to focus on the brigade level and up, rather than on battalions and brigades, a direct response to those who disliked the 1976 version.[8] The result was termed "AirLand Battle." Two officers assigned to the writing team, Lieutenant Colonels L. Don Holder and Huba Wass de Czege, were key contributors.[9]

Initially, there were no plans to integrate either an operational level of war or operational art. In fact, the writing team had misgivings about the concepts, but General Starry's successor, Glenn K. Otis, overruled them.[10] Then, in 1980, as the revision team was still at work, Edward Luttwak published an influential article, "The Operational Level of War," in *International Security*. Luttwak refers to the operational level as an independent level, but it is not formally defined. Instead, he presents the operational level as the realm of tactical concepts or schema such as the German blitzkrieg. His "level" bears little resemblance to the level of subsequent American doctrine, still less (as we have seen) to any actual conception of warfare held by the Germans or Soviets themselves.[11] The term "operational art" does not appear.

General Starry actually began the practice of using the terms "operational level of war" and "operational art" interchangeably as synonyms. As we have seen, this was not reflective of Soviet doctrine. Yet even in Starry's own writings, there is no clear elucidation of the concept. The general routinely conflated tactical and operational levels in articles, letters, and speeches, only rarely pegging the concept to command level and never to scale.[12] On other occasions, he ascribed the concept to the Wehrmacht (which did not use it). And elsewhere, he described it as "theater-level and above," "the theater level," and the corps level and above.[13]

The result of these efforts was the 1982 revision of FM 100-5, now titled *AirLand Battle*. In it, the operational and tactical levels are both specifically tied to command level, not to scale, function, or logic.[14] The term "operational art" does not appear.[15] The definition of strategy is less that and more a definition of war.[16] This revision retained the heavy influence of German mechanized warfare, despite the fact that the Germans used no operational level.[17]

The issue was further confused in the 1986 revision of FM 100-5. This version replaces the operational level with operational art.[18] Tactics is now the actions of corps and smaller units (which is essentially all units).[19] But operational art is still transposed between the definitions of strategy and tactics as if it were an independent level, and the term "operational level" remains elsewhere in the document despite having no formal definition. Despite these issues, definitional and conceptual, by the mideighties, the operational level of war was accepted as canon, with operational art crystallized as a synonym, and the now-American concept began to influence other branches of service.

By the 1993 revision of FM 100-5, the operational level reached its zenith in U.S. Army doctrine. Its definition at this time is highly tautological, almost to the point of absurdity. The operational level of war is where "joint and combined operational forces within a operational theater perform subordinate campaigns and major operations and plan, conduct, and sustain to accomplish the strategic objectives of the unified commander or higher military authority. . . . The focus at this level is on conducting joint operations . . . to achieve operational objectives."[20] The operational level of war is where operations occur for operational objectives in an operational place. It is also defined as a "link" between tactical forces and strategic goals. Operational art is also defined as a way to "ensure [that] commanders use soldiers, matériel, and time effectively."[21] One wonders why it is only at the operational level that soldiers, matériel, and time should be used effectively.

PAST AND PRESENT

In 1989 the U.S. Marine Corps released FMFM 1, *Warfighting*, a work heavily influenced by then–commandant of the Marine Corps General Alfred M. Gray. The slim document is less a work of doctrine and more a philosophical treatise, but it does include a short introduction to the operational level of war (but not operational art). The Marine Corps version of the operational level was expanded in FMFM 1-1, *Campaigning* (1990). This version is far more conceptual. It is not linked to scale or command level but more to the linking and support of multiple tactical actions over time: "Without this operational coherence, warfare at this level is reduced to a series of disconnected and unfocused tactical actions with relative attrition the only measure of success or failure."[22] Originally, FMFM 1-1 was supposed to be titled *Strategy* and *Campaigning* was supposed to be FMFM 1-2's title (and focus). No publication was written for strategy until the 1997 doctrinal realignment under Commandant of the Marine Corps General Charles Krulak. Both FMFM 1 and FMFM 1-1 were updated in 1997 and renamed MCDP 1, *Warfighting*, and MCDP 1-2, *Campaigning* (with MCDP 1-1, *Strategy* taking its planned place in the series), but the operational level was retained.[23]

In 1992 the U.S. Air Force released Air Force Manual 1-1. The publication was the output of a sustained intellectual effort by Air Force command and integrated lessons from the Gulf War of 1991. The 1992 version included the operational level of war along with strategy and tactics, whereas the previous version (1984) did not discuss levels of war at all.[24] The document mentions the operational level (with the other two) but then focuses more on operational art. For the Air Force, operational art was "the planning and employment of air and space assets to maximize their contribution to the combatant commander's intent."[25]

The U.S. Navy did not officially adopt the operational level of war until 1994—and only then at the urging of the Marine Corps. The 1994 version of NDP 1, *Naval Warfare*, was the first Navy publication to define it, and the definition largely matches the conception found in FMFM 1, *Warfighting*.[26] To a far greater extent than the Army, the other three services have focused more on planning, preparing, conducting, and sustaining tactics than on definitions based on scale, distance, or command level.

Subsequent to the adoption of the operational level of war in U.S. doctrine, historians began projecting the concept backward into American military history. In his book on American operational art, Michael R. Matheny defines operations and operational art as determined by size, even though the original Army version defined it as a command level. For Matheny, large amounts of troops moving vast distances within a large area such as a theater is operational, further confusing the issue.[27] (The idea of the operational level being primarily logistics will be examined further in a later chapter.)

James J. Schneider pegs the creation of U.S. operational art to the American Civil War for a scattershot collection of reasons, from the creation of army groups to large-scale battlefields to the "operational vision" of commanders like Ulysses S. Grant. What Schneider misses—indeed he does not even mention them at all—is the pseudoprofessional military staffs that were key to Civil War combat. The litany of "new" aspects of warfare Schneider identifies are the early aspects of its industrialization that required the modernization of staffs.[28] The American Civil War was the point where operational art began to appear in the United States because it was when staffs began to be truly institutionalized. Elsewhere, Schneider has defined operational art as "the creative use of distributed operations for the purpose of strategy."[29] But the distribution of forces in time and space is clearly a tactic, and an ancient one at that.

Fortunately, the U.S. Army's view of the operational level of war seems to be changing. The 2011 version of ADP 3-0, *Unified Land Operations*, purposely does not describe levels of war, instead using the term "operational art" and specifically mentioning that it is not limited to any specific level or echelon.[30] Unfortunately, the operational level has since crept back into Army doctrine. In the most recent operational doctrine, ADP 3-0, *Operations*, published in July 2019, the operational level of war is mentioned only seven times. Twice it appears as "strategic-operational level" and once as "operational-tactical."[31] This is eerily reminiscent of early Soviet doctrine. By contrast, operational art appears as an independent concept many times. That the operational level of war cannot be communicated without recourse to hyphenated connections to strategy and tactics is an indication both of the concept's inadequacy and the Army's willingness to rethink it. Army doctrine thus remains confused and contradictory.[32] This has prevented a true and useful organizational understanding of operational art.[33]

ANOTHER WAY: THE NAVY'S GENERAL BOARD

Adopting the operational level of war, as poorly conceived though it may have been, was an organizational response on the part of the U.S. Army to the changing character of warfare and a recognized need to adapt to new conditions. Rather than looking to the Soviet Union for answers, however, it could have looked closer to home—to the U.S. Navy.

Much like the Army had to conceptualize ground warfare in an atomic era after World War II, the Navy had faced a similar challenge earlier: the transition from sail to steam and the integration of subsurface and aerial platforms into naval operations. Much like the Royal Prussian Army under Scharnhorst, the Navy navigated the transition through a number of institutional, rather than conceptual, means.

The first was the establishment of the Navy Board, the first attempt at a true general staff in the American system. First termed the Naval War Board in 1898, it has gone through a number of iterations and changes since that time, and its influence has waxed and waned.[34] It was a key component of the Navy's ability to simultaneously adapt to circumstances, win multiple difficult naval wars, maintain a global presence, and ascend to become the most powerful navy in the world.

Other institutional responses included the creation of the Naval War College, the creation of the Office of the Chief of Naval Operations, modernization of the staff of the Secretary of the Navy, and modernization of training, especially in terms of naval gunnery. And while the Army had some equivalent organizations, the interactivity between these systems in the Navy was the key to success. The interaction of these institutional organs created an environment in which new concepts and doctrine were worked out, tested, adopted, and disseminated across the Navy. Concepts could not just be mandated from the top down through personal influence. The system produced key doctrines and tactics before and during World War II that enabled the Navy to wage the campaign in the Pacific theater.[35] The system as a whole, like the Scharnhorst Model, was a complex adaptive system capable of identifying and testing emerging concepts from the bottom up—like infiltration tactics or the use of the Combat Information Center—which were later adopted by the institution as a whole. The system never became a full general staff–like system, however, despite efforts on the part of the Theodore Roosevelt and Taft administrations to make it so. This was due to congressional fears of losing civilian control of the military.[36]

CONCLUSION

In effect, AirLand Battle was a potent mix of German concepts—such as mission tactics, mechanized warfare, and the *Schwerpunkt* adopted from the Bundeswehr, and earlier German doctrine—and ideas such as the Division 86 and Corps 86 studies and parts of Active Defense doctrine. For the most part, it was an effective response to the Soviet deep-operations concept, although it is fortunate that the two were never put to the test head to head. The Russian concept of operational art and the American operational level of war both seem grafted on. In essence, the Army did most of its homework on *AirLand Battle*, then copied the answer to one question from the Soviets. The doctrine informed the execution of Operation Desert Storm in Kuwait and Iraq in 1991, which featured its own deep operations–like envelopment complete with deep fires and air-assault operations.

We know now that the drafters of the doctrine were not in total agreement about adopting the operational level of war. One of its primary writers, Brigadier General Huba Wass de Czege, who later founded the Army's School of Advanced Military Studies, has explicitly stated that "operational art is not a 'level of war' as our current western military doctrines assert."[37] The general points to a translation error as the culprit behind its adoption.

Despite its strange origins, subsequent mistranslations and misapplications, and the fact that it did not even exist in the German and Soviet doctrines it was supposedly found in, the operational level of war remains in U.S. doctrine. Yet these same issues do not exist for operational art, a more well-formed concept that actually did exist. Conflation of the two concepts has prevented the U.S. military from applying operational art to its full potential as a discipline for planning, preparing, conducting, and sustaining tactics in support of strategy.

5 THE OPERATIONAL LEVEL AND THE CIVIL-MILITARY RELATIONSHIP

A standing military force, with an overgrown executive will not long be safe companions to liberty.

—JAMES MADISON

In 1827 two young Prussian General Staff officers sent a tactical-decision game and their competing solutions to Clausewitz, then the director of the War Academy. Clausewitz gave his advice on the merits and demerits of both solutions, but first he admonished the younger men. "Forgive me if I start at the beginning," he wrote. "War is not an independent phenomenon, but the continuation of politics by other means. Consequently, the main lines of every strategic plan are *largely political in nature*, and their political character increases the more the plan encompasses the entire war and the entire state." He continued that such problems, stripped as they are of political context, may be "useful exercises" but have little or no resemblance to reality, as war cannot be understood absent its political nature. "But such a view," Clausewitz concluded, "would summarily reject all of the earlier history of war, which is absurd."[1]

That it was even necessary for Clausewitz to say this to an officer of the general staff is evidence that the Prussians were already on a path to sever war from politics. The previous chapters have alluded to the problematic relationship between the operational level and civil-military relations but focused more on the implications for theory. The implications of theory for practice, through the lens of civil-military relationships, however, reveal the depth of the problem. Since strategy is inherently political, doctrinal conceptions of the strategy-tactics relationship have implications for the civil-military relationship.

THE GERMAN CASE

Clausewitz's admonishment failed. It was not that his correspondents ignored him, but rather the groundswell in Prussian culture for military domination predated his own work and would rise to terrifying heights after him.

The posthumous publication of *On War* did nothing to stem the tide for one major reason: the manuscript was changed to support those who wanted more military control over government than the original ever intended. Clausewitz's brother-in-law, Friedrich Wilhelm von Brühl, edited the text for the second publication specifically to make it seem like Clausewitz believed that the military should have a greater say in war and foreign policy than civilian policymakers. These modifications were not discovered and corrected until the 1950s by Werner Hahlweg.[2] Many English translations were produced from the erroneous translation, however, and still carry these modifications. The earlier Scharnhorst Model, which Clausewitz helped develop, created the general staff but purposefully left it subordinate to the War Ministry, the civilian component of the military.

During the Danish War of 1864, this began to change.[3] Raised to chief of staff during the course of the war, Helmuth von Moltke was given the authority to transmit orders directly to troops in the field, rather than transmitting them through the War Ministry. Moltke himself chafed at political interference in war, leading to friction between himself and Bismarck, then minister president of Prussia.[4] Bismarck at times overruled Moltke, who tended to think apolitically. By the Franco-Prussian War, German military leaders, including Moltke, began excluding or attempting to exclude civilian policymakers from planning meetings, including Bismarck and War Minister Albrecht von Roon.[5] Thereafter, the now Imperial German Army took progressive steps to increase the power of the army and the general staff at the expense of civilian authorities, transferring important functions from the war ministry to the general staff itself and other more-controllable entities. This was an effort not just to gain more power but also to forestall democratic reforms that could reduce the army's privileged space. Thus, the army became a "state within a state."[6] Once the Nazis took power and coopted a willing Wehrmacht, the state within the state simply became the only state.

THE RUSSIAN CASE

The Soviet case is almost the opposite. Russian staff officers were never well respected until the very end of the imperial era. Leo Tolstoy famously lampooned these men in *War and Peace*, including Clausewitz, who served with Russia against Napoleon's invasion in 1812.[7] A general staff and a quartermaster were appointed during the reign of Peter the Great, but few subsequent tsars had much use for them, and Paul I even abolished them.[8]

Although the name was copied, the Imperial Russian General Staff never took on the large role of its Prussian cousin.

The tsarist general staff was always a creature not of Russia nor of the Imperial Russian Army, but of the Russian aristocracy and thus the political establishment. The military modernized only late; the Miliutin reforms of the 1860s and 1870s essentially brought the Napoleonic Revolution to Russia at long last.[9] When the general staff was copied by imperial Russia, it was split into three departments at first, finally united by Miliutin.[10] It was only at this point that Russian staff officers began receiving specialized education, duties, and uniforms. Not until the late 1870s did Russian general-staff officers, called *Genshtabisty*, become an elite service within the army.[11] Even after the reforms, however, promotion and billets were determined more by social station than anything else.

The Russian Revolution did not immediately sweep away the general staff for the simple reasons that its services were needed during the Russian Civil War and it never had enough power for the Bolsheviks to see it as a threat.[12] Afterward, however, as its power increased and Stalin's paranoia increased in the 1930s, the general staff became a target. By then, though, it was thoroughly enmeshed in cutthroat Bolshevik politics. Although the purges sealed the primacy of politics over the military, it left the Red Army hobbled by a lack of direction and bereft of talented staff officers when Nazi Germany turned on its ally in 1941. Stalin and General Zhukov, who began the war as chief of the general staff but held a variety of more powerful posts throughout the war, had to hastily reconstitute an effective staff-officer corps.

THE AMERICAN CASE

In United States, neither of these experiences have occurred. Whereas the Germans purged civilian influence from below and the Soviets purged military influence from above, the U.S. military purged itself. What happened in the American case was a military retreat from strategy.

Vietnam was a searing and traumatic experience for the military, and not just because of the defeat. Military leaders had an uneasy relationship with President Lyndon Johnson and found no improvement with the election of Richard Nixon as his successor.[13] Both presidents made military decisions based on domestic political desires. This practice tarnished the U.S. military through ill-considered purges of South Vietnamese leaders and illegal invasions of neighboring countries that had to be concealed from the public.

This is not to say the military did much to cover itself with glory. Although the fighting qualities of the U.S. military were as viable as ever, neither General William Westmoreland nor General Creighton Abrams ever got a handle on understanding the war they were in, let alone prosecuting it effectively. While the North Vietnamese were winning the war politically in South Vietnam and in the United States, the American military was almost completely absent, focused solely on the tactics of fighting the Viet Cong and the North Vietnamese Army. After the war, U.S. military leaders believed that they had won the war and the politicians or the media had lost it. Hagiographic defenses of the army's performance appeared, featuring fantastical alternative strategies that were just as politically naive as the actual ones.[14]

The combination of policymaker malfeasance and military mythmaking prevented a proper diagnosis of what went wrong with Vietnam, as both the military and civilian sides failed. At no point did civilian policymakers or military leaders understand the limitations of military force; no amount of American violence could address the political differences between North and South Vietnam. The experience could have been the impetus for the military to examine its side of the civil-military relationship. Instead it beat the retreat.

It is not a coincidence that the adoption of the Soviet-style apolitical operational thought occurred immediately after Vietnam. It offered a convenient lever to shift blame entirely onto the political side of the civil-military relationship. Strategically, the U.S. military had lost, but the operational level offered no reason to care about that. Operationally, the Army had performed its job. The Army pulled into itself, then pulled the other services with it. The American military also ignored Clausewitz's admonishment, but instead of one side or the other dominating, one side simply crossed its arms, stomped its feet, and refused to participate.[15]

CIVIL-MILITARY RELATIONS TODAY

Today, the American civil-military relationship is not so much broken as it is adrift. Rather than one side or the other seeking to dominate, both seem to defer to the other. Policymakers put a great deal of trust in military leaders, who, in exchange, uncritically lend their support and credibility. Policymakers show little interest in understanding the military side, and military leaders show even less interest in understanding the political side. The tendencies are reinforced by the influence of Samuel Huntington's objective-control model where policymakers and military officers have clear, distinct areas of responsibility, an outdated and problematic conception.[16] Strategy, as the interface between these sides, is left an orphan.

Abroad, the two "surges" of additional troops and resources, one in Iraq and one in Afghanistan, offer a convenient lens into the civil-military relationship. In both cases, policymakers had no answer for rising insurgent and terrorist violence in the countries and no plan whatsoever to extricate U.S. forces from the regions. The military plan in both cases was the same: more troops. The Iraq surge occurred from 2007 to 2009 and featured five additional brigades of U.S. troops. The Afghanistan surge featured 30,000 additional troops, plus enablers, beginning in 2010.[17]

But one worked and the other did not. The Iraq surge worked because it coincided with the "Sunni Awakening," when Sunni leaders in Iraq turned against the insurgents and terrorists and began to assist the United States and the fledgling Iraqi government. This was a political change that was then exploited by the increased number of U.S. forces in the country. But this was sheer luck—at no point was it the plan. When military leaders later convinced President Barack Obama to run the same play elsewhere and expect the same results, it failed. No such political change occurred in Afghanistan, so there was no opportunity for the increased number of troops to seize and exploit. Military leaders did not understand how to recreate the success of the Iraq surge because they did not understand why it was successful in the first place. It had been a plan of "first would come increased security [through the additional five brigades]. Then would come political progress, and with it, the building of a reliable army and police force."[18] The opposite actually happened: political progress *produced* security. The misdiagnosis of the Iraq surge—rooted in the staunch apolitical stance of American military leaders—produced the erroneous assumption at the core of the Afghanistan surge: that a sudden increase in troops would bring security, within which political progress would magically occur. Both generals and policymakers had a responsibility to know better. Too often, the U.S. officer corps uses the operational level as a shield behind which it deploys "best military advice." But no military advice can be beneficial if it is stripped of its inherent political nature.

CONCLUSION

Prussia and then Germany's failure to heed Clausewitz's admonishment took the form of the military side of the civil-military relationship dominating the other. The Soviets failed in the only way Marxist-Leninists could, predictably and through the complete subjugation of the military professional to totalitarian might. The American system is failing in a completely different way, with both sides of the relationship retreating from responsibility and the inherently political nature of strategy. A healthy civil-military relationship features balanced authority and responsibility.

As of the time of this writing, the United States has yet to produce political progress in Iraq or Afghanistan and has added Libya and Syria to the list of astrategic interventions followed by years of chaos. The Trump administration, which claimed to rebuild the U.S. military, did nothing but exacerbate the toxic civil-military relationship, viewing the military largely as props to bolster its image and even deploying troops domestically for dubious reasons. Policymakers are ill informed about what the U.S. military is doing and where, if they are even aware that the military is doing anything at all.[19] For its part, the apolitical military has been an enthusiastic accessory, confusing compliance with professionalism.

The U.S. officer corps' ongoing retreat from the inherently political nature of strategy, aided and abetted by the operational-level-of-war redoubt, continues. The military as a whole should not be partisan, taking the side of no political party, but it cannot be apolitical. This is also not to say that military officers should hold no partisan opinions; studies have shown that they do and that the idea of nonpartisan officers is largely a myth.[20] Rather, the military must embrace, rather than retreat from, the political nature of war and warfare just as much as policymakers must be willing to do the work of understanding the tactics and campaigns that they expect the military to carry out.

6 A THEORY OF OPERATIONAL ART

To a mind that artfully combines discipline with intuition, theory offers the opportunity to roam freely back and forth between the general and the particular.

—HAL WINTON

Thus far, this book has been destructive. It has examined some of the arguments for and against the operational level of war, then the history of its development since the Napoleonic Revolution that ushered in modern warfare. We have found that the operational level of war never existed in the Prussian and German systems. We have found that it existed only in nascent form in the Soviet system, where it was tied to Marxist-Leninist military ideology. And we have found that the U.S. Army mistranslated the Soviet version, conflated it with other concepts, misapplied it, and then accepted it without examination. At this point, the operational level of war can be safely and happily discarded.

But we have also found that the complexity of modern war, to which the development of the operational level of war was a response, is real. We have found that other ways of coping with that complexity, namely institutional methods like professional staffs vice conceptual methods like the operational level of war, were both necessary and effective. Specifically, we have found that the development of military staffs was one of those methods, that the Scharnhorst Model was a superior way to do so, and that operational art—as a description of what military staffs do—is useful and does not suffer from the same defects as the notion of an operational level.

These ideas, having survived the destruction of the previous chapters, now offer a foundation for a theory of operational art.

RESTORING THE TACTICAL-STRATEGIC DIALECTIC

Arguments for the operational level of war based on scale, complexity, or command level fail because the other two levels—tactics and strategy—are based on none of them. Neither the Red Army nor the U.S. Army adopted the operational level of war based on an argument of function. The argument that the operational level "links" the two other levels came later, but it also fails: tactics and strategy are inextricably connected to the point where they are not truly distinct. Strategy can only be accomplished through tactics, while tactics without the purpose provided by strategy is merely random violence. To do one is to do the other and vice versa. The gap that needs to be bridged is not between tactics and strategy, but between tactics and policy, and strategy is the interface between them.[1]

Clausewitz's framework for defining war features a dialectic between strategy and tactics that is a component of conceptualizing warfare—that is, how wars are fought. As mentioned in the introduction, he used a logic to differentiate strategy and tactics—not scale, not command level, and not size.

The logic of tactics is "the use of armed forces in engagements."[2] Anytime a military force is engaging an opposing military force, the logic of tactics pertains: that is, the defeat of the opposing force.

The logic of strategy is "the use of engagements to attain the object of the war."[3] Here, Clausewitz specifically means the results of combat. The goal of any war is to impose a political end state on the opponent. The principal means for that imposition is a successful engagement. Strategy is inherently political and thus follows a political logic. Although Clausewitz was famously dense and opaque in the unrevised *On War*, in personal correspondence, he was unequivocal about strategy: "War is not an independent phenomenon, but the continuation of politics by different means. Consequently, the main lines of every major strategic plan are *largely political in nature*, and their political character increases the more the plan encompasses the entire war and the entire state."[4] The logic of strategy is political. The logic of tactics is combat.

Tactical logic and strategic logic do not always agree; in fact, they often clash. For example, Germany's use of unrestricted submarine warfare during World War I may have made sense tactically, but it had dire strategic consequences, bringing the United States into the war (see Case Study 3). For Germany, the logics—tactics on one side and strategy on the other—never aligned. On the Allied side, the logic of tactics and the logic of strategy did align. Defeating Germany's armed forces would simultaneously remove its ability to engage in tactics and remove the only barrier preventing the Allies from imposing their political will. This is admittedly a simplification, but it suffices to illustrate the tactical-strategic dialectic.

Such contradictions between the logic of tactics and the logic of strategy are part and parcel of Clausewitz's theory as not just a dialectic theory of war, but specifically a Hegelian dialectic theory of war. For both Clausewitz and the German philosopher Georg Wilhelm Friedrich Hegel, contradictions provide the dialectic with a dynamism produced by the opposition but then synthesis of two conflicting elements.[5] The interaction of tactics and strategy, though oppositional at times, is what produces a synthesis (a way to impose a political end state on the opponent). It is easy to see why the interpolation of an artificial level between the two components of a dialectic causes them to cease functioning: it prevents their interaction.[6]

Understanding this dual logic is key for understanding war, for it is here that war gains its paradoxical nature. What makes tactical sense may make no strategic sense. Achieving a synthesis of tactics and strategy is the key to the use of military force to achieve policy goals.

There is yet another reason to eject the operational level of war from strategic theory: achieving simplicity and symmetry. Tactics, although influenced by the desired political end state, is primarily about combat. Strategy, because it is about achieving the political end state, is inherently political. The operational level must either be political, apolitical, or involve more political consideration than tactics but less than strategy. Two apolitical levels are unnecessary, as are two political levels. The last option, some apolitical-political hybrid, is nonsensical on its face, especially since proponents insist the operational level of war is entirely apolitical. Such an idea can only lead to more confusion. Understanding of war as a phenomenon or as a specific event must derive from the political aim, as that is what gives it its character.[7] The operational level of war is not logically derived from any framework in which war is political in nature, as a continuation of policy by additional (violent) means.

This leaves no room for an operational level to have its own logic and thus be useful. Proponents who address a logic for the operational level at all usually just commandeer that for either tactics, strategy, or both as their own support. In other words, the operational level has no function of its own. In a campaign, combat is occurring to achieve a victory over the opponent's armed forces (making it tactics). This logic applies equally to an insurgent cell of two people as to an army of tens of thousands. It does not change with scale, numbers, or command level. When it comes to the use of that victory, it is and can only be strategy.

This validates Justin Kelly and Michael Brennan's thesis that the inception of the operational level of war destroyed the U.S. military's ability to manage tactics supportive of strategy, as the two were no longer connected. It also validates William F. Owen's thesis that the art of tactics has suffered since the operational level of war was promulgated.

Additionally, the concept of "levels" is no longer necessary either. One of the insidious effects of the operational level of war is that it crystalized a view that tactics and strategy are discrete activities. This discreteness is never effective: tactics absent strategy achieves nothing; strategy absent tactics is impossible. Tactics and strategy are activities that, when synthesized to resolve their inherent paradox, enable the achievement of policy objectives. The idea of levels segregates what should be considered holistically. As Professor Thomas Bruscino of the U.S. Army War College puts it, "Theory, in order to be sound, must first be accurate in its description of a phenomenon before it can say what it all means. Any description that implies a fixed hierarchical relationship between policy, strategy, operational art, and tactics is not accurate, and therefore theoretical analyses based on that implication will be flawed. Levels of war imply fixed, logical, and sequential connections between levels. By ignoring reciprocal influences among policy, strategy, operational art, and tactics, levels of war have led to flaws in analysis and problems in application."[8]

Tripartite depictions of war along a tactical-operational-strategic progression impose an artificial linearity on war that is not—indeed cannot be—true. It reduces the study of war, strategy, and theory to a series of if-then statements. If the tactics work, then operations will work; if the operations work, then the strategy will work. This is very easy to teach in professional-military education courses and easy to depict in doctrine. It is also easy for commanders to fall back on such training when confronted with the inherent complexity and nonlinearity of war outside the classroom. But it is not only wrong—it cannot succeed in the real world.[9]

Lastly, it has been said that the operational level of war performs a vital interfacing function between events on the battlefield and the concerns of policymakers, essentially between tactics and policy. This function is vital, but it is the function of strategy. As Martin Kornberger and Anders Engberg-Pederson have written regarding Clausewitz's conception of strategy, "Strategy does not consist in fighting battles nor in making policy, but as the mediating element between them."[10] Removing this vital interfacing function of strategy and cutting its connection with politics, which the operational level of war is designed to do, has dire effects on the working of strategy.

OPERATIONAL ART—THE ACTUALIZATION OF TACTICS

Recognizing the theoretical problems of the operational level is important, but the practicalities of executing tactics in combat is also necessary. Since the Napoleonic Revolution, the problem has become larger than any one individual. Tactics is now a team effort.

This is where the concept of operational art comes in as a way to describe the disciplines necessary to enable tactics. Worth repeating here is Milan Vego's definition of operational art as "a component of military art concerned with the theory and practice of planning, preparing, conducting, and sustaining campaigns and major operations aimed at accomplishing strategic or operational objectives in a given theater."[11] Limiting planning, preparing, conducting, and sustaining to only campaigns and major operations, however, would be folly. Any military operation, no matter the size, must be planned, prepared, conducted, and sustained. Trimming Vego's definition gets closer to the mark. Restoring the tactical-strategic dialectic, specifically with Colin S. Gray's concept of strategic effect, yields the following definition: Operational art is the planning, preparing, conducting, and sustaining tactics aimed at accomplishing strategic effect.

Here, tactics is, again, "the arrangement of military forces in such a manner as to defeat the enemy."[12] And strategic effect is "the cumulative and sequential impact of strategic performance on the course of events."[13] Tactics executed and grouped over time to accomplish a single objective is a campaign.

Recognizing that such a task is too complex and expansive for any one individual, military organizations began forming military staffs to perform these management functions. While there are many works on the theory of operational art, few attempt to produce a theory of how a military staff should be trained, organized, and equipped to perform it. The rest of this book will do just that.

THE DISCIPLINES OF OPERATIONAL ART

Modern commanders require a military staff to perform a variety of functions that enable tactics. These include managing the military forces available; managing information about those friendly forces, enemy forces, and the operating environment; coordinating tactical actions across time and space; managing supporting arms; arranging logistics and sustainment; and managing the means and processes of command and control.

Operational art thus requires a number of disciplines. These, much like the tactical tenets, are already codified among current military doctrine, although in a haphazard way. In addition, they do not occupy a place in doctrine that places them in the context of dialectical tactics and strategy. These disciplines are usually known as the "warfighting functions" and typically include intelligence, maneuver, fire support, command and control, logistics or sustainment, and force protection. They also closely, but imperfectly, map to the major sections of modern staffs. This has created gaps and confusion. Like the tactical tenets, a close examination and elucidation of the warfighting functions as principles of operational art requires some modification, consolidation, and rejection.

First, an operational discipline enables tactics. The U.S. Army's most recent ADP 3-0 provides a good description of the role of the warfighting functions: "The purpose of warfighting functions is to provide an intellectual organization for common critical capabilities available to commanders and staffs at all echelons and levels of warfare."[14] Until 2007, Army doctrine referred to the warfighting functions as "Battlefield Operating Systems" or "Battlefield Functional Areas."[15] Whatever the term, the commonality is their usefulness as a cognitive framework to describe necessary force multipliers or tactical enablers. This implies the facilitating function of the disciplines.

Importantly, the disciplines are not bins in which to organize tactical forces, although sometimes it seems that way. They are functions that the staff performs for tactical commanders. A combat-engineer unit, for example, may conduct missions that enable the operations staff's plan, enable fire support by hardening battery positions, or maintain logistics lines of communication through the construction of fortifications and route clearance. Dividing operational art into operational disciplines does not necessarily mean that the categories are impermeable, or that military forces should be organized on those lines.

The first discipline is administration, the management of available friendly forces. **Administration enables tactics by sustaining the human resources of the military organization physically, mentally, and morally.** This is given little attention in strategic theory and historical literature, but it is vital to the functioning of any military force. Administration is so vital that adjutants used to perform the functions of an operations officer, and in some militaries, the post of personnel officer was considered higher than that of an operations officer (or equivalent). Every commander must know how many personnel are available, see to their needs, and ensure that they are paid and compensated. The role of fair and effective administration in sustaining moral cohesion cannot be overstated.

The second discipline is information. **Information enables tactics by ascertaining relevant facts, figures, and knowledge regarding friendly forces, enemy forces, civilian populations, and the environment while preventing the opponent from doing the same.** A force that does not manage, acquire, process, or analyze information to produce intelligence is blind. Manipulation of information, especially information available to the opponent, is an element in producing surprise, deception, confusion, and shock.

The third, albeit the first among equals, is coordination, more commonly referred to as operations. **Coordination (or operations) enables tactics by conducting and synchronizing tactical actions and operational disciplines across time, space, and forces available.** Individual, disconnected tactical actions can only accomplish limited goals. Instead, combat units that perform tactics must be orchestrated in time and space to produce an effect larger than the sum of their parts. Coordination is the focal point of operational art, tying the other disciplines together simultaneously with the actions of tactical forces.

The fourth discipline is fire support, the management of supporting arms. **Fire support enables tactics by applying the force's long-range, standoff, and heavy weapons in support of its other components.** The technical means of fire support, at least since cannon artillery was developed, requires specialist units and specialist troops. These fire-support specialists are a vital part of the commander's staff.

The fifth is logistics, the management of the transportation and sustainment of military forces. **Logistics enables tactics by facilitating the movement and sustainment of tactical forces.** A force cannot fight if it cannot move, maintain its equipment, resupply its munitions, and feed itself. It cannot continue to operate if supplies are not replenished and equipment is not repaired. Logistics is the foundation of operational art.

The sixth discipline is command and control, the management and maintenance of vital communications between the commander and the commanded. **Command and control enables tactics by establishing a feedback loop between the commanders and subordinate commanders and their staffs, providing direction down and awareness up.** The command function enables the commander to give direction to subordinate commanders. The control function provides the feedback on the actions taken to enable the commander to update or redirect them.

For most of premodern military history, the commander largely had to manage these six disciplines himself. As the character of warfare has trended toward an ever-larger scale, the increasing articulation of military forces, and a greater tempo, staffs are required to manage these areas for the commander.

CONCLUSION

The preceding theory can be summarized simply and succinctly. Warfare is a strategic competition between two or more political entities. Political goals can only be realized through strategy, which can only be accomplished through tactics. Tactical actions are grouped into campaigns, which must be planned, prepared, conducted, and sustained. Operational art is the planning, preparation, conduct, and sustainment of tactics aimed at accomplishing strategic effect. The major disciplines required by operational art are administration, information, operations, fire support, logistics, and command and control, although special staff should not be excluded. These statements, along with the theory of tactics in my previous book (*On Tactics*) encompass everything military organizations are formed, trained, and equipped to accomplish.

7 ADMINISTRATION

The more I see of war, the more I realize how it all depends on administration and transportation.

—A. C. P. WAVELL

Historians and military thinkers have paid little attention to the administration of military forces as organizations. Bureaucracy is inevitable in any organization, but in war, inefficient and ineffective management of military forces can be lethal. It is therefore necessary to place administration in the context its importance demands, as an operational discipline managed by staff officers. While military administration is ubiquitous, it is varied and has not been well documented. Nevertheless, every operation in history has hinged on the management of the humans involved.

Although the term "administration" is used here to align with current military practice, it should rightly be understood as "human resources," a term common in commercial organizations to describe the functions related to the management and development of employees.[1] No commercial organization can succeed without employees who are willing to do the work necessary for it to compete in the marketplace. The consequences for a military force that neglects its personnel are even more dire. Soldiers who are not consistently paid, promoted, and recognized for their efforts will not fight as hard as those who are. Soldiers who are neglected long enough will turn their swords on their leaders, and justifiably so. Thus human resources, despite the relative recency of the term, has been a primary concern for commanders throughout military history. Better administered forces perform better in battle.[2]

Administration enables—or disables—operations because it is directly connected with the morale of the fighting forces themselves. Few, if any, active or former service members reading this will not recall an administrative debacle that delayed pay, benefits, travel, promotion, or leave. No good commander can ignore these issues. Staff members who manage administration are as vital as the others, ensuring that the human resources of the military force are ready and willing to execute orders. **Administration** enables tactics by sustaining the human resources of the military organization physically, mentally, and morally.

ADMINISTRATION IN HISTORY

Although commanders throughout history have been concerned with the human capital available to them and needed assistance to manage them, modern military administration arose with bureaucracies that managed forces for sovereign governments. Before the development of defense ministries, at least in Europe, the administration of military forces was delegated either to feudal nobility or to mercenary captains. Once militaries were nationalized, governments were obliged to take on their administration. While Western European–style military bureaucracies are the most widely known today, nascent forms arose in ancient Persia, ancient Rome, and medieval China.

The French experience is exemplary of the relationship between effective military forces and effective military administration. At the height of the Thirty Years' War (1618–48), France found itself bankrupt, unable to rely on mercenaries and proxy forces, and in possession of a corrupt and moribund army. The government solved this problem through the creation of a modern civil service to administer the army, organize and regulate it, and better support it through regular management and logistics. The result, by the end of the seventeenth century, was the most powerful, professional, and advanced military in Europe.[3]

France did not stop there. Marc-Pierre de Voyer de Paulmy, comte d'Argenson, minister of war under Louis XIV, began introducing Enlightenment-style rational policies after the War of Spanish Succession (1701–14), including a route for commoners to gain nobility through military service.[4] The latter was key, as the skill sets necessary for jobs like the artillery and supply were not available among the nobility, only among lower classes. Diversifying the recruitment pool increased capability. Subsequent ministers aimed to alleviate financial stress on the part of soldiers, began to curtail the purchasing of commissions, and introduced merit-based promotions.[5] There were similar reform attempts in the ministry of the navy, but it had far less influence and prestige and was less successful.

These reforms were not enough to stave off the French Revolution, of course. Nor were they limited to France; every neighbor and adversary adopted similar reforms, more or less. But regular, rational, noncorrupt management of military forces contributes to success in combat wherever the administration discipline is performed well.

THE ADMINISTRATION DISCIPLINE

For whatever reasons, none good, the art of military administration has lost prestige since its modernization, as have the rest of the disciplines. It was originally seen as a highly prestigious, important, and technical post. During the two world wars, some military forces began recruiting women specifically for administrative positions to "free a man to fight." This may have begun a process of gendering military administration, making it seem effeminate or subservient to more "masculine" activities. This, of course, is preposterous. Military administration is as vital as any other operational art.[6]

The adjutant or adjutant general, along with administration, originally performed many of the roles now carried out by the operations staff. German staffs had a unique billet, the chief of military personnel. This person was a trusted, accomplished officer, chosen by the commander, whose primary duty was the "rehabilitation" of officers who had failed because of "matters of honor," including such things as public drunkenness, insubordination, gambling debts, and dueling (after it became illegal).[7] This mentorship and protégé program prevented the loss of otherwise talented personnel who had made mistakes and allowed them a chance to get back on track, preserving the human resources of the institution. Simultaneously, it trained the mentor in the kind of personal leadership necessary for later command of their own unit.

Few theorists have turned their gaze to administration, but in a 1903 essay, American naval strategist Alfred Thayer Mahan took on the subject directly. His essay "The Principles of Naval Administration" specifically examines the navies of advanced, democratic societies, but Mahan's principles apply equally to organized armies and navies across history. He defines administration as "an office committed to an individual, or to a corporate body, by some competent authority, to the end that it may supply a particular want felt."[8] Administration is necessary for anyone appointed to an office, or billet, for some specific purpose by legal authority. This applies to literally everyone in uniform. When it comes to military administration, Mahan believed that, in some respects, it resembled civilian-style management, such as business administration. But in other ways, it was different.[9]

The major difference between military administration and all other types, Mahan says, is its dual nature. Military administration is not just responsible for the internal efficiency of its particular organization but also to external entities, such as the government as a whole. In other words, military administration is composed of internal and external administration.

It is incumbent upon both commanders and staff officers to responsibly administer the public trust. Mahan uses the analogy of an engine to demonstrate the need for both good administration and good administrators: "The engine will be good, but the engineers must also be good."[10]

INTERNAL ADMINISTRATION

The first function of administration is internal administration, or the orderly and efficient management of the needs of the members of the command. The staff officer charged with this discipline is usually referred to as the adjutant. When military staffs were beginning to develop, the adjutant general performed the functions of both a modern S-1 and S-3 officer, combining administration and operations. In the U.S. National Guard, the top officer for some states still holds the title of adjutant general.

No military organization can exist without bureaucracy, as distasteful as it may be, and no professional organization should tolerate inefficient administration of bureaucratic requirements. As mentioned above, such problems deplete morale and are a true risk to the operational effectiveness of a command.

The primary function of the administrative staff is personnel tracking: how many people are on hand at any given time and able to perform full or partial duty. No commander can effectively plan an operation without a detailed accounting of how many troops are available to execute it. Personnel tracking also involves compiling casualty lists, a vital feedback mechanism for any commander.

Perhaps the most important aspect of administration that must be managed effectively by the staff is pay. An army may march on its stomach, but the troops will not even show up for the march without pay. For centuries, few military organizations could reliably pay their soldiers on a regular basis. Soldiers were not even provided food but had to forage or loot it. The precedent that the state should provide its soldiers with, at the very least, daily food was not established until the late seventeenth century by the French army under Minister of State for Military Affairs François Michel Le Tellier.[11]

Although they are generally considered special staff—unaffiliated with the full staff section—medical, spiritual, and mortuary affairs should rightly be considered part of human resources and fall under the adjutant's oversight. The medical staff is concerned with the physical sustainment of the troops; mental-health professionals (where they exist) are concerned with the mental sustainment of troops. Chaplains, mortuary affairs, and judge advocates are concerned with the moral sustainment of troops. Nowhere else is the staff organized to enable these professionals to operate or to coordinate their efforts, as they all are relegated to semi-independent special staff sections, nor can the commander depend on one professional to have oversight of these officers. These staff members, however, do perform a similar role.

EXTERNAL ADMINISTRATION

Staffs can rarely meet all of the administrative requirements of their units without interfacing with external entities. This may be a higher headquarters, joint or combined partnered units, intelligence and diplomatic agencies, or host-nation organizations. For example, U.K. units have an "information and outreach" section that manages, in addition to information operations, a variety of functions that revolve around the unit "reaching out" to other organizations. These functions have become even more important in modern warfare, and they can be overwhelming for a staff that is not designed to manage them.

Some of these functions include public affairs; protocol and key-leader meetings; liaison with joint, combined, or coalition forces; and local contracting. These are all classic staff functions that continue today and must be managed. They comfortably fit within a staff section well versed in liaison and administration.

Recall Napoleon's staff and how it included personnel who managed the administration of the country while he was on campaign. As the sovereign of France, he could not ignore external administration. The situation is different for modern commanders, but they also cannot ignore external agencies and organizations. Whether they are enablers, key allies, or just coactors on the battlefield, the staff must conduct outreach. This includes interagency outreach to other governmental organs, just as Napoleon had to do, but also to nongovernmental organizations, such as humanitarian assistance groups, economic agencies, and aid and development organizations, as well as to other civilians who live in and around the operating area. A study of division command found that this type of outreach was so important that it may be required, but even subordinate commands will interact with their local environment and require similar effective contact.[12]

But external administration can have direct effects on the battlefield as well, through liaison officers. Coalition warfare is increasingly common, and most coalitions at war depend on liaison officers, rather than integrating staffs, for coordination. The coalition that finally defeated Napoleon, for example, was tied together through the liaison officers of the Prussian General Staff.[13]

MOTIVATOR-HYGIENE THEORY

Concepts from the business world should always be viewed with skepticism when translated to the military realm, but one theory in particular applies to administration, which, one could argue, is the operational discipline most similar to business. This is psychologist Frederick Herzberg's motivator-hygiene theory.

Motivator-hygiene theory is primarily built on the idea that employee satisfaction is not a single sliding scale, with dissatisfaction on the one end and satisfaction on the other. Rather, each extreme exists on its own separate "scale." Workplace dynamics such as company policies and administration, supervision, interpersonal relationships, working conditions, salary, and status increase employee dissatisfaction if they are not well administered. But good administration does little to increase satisfaction, it only maintains it. Other aspects of management such as recognition for achievement responsibility, growth, and advancement (that is, promotions) have a greater influence on increasing employee satisfaction.[14]

This theory applied to military organizations illuminates how administration can contribute to morale, unit cohesion (the sense of an individual belonging to the unit), and institutional cohesion (a sense of an individual belonging to a particular branch of service). Poor policies, or good policies poorly administered, will decrease morale, unit cohesion, and institutional cohesion, therefore reducing combat effectiveness. Rewards, recognition, and promotion, however, can increase it. Administration of a military-rewards system is of critical importance to maintaining morale. The receipt of awards is not only emotionally charged but also tied to promotion and recognition. The awards process must be administered in an efficient and, most importantly, fair manner, preventing senior leaders from playing favorites; rewarding friends or high-ranking, influential individuals; or distributing awards unequally between officers and enlisted personnel.

ADMINISTRATION AND THE PACIFIC THEATER

Some may disagree that administration can have a tangible effect on combat effectiveness. The following vignettes from the Pacific theater of World War II demonstrate that this is not the case, providing examples of both poor administration creating risk and good administration underpinning successful tactical action. This effect on combat effectiveness warrants the inclusion of administration in any list of operational disciplines. Proper management ensures that the right people are in the right job at the right time and strives to prevent the disruption inherent in frequent or unnecessary changes in command personnel, except when absolutely necessary. Sometimes, administrative moves are overdue even if motivated by increasing effectiveness. Other times, they are motivated by political or institutional desires that have nothing to do with military effectiveness.

GHORMLEY VERSUS HALSEY

At the outset of the Guadalcanal Campaign, the U.S. theater commander in the South Pacific was Rear Admiral Robert L. Ghormley. Although he was an intelligent and experienced officer, there were still some questions about his suitability to oversee a campaign as complex as Guadalcanal. As commander of the South Pacific, he personally worked long hours in spartan conditions to support Allied operations in that theater. In October 1942, a few months after the landing at Guadalcanal, Admiral Chester Nimitz toured the theater and was not satisfied with the level of support provided to the 1st Marine Division, then holding a small portion of the island that included a key airfield. He concluded that Ghormley did not have the aggressive leadership style necessary to spur air and naval efforts to support the embattled Marines. On 16 October, Nimitz relieved Ghormley of command and ordered him to await his replacement for a turnover of command.[15]

Enter Vice Admiral William "Bull" Halsey Jr., a brash and aggressive naval commander. While he would make some questionable decisions later in the war, Halsey was exactly the right commander for the South Pacific in October 1942. Soon after taking command, he summoned Major General Alexander Vandegrift, commander of the ground forces on Guadalcanal, to a conference and promised him all the support he could provide.[16] Halsey's naval forces more than lived up to the promise (as described in Case Study 5). The administrative relief of Ghormley and replacement with Halsey had direct, beneficial consequences for Vandegrift's Marines.

VANDEGRIFT VERSUS PATCH

Vandegrift himself was no slouch when it came to ensuring that military administration contributed to, instead of detracted from, combat effectiveness. Despite the tenuous position of 1st Marine Division on Guadalcanal in

September 1942, the general was still called upon to attend to administrative matters. A number of promotions had occurred for officers of the division. So despite strenuous Japanese resistance, Commandant of the Marine Corps Thomas Holcomb requested that Vandegrift send some of those men, the ones now too senior for their combat billets, stateside to help form and train new units. In execution, Vandegrift used this policy to send home some officers whose performance in combat was less than ideal, reasoning that their on-the-ground perspective would still be valuable in training.[17] Meanwhile, he retained senior officers who had performed well in action, despite their seniority. Vandegrift deftly exploited this administrative burden as an opportunity to get the right people in the right place at the right time.

Later in the campaign, after Vandegrift was relieved by Major General Alexander Patch of the U.S. Army, administration of the ground forces on Guadalcanal was less efficient. One of the subordinate units of Patch's XIV Corps was 2nd Marine Division, sent in relief of 1st Marine Division. Second Marine Division, which had already been deployed to Reykjavik, in the European theater of operations but was new to the Pacific, was commanded by Major General John Marston IV. But because Marston was senior to Patch, and since the Army provided the majority of ground troops on Guadalcanal by that time, he was barred from accompanying his division to the island. Instead, command of 2nd Marine Division devolved to Brigadier General Alphonse DeCarre. For no tactical reason whatsoever, these Marines were deprived of the services of the commander they had formed and trained under.[18]

This was not the end of weird administrative arrangements during Patch's tenure on Guadalcanal. In January 1943, during the final offensive as the Japanese were withdrawing from the island, Patch detailed 147th and 182nd Army Regiments, along with 6th Marine Regiment, to form a division-sized unit under 2nd Marine Division Headquarters, reporting to General DeCarre. Rather than just attaching 147th and 182nd Regiments to 2nd Marine Division, Patch instead created a hybrid unit and essentially renamed DeCarre's division as the Combined Army-Marine Division, or CAM Division.[19] Fortunately, the Imperial Japanese Army units left on Guadalcanal, starving and employed in desperate rearguard actions, were in no position to exploit the time American commanders wasted on such bureaucratic niceties.

BUCKNER, GEIGER, AND STILWELL

It would not be the last time that administrative measures were employed in nonstandard ways in the Pacific theater. The initial landing-force commander during the Battle of Okinawa in 1945 was Lieutenant General Simon Bolivar Buckner Jr., USA. The Japanese defense on the island was one of the toughest yet encountered, stalling the American offensive. Whether this was due to Buckner's leadership is debatable, for as the battle wound down, the general was killed in action by Japanese artillery fire.[20]

Buckner was succeeded by Major General Roy Geiger, USMC, a tough and experienced veteran of Guadalcanal, Bougainville, Guam, and Palau Islands. Few Americans had seen more combat in the Pacific than Geiger. He commanded American forces on Okinawa for the remainder of the battle. Despite his success, and with the battle all but over, Geiger was replaced by an Army officer—General Joseph W. Stilwell—who had been pushing General Douglas MacArthur for command since before Buckner was killed, despite the fact that he was too senior for field command and had not held any command in the Pacific War.[21] Indeed, Stilwell had earlier been removed from his operational billet in China due to a consistent inability to work with other Allied commanders. Once again, service insecurity had taken precedence over administrative efficiency and combat effectiveness.

CONCLUSION

These vignettes demonstrate that the administration of military forces does not stop for combat operations and, therefore, cannot help but influence the warfighting capabilities of those forces. Like the other operational disciplines, administration can enhance—or diminish—combat effectiveness and pervades tactical actions throughout a campaign.

Administration is simultaneously an analytic- and a people-driven activity. The science of discipline is usually clear, but its application requires an understanding of humans individually and in aggregate. It requires judgment. The management of such processes does not stop when bullets stop flying. In fact, administration is even more important in combat, as the documentation of combat actions has real implications for the people involved who may later require medical or other kinds of support.

These are not unimportant functions. Indeed, they are vital. They have been left off the list of warfighting functions for too long. A commander must be concerned with internal and external administration and needs a competent staff able to efficiently and effectively administer to enable that officer to focus on the fight.

8 INFORMATION

We have found the tracks of 32 men and 3 donkeys.
— EGYPTIAN BORDER-PATROL REPORT, CIRCA 2000 BC

Combat runs on information. Without it, there would be no tactics, just wild, careening movements and random encounters. Commanders must at least know, or think they know, where the opposing force is likely to be, who it will be, and how they are likely to fight. From dust clouds to foot trails to targeting data pulled from satellites in orbit, information guides combat forces before, during, and after a fight.

Edward Luttwak has characterized combat between two similarly equipped forces—NATO and Soviet forces in a hypothetical battle in central Europe—as a competition to analyze the situation, make decisions on how to proceed, and then execute those decisions faster than the other side.[1] All things being roughly equal, such as in this head-on collision between the best and heaviest forces of two superpowers, the ability of one side to act and react faster than the other might well prove decisive. But the need for information to drive the actions and operations of military forces is imperative whether or not they are similarly equipped. John Boyd is another theorist who developed an entire theory of war around this idea.

As will be seen below, Boyd developed a model of competitive decision-making called the "Observe-Orient-Decide-Act Loop" (OODA Loop). At its core, it is a model of how an individual or an organization (such as a military staff) takes in information (observe), analyzes it (orient), makes a decision based on that information (decide), and then acts on it (act), which in turn changes the state of the information. Without intending to, Boyd produced a model of the information discipline.

For centuries, the information activity of military forces was focused on intelligence and counterintelligence. There is little more to say about it than what was captured in Sun Tzu's chapter on the employment of secret agents, what today is called human intelligence. Yet intelligence does not cover nearly all of the ways information is important to military forces, nor all the ways that they can exploit it today. The Napoleonic Revolution expanded the information requirements of military forces, and they have only grown larger since. **Information enables tactics by ascertaining relevant facts, figures, and knowledge regarding friendly forces, enemy forces, civilian populations, and the environment while preventing the opponent from doing the same.**

HISTORICAL SURVEY

ANCIENT

What is today known as information warfare, information operations, or influence operations (hereafter information warfare) is ancient. One of the earliest examples on record is Assyrian epic war poems. These were not mere artistic works, but rather meant to influence friendly and hostile populations to accept Assyrian rule. One of the earliest was that composed by King Adad-nirari I, which depicted not only military successes but also mercy toward the defeated, like the Kassites. These poems were displayed in palaces and also designed to be recited.[2] Some described recent operations in a twisted blend of public affairs and information operations, such as the epic of Assurnasirpal II:

> I built a pillar over against the city gate, and I flayed all the chief men who had revolted, and I covered the pillar with their skins; some I walled up within the pillar, some I impaled upon the pillar on stakes, and others I bound to stakes round about the pillar; many within the border of my own land I flayed, and I spread their skins upon the walls; and I cut off the limbs of the officers, of the royal officers who had rebelled. Ahiabab [the rebel leader] I took to Ninevah, I flayed him, I spread his skin upon the wall of Ninevah.[3]

The brutality depicted had a purpose and a message: resistance is futile. This is not just pure braggadocio. The political violence employed by Assurnasirpal was political communication, amplified after the fact through oral and architectural means. Assyrian war poems are an early example of information operations—communication to nonmilitary audiences meant to deter the need for warfare.

While spreading information is ancient, so is gathering it. In recent years, the U.S. military has had to create a system for gathering and assessing economic, regional, and ethnographic information about the various areas of operations within which it operates. But this need, too, is ancient. Alexander the Great did this for his campaigns, as did Julius Caesar. In fact,

Roman military forces had a well-developed information system, including specialized three-tiered reconnaissance forces: *procursatores* for close reconnaissance, *exploratores* for long-range reconnaissance, and *speculators* for even longer-distance investigations.[4]

Caesar is notable because he professionalized this system and valued information so highly that he granted such scouts the right to report directly to him rather than to subordinates. The effectiveness of his system was evident in his Gallic campaigns, in which he played tribes against each other and attacked not just military forces but also supply depots and lines of communication.[5]

Earlier Roman commanders also knew how to use information, especially to attack an opponent's morale. During the Second Punic War (218–202 BC), Roman forces had Hannibal's army besieged in southern Italy. Another Carthaginian army under his brother, Hasdrubal Barca, was en route through northern Italy to raise the siege. But unbeknown to Hannibal, a portion of the Roman forces left the siege, marched north, and annihilated Hasdrubal's army, then marched back to reinforce the siege lines. Hannibal and his men learned that no help would arrive when the Romans launched Hasdrubal's severed head into their camp.[6] One can imagine the effect on morale.

MEDIEVAL

Information was no less important to medieval militaries. Teutonic Knights employed scouts to travel roads in their area and write reports on navigation, terrain features, and other local conditions that were then compiled into guidebooks.[7] During the Hundred Years' War (1337–1457), both the English and the French employed networks of local spies in each other's territory.[8] Saladin, the twelfth-century Kurdish general, won territory using information alone. In a rapid campaign in 1174, he sent letters to opponents presenting himself as working in the interests of the legitimate emir, although this was not true. He took Damascus without resistance, then shortly thereafter Homs and Hama.[9] His expanded territory allowed Saladin to proclaim himself a sovereign in his own right.

The importance of information in warfare was enhanced during the Thirty Years' War, when the advent of the printing press and increasing literacy allowed the greater spread of information. The seventeenth century also saw the beginning of rudimentary newspapers and postal systems, spreading information about the movements of military forces and the outcomes of battles. Propaganda, distributed as posters and leaflets, immediately appeared, and civilians became more involved in warfare through commentary on the events, twisting information to benefit one side or the other.[10] Leaders' personal letters were released to embarrass and delegitimize them, and Gustavus Adolphus, one of the best generals of the age, wrote a public manifesto justifying his invasion of German lands to maintain popular support.[11]

The role of propaganda and information used to influence populations in support of military action skyrocketed during the English Civil War (1642–46). The British Library houses only four examples of newspapers from the country for 1641. By 1645, there were 722 publications.[12] The potential to use media as a form of information warfare ascended to a high art by the American Revolution. Both sides used media outlets to persuade colonists to join one side or the other. Some efforts, like Thomas Paine's *Common Sense* and *American Crisis*, had decisive effects that tilted support toward independence.[13] Benjamin Franklin succinctly summed up the potency of information: "Now, by the press, we can speak to nations; and good books and well written pamphlets have great and general influence. The facility with which the same truths may be repeatedly enforced by placing them daily in different lights in newspapers, which are everywhere read, gives a great chance of establishing them."[14]

Napoleon himself was a frequent employer and victim of information warfare. During his Egyptian campaign, the Royal Navy intercepted many of the expeditionary force's letters, including Napoleon's own. The British government simply reprinted any embarrassing letter from him and many of his officers in yearly published volumes to undermine the French effort.[15] During the Siege of Acre (1799), Royal Navy commodore Sydney Smith sent Napoleon recent newspapers from throughout Europe detailing the collapse of French military fortunes, even of revolts in France itself. Napoleon, realizing that he could expect no further help, abandoned the siege. The newspapers were not a deception; the reports were all true.[16]

During the American Civil War, Maj. Gen. Thomas J. "Stonewall" Jackson's Valley Campaign is frequently pointed to as an example of expert maneuver. In fact, Jackson's success was due more to excellent information. His small Confederate army was weak in everything except information. Jackson had lived in the Shenandoah Valley before the war and knew the ground.[17] He also employed on his staff a local civilian mapmaker, Jedediah Hotchkiss.[18] Finally, he had an excellent, if undisciplined, cavalry commander who understood reconnaissance.[19] Jackson's ability to rapidly outmaneuver Union forces was grounded in his more accurate understanding of his opponent and the environment.

Although Jackson did make mistakes, some based on faulty intelligence, Union commanders in the Shenandoah had little in the way of an intelligence system at this point, outsourcing it to an incompetent private firm. Jackson's principal opponent, Maj. Gen. Nathaniel Banks, continually operated on faulty and outdated information.[20] Utilizing a basic method of information operational art was the difference between the Confederate and Union forces in the Valley, not Jackson himself.

MODERN

As we have seen, Napoleon's staff system began the professional management of military information. For example, he was famous for being obsessive about maps, which are just codified information about terrain. But since his time, the number of information assets available to the commander have increased, and the influence of geography has in no way diminished.[21]

By World War I, new forms of information transmission enabled new forms of information warfare, such as electronic warfare and signals intelligence. The Eiffel Tower was even used to jam German wireless transmissions on the western front.[22] Wireless transmission also had drastic effects on naval warfare. Before this time, warships could almost disappear when at sea; they could not be contacted or found without wide area searches. Now, the signals of their communications could be detected and their locations ascertained and passed along to other ships.

For instance, Royal Navy ships under Rear Admiral Sir Christopher Cradock used electronic warfare when assigned to disrupt German naval activity. Their task was to find and defeat German cruisers, notably the *Scharnhorst* and *Gneisenau* under Vice Admiral Maximillian von Spee, in or around the Magellan Straits.[23] Cradock initially looked on the Pacific side, off the coast of Chile.[24] But when a wireless station on Suva in the Fiji Islands picked up a German transmission indicating the whereabouts of von Spee's squadron, Cradock was able to narrow his search.[25] On November 1, 1914, both the British and German squadrons found each other off the Chilean coast near Coronel via wireless signals. Von Spee knew that a British squadron was in the area. Cradock, however, believed that he had found an isolated enemy cruiser because the Germans were using only one ship's wireless set to hide the strength of their force.[26] The British ships, although outdated, could have defeated one of the more modern German cruisers had they caught it alone.

Both squadrons formed open formations to search for each other, then battle formation upon sighting each other.[27] The outdated British ships sailed directly into an ambush in which they were outgunned. The German squadron not only had the better position, with Cradock's ships silhouetted by the setting sun behind them, but also the longer reach, as *Scharnhorst* and *Gneisenau* outranged the available British guns. Two British ships, the *Good Hope* and the *Monmouth*, were sunk; a third fled to carry a warning to other British ships in the area. Sixteen hundred British sailors perished, while only three German sailors were wounded.[28]

While intelligence—processed and analyzed information about the enemy force—is just one component of the information operational art, it is a vital one. Intelligence has always been a key element of military operations, and not just for the inherent advantage of gaining information about the opponent. Intelligence also enables other aspects of information warfare, such as military deception. Regarding the Normandy invasion in 1944, it enabled the Allies to plan an effective military-deception operation in advance of the landings and check to see that it had worked.

In the Pacific theater, American decryption of Japanese codes enabled the victory at Midway (1942), which was decisive for regaining control of the Pacific. This intelligence work identified the date on which the Japanese fleet would attack Midway Island, allowing Admiral Nimitz to deploy forces to attack them as well as use ships in the Coral Sea to transmit fake radio traffic to convince the Japanese that an entire carrier group was still there.[29]

While ensuring that information can be acquired and preventing the enemy from doing the same are important, corrupting the quality of the information gained by the opposing force is also key. From the Trojan horse to today, military deception is a function of information operational art that must be managed by the staff.[30] Nor has the advance of surveillance and digital awareness reduced the opportunities for such trickery. In Kosovo during the 1990s, NATO warplanes dropped three thousand precision-guided munitions on Serbian targets. Only fifty actual targets were hit, but NATO destroyed five hundred decoys.[31]

THE INFORMATION DISCIPLINE

Clausewitz took it as a given that it is difficult for military organizations to acquire, process, and exploit information, and he was right. He had an expansive definition of intelligence—"By the word 'information' we denote all the knowledge we have of the enemy and his country; therefore, in fact, the foundation of all our ideas and actions"—that is more inclusive of information than it is strictly military intelligence.[32] Nor did information warfare escape his eye. In his *Principles of War*, a much earlier publication than *On War*, Clausewitz identifies three motivations—objects—of war, the third of which is "to gain public opinion."[33] Notions that he would not understand war in the information age, or that *On War* no longer applies in a "newly" information-saturated battlefield, are misguided.

There are numerous and competing definitions of information warfare, but the definition presented herein, following Clausewitz's lead, is a broad one: information warfare consists of everything a military force does to accurately sense and make sense of its interactions with its environment and enemy forces, preserve its ability to do so, and prevent the enemy from doing the same. It involves intelligence (gaining and analyzing information), operational security and secrecy (preventing the opponent from doing so), and deception and disinformation (corrupting the opponent's information). It is means agnostic. Signals intelligence, human intelligence, electronic warfare, and cyberwarfare, to name just a few, are means to gain, deny, or manipulate information.

ANALYSIS AND INTELLIGENCE

In current U.S. doctrine, intelligence remains a separate warfighting function from information. Actually, at the very least, they are too interconnected for that. Whether intelligence is a subcomponent of information is a different issue. Intelligence is not just information—it is information that has been acquired, processed, and analyzed based on its relevance for the commander, the staff, or the mission. The practice of intelligence is also not just gathering information. It is using information for prediction; making a judgment call on what the enemy will or will not do based on the information at hand. Its predictive nature distinguishes intelligence from information. But because it is dependent upon information, intelligence remains a subset of it.

The idea of what intelligence is has expanded since the Napoleonic Revolution. Today, information about almost anything could prove relevant to military operations. There is also no sure way to ascertain what information will be relevant and what will not, hence information must be gathered and then analyzed for its intelligence value. Traditional military staffs did not usually take such a broad view of information, believing in simply filtering out everything that was not obviously intelligence. Since military staffs have not evolved significantly since the creation of the general staff, neither has this conception of intelligence.[34]

This is not to diminish its importance. Military intelligence can and should have pride of place in any theory of information warfare; neither offensive nor defensive information warfare can be employed effectively without it. Yet it is important for staff officers to understand what intelligence is: information that has been analyzed to draw relevant conclusions. Lastly, while Western military doctrine generally views intelligence and information warfare as two different disciplines, this is not true of other militaries. The People's Liberation Army, for example, views intelligence as one of four subcomponents that compose information warfare.[35]

INFORMATION WARFARE

Information warfare is a dynamic competition. Both opponents engage in this process, can affect the other's process through offensive information warfare (such as military deception), and can protect their own process through defensive information warfare (such as operational security, cryptology, and so forth). Offensive information warfare is any use of intelligence to degrade, corrupt, deceive, or undermine the opponent. Defensive information warfare is any use of information to protect, conceal, mask, or deny the use of information by the opponent.

There are as many forms of information warfare as there are means of transmitting information. They include military deception, electronic warfare, cyberoperations, and psychological warfare, among others. It is important, however, not to confuse the means—such as radios or computers—of information warfare with the use of that information itself.

One way to conceptualize information is Boyd's OODA Loop. This was not its intended purpose, but a glance at the OODA Loop shows just how much Boyd was focused on information and the perception thereof.

This model is already suffused with the information aspects of military operations, and its greatest strength is its integration of perception and processing information to produce an action.

Adding some of the ways that military forces can perceive their environment on the front end—to the "observation" step—and some of the ways information can be exploited for comparative advantage to the end—under the "action" step—yields the following:

The OODA Loop was intended to show how military forces decide and act based on the supposition that acting and reacting faster than the opponent will yield victory. Perhaps unintentionally, Boyd has provided us with a solid explanatory framework for information warfare as the way in which

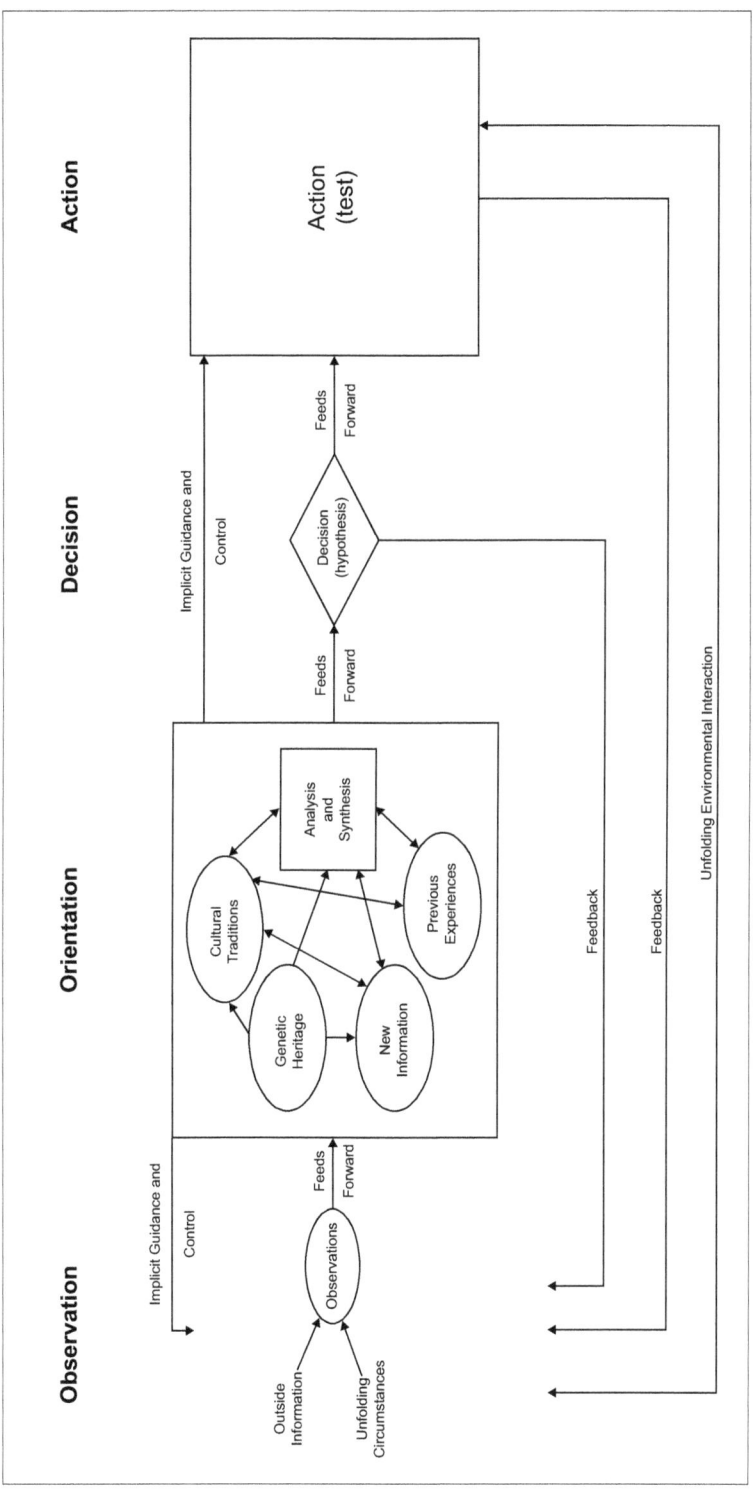

John Boyd's OODA Loop
Courtesy of Chris Robinson.

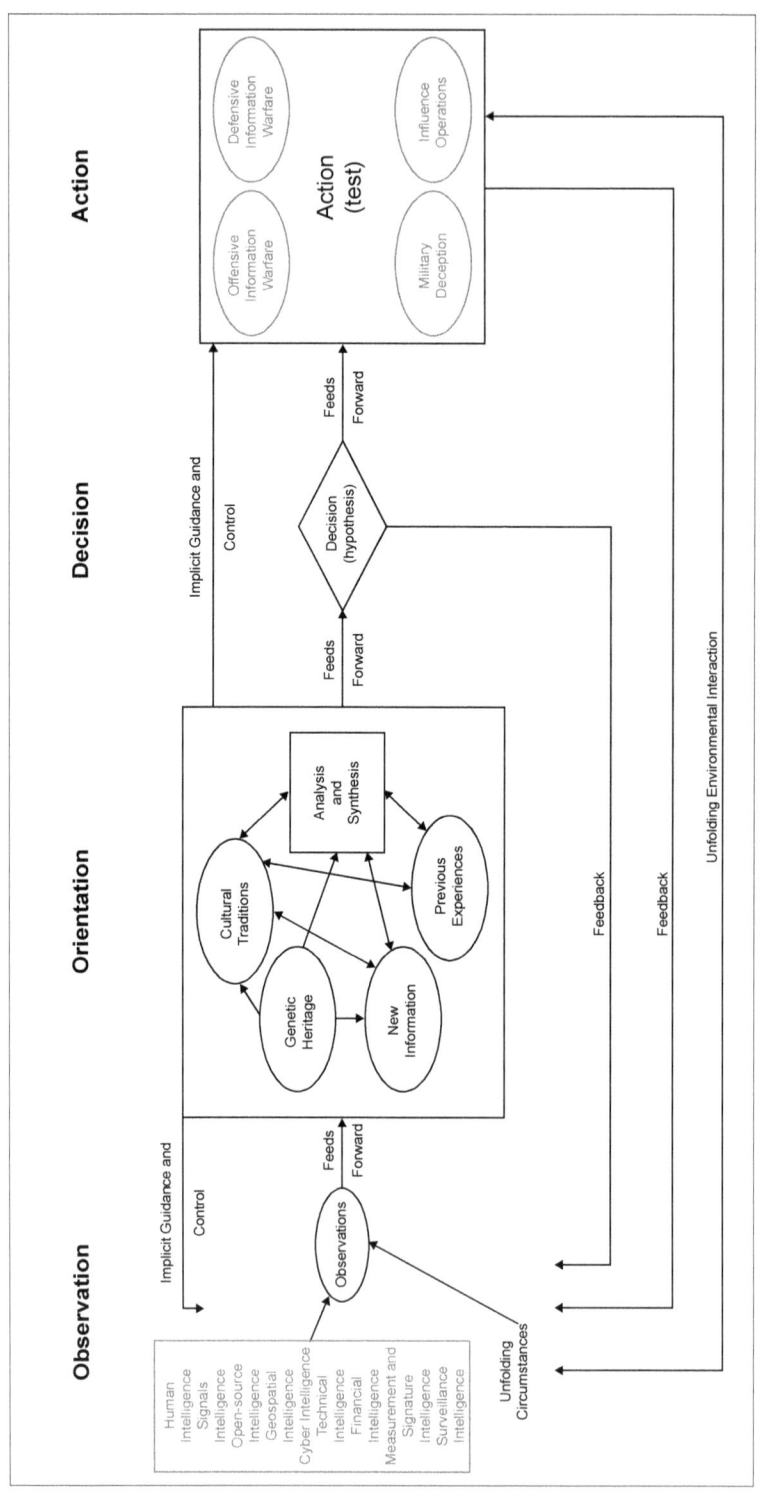

John Boyd's OODA Loop (Notated)
Courtesy of Chris Robinson.

military forces perceive their environment, the opponent, and themselves and manipulate the perceptions of the opponent and other audiences.

The idea of "outlooping" an opponent is clarified by these additions. The better an actor is at gathering, analyzing, and synthesizing accurate information through various means, the more effective the decision making and, consequently, the more effective the employment of offensive and defensive information warfare, military deception, and influence operations, as well as other combat arms. The longer this process goes on, and the faster it occurs, the further the opponent falls behind in the competition to execute decisions based on accurate information. There is a common misconception that the point of the OODA Loop is simply to charge through the process faster than the opponent. In reality, the quality of the process is what matters: speedily generating decisions and actions based on faulty information or poor processing thereof is a recipe for disaster. Protecting the quality of the process and, better yet, corrupting the opponent's process is the goal of the information staff.

Like most other military capabilities, information can be used offensively and defensively. Offensive information warfare involves the acquisition of information relevant to the campaign as well as attempts to distort, deceive, manipulate, or otherwise corrupt the information available to the opponent. Defensive information warfare involves the protection of information about friendly forces and the denial of that information to the opponent.[36]

MEANS OF INFORMATION WARFARE
RECONNAISSANCE AND COUNTERRECONNAISSANCE

Usually seen as an aspect of maneuver, reconnaissance and counterreconnaissance should be seen as a competition for information that, in turn, facilitates maneuver. The forces involved in conducting reconnaissance, or those conducting counterreconnaissance missions such as screening, are usually not the same ones that will perform a maneuver. They should also be designed for such missions. Recall that light cavalry forces were generally used for reconnaissance, while heavy cavalry forces were used for decisive attacks.

The number of military platforms capable of conducting reconnaissance, such as unmanned aerial systems, has multiplied in recent years. Although these capabilities tend to be used in permissive environments where opposing forces lack air-defense capabilities, the trend toward pervasive and persistent reconnaissance in modern warfare is clear. Counterreconnaissance capabilities, therefore, are becoming more important.

PUBLIC AFFAIRS

Public affairs is a vital tactical enabler, although it is not used for deception or manipulation. No military force can operate without the observation of local audiences and, in the modern era, global audiences. Absent a public-affairs effort, civilians will naturally form their own speculative impressions of what a military force is doing. These impressions, inevitably inaccurate, can then be manipulated by the opponent. A military force must forestall this through a planned and coordinated public-affairs effort to counteract both speculation and manipulation. Failing to do so cedes maneuver space and initiative to the opponent's information-warfare efforts. While this remains solely a defensive information-warfare capability, it is no less important.[37]

Although lacking many, but not all, of NATO's technological advantages, the Taliban since 2001 has waged a cohesive and sustained public-affairs campaign in Afghanistan that has stymied Western operations there. Using means as simple as letters and leaflets, it has controlled the information space from the beginning, a vital aspect of warfare for terrorist groups.[38]

CYBERWARFARE

Cyberwarfare is perhaps the only truly new form of information warfare. Its most obvious application is, of course, the acquisition of enemy information through the infiltration of digital networks, although there are myriad applications for deception and misinformation as well as simply attacking those systems to stop them from functioning. Defensive cyberwarfare involves the protection of friendly digital networks from the acquisition of information, deception, and denial of service. Cyberwarfare capabilities are generally classified at a high level, which makes public description difficult.

ELECTRONIC WARFARE

Electronic warfare is extremely important today, although this has been true for quite some time. Recall the French use of units on the Eiffel Tower to jam German transmissions during World War I. A number of effects can be achieved through electronic warfare. Jamming can shut down the opponent's command-and-control networks, for example, while electronic transmissions can be used to flood the information space with inaccurate or deceptive broadcasts.

Both offensive and defensive electronic warfare evolved along with aviation. During the "Battle of the Beams," the Luftwaffe developed a way to use radio beams to guide bombers to their targets. The British quickly learned to jam these transmissions.[39] During Vietnam, the U.S. Air Force began wide-scale suppression of air-defense radars by using "wild weasel" missiles that homed in on the units' electronic signature.[40] The development of such missiles and decoys led to ever more complex and integrated air-defense systems, combining layered antiaircraft missiles and detection measures to stave off aerial attacks.[41] Countermeasures to such systems appeared almost immediately. In 1982 the Israelis used unmanned aerial vehicles to force Syrian air defenses to fire, which revealed their positions to electronic detection, allowing the Israeli Air Force to target and destroy them.

MILITARY DECEPTION

Deception was covered in greater depth in *On Tactics*, but the information staff has a large role to play in a commander's ability to achieve it.[42] Although traditionally viewed as a function of intelligence, deception also depends on information, requiring knowledge of the opponent's ability to obtain information, likely interpretation of the deceptive information, and likely actions based on it. At its core, military deception is a corruption of the adversary's information processing. Although emergent technologies to obtain accurate information promise to reduce the possibility of deception, increasing the means to obtain accurate information also increases the vectors that can receive inaccurate information. Military deception, therefore, is likely to play a larger role in the future than in the past.[43]

The influence, importance, and potency of information in warfare will only increase as emergent technologies such as artificial intelligence, quantum computing, and data science continue to mature. These advances will likely offer both threats and opportunities for military forces, even replacing some of the simpler processes currently performed by humans. The potential for these technologies to increase the speed, efficiency, and accuracy of the vital information analysis that yields intelligence is great, but it remains to be realized.

CONCLUSION

Intelligence drives operations, and it takes information to generate intelligence. The information discipline is as unwieldy as it is critical, but separate disciplines for information and intelligence make little sense. Keeping the two aspects conceptually divided prevents deep coordination and integration, both within the discipline and with other disciplines, especially operations. No amount of technical means can foster integration without first getting the theory of their interaction correct. For all its technological wizardry, the United States has struggled with information warfare in Afghanistan, where the Taliban routinely uses "night letters" to influence the environment.[44] An understanding that information is an ancient operational art can help frame the problem and prevent distraction by the modern technological means to conduct it.

Almost everything that occurs on, near, or connected to combat involves information, whether military organizations recognize it or not. Even pure violence sends a message. The most important principle, of course, is that actions speak louder than words. Events on the battlefield can be "spun," though only to a degree.

British general Nick Carter, who has had extensive experience in command in Bosnia, Kosovo, Iraq, and Afghanistan, has observed, "As a commander you now live in a fish bowl; war is a theatre and you are a producer of a spectacle that must appeal to a range of audiences. For success is invariably defined by the triumph of the narrative."[45] As the world becomes increasingly suffused in the information revolution, the information discipline and information staff officers will become more and more important as commanders navigate the modern battlefield.

9 OPERATIONS

The plan of the battle fixes for each Division where, when, and how it is to fight—that is, it fixes <u>time</u>, <u>place</u>, and <u>form</u> of the combat.

— CARL VON CLAUSEWITZ

Maneuver is typically one of the warfighting functions, but the operations staff is often more concerned with the coordination of tactical units and supporting arms in many ways, not just in this one aspect of tactics. The other problem with considering maneuver an operational discipline is that it implies a focus on offensive means. The staff and its commander, however, must be concerned with both offense and defense. Maneuver fits better as a tactical tenet.[1] Additionally, the job of the operations staff is not just to coordinate maneuver but also other tactical tenets and the other functions of the staff. The coordination they perform is the art of ensuring that all friendly forces involved employ tactics at the appropriate time and place by orchestrating the efforts of the other staff functions.[2] The discipline of arranging time, space, and forces for advantage in combat appears in Clausewitz's early works (as quoted above) and is further developed in *On War*. This discipline could be called "coordination," but "operations" is used here in accordance with modern naming conventions for clarity.

The operations officers have the most tactical function on the staff; their responsibility is to position forces to execute the tactical movements desired by the commander, though always with an eye on the strategic goals. Thus, they are primarily concerned with time, space, and forces, ensuring that different tactical forces are employed at the right time and place to maximize their advantages and mitigate each other's disadvantages, that they are coordinated, and that they are sustained so as to ensure that their combination is greater than the sum of their parts. Operations is the discipline responsible for the employment and coordination of combat forces across time and space. Planning is the primary way this is accomplished, and combined arms is the goal. This is why the production of written orders resides with the operations staff, with the operations officer usually delegated tasking authority over subordinate units and staff sections by the commander. Operations as a discipline encompasses both the planning and synchronization functions as identified by Milan Vego.

The province of the operations staff is to design the array of forces available to support the plan, whether that array be focused on mobile, positional, or guerrilla warfare; offense or defense; methodical, plodding attrition or dynamic, maneuver-focused annihilation. No one mode is better or worse than any of the others, some are just more or less appropriate for the situation, mission, strategy, and the capabilities of the opposing forces. The coordination discipline of operational art is most directly related to tactics—that is, combat. Perhaps most importantly, the operations staff focuses the other disciplines of operational art. In the words of Clausewitz, "Every activity in War . . . relates to the combat directly or indirectly. The soldier is levied, clothed, armed, exercised, he sleeps drinks, eats, and marches, all merely to fight at the right time and place."[3] **Coordination (or operations) enables tactics by conducting and synchronizing tactical actions and operational disciplines across time, space, and the forces available.**

HISTORICAL SURVEY

A historical outline of the operational/coordination function as a whole would be an entire book, or many books, of which there are several examples. It will suffice here to summarize Archer Jones' concept of major "weapon systems" throughout the history of warfare. Jones identifies four major ancient weapon systems: light infantry, heavy infantry, light cavalry, and heavy cavalry. Although the details and equipment vary across time and cultures, this taxonomy captures the general unit types that could be employed.

Light infantry were lightly armored and armed with either a melee or a missile weapon. Such troops enjoyed greater mobility than more stoutly equipped counterparts but could not go toe to toe with them. Heavy infantry used stronger armor and shields and carried various kinds of melee weapons. They were, of course, slower, but when they fought in a dense formation such as a phalanx, they could not be easily attacked and overcome. The parameters are roughly the same for light and heavy cavalry but for the addition of a horse. Light cavalry forces were better for reconnaissance, skirmishing, and screening. Heavy cavalry forces delivered shock attacks.

Much of ancient warfare can be understood as the need to maneuver combinations of these four weapon systems so as to apply their strengths against the weaknesses of another unit. For example, light cavalry archers were strong against heavy infantry because they could fire their missile from range and the heavy equipment of the foot soldiers would prevent them from closing the distance.[4]

If a unit met one over which it had the advantage, it would almost always win the engagement so long as it played to its strengths. Heavy infantry would defeat light infantry if they fought hand to hand, but if light infantry used its mobility to avoid such combat, it would not. Cavalry usually always had an advantage over foot, except when heavy infantry stayed in densely packed formations.

These four weapon systems pertained during the Middle Ages. The exception was the ascendancy of heavy cavalry in the West, where knights on horseback became the dominant weapon system due to a number of political, not just military and technological, reasons. There were also a number of other exceptions. The Arab armies that confronted the Crusaders used both light cavalry and light infantry—although not exclusively—to great effect. Swedish troops mimicked the Greek phalanx, deploying tightly packed formations of infantry armed with eighteen-foot-long pikes.[5] The Germans soon copied them. English light infantry armed with the longbow proved to be another successful deviation. All of these alternative methods were dominant—for a time—until units and tactics were developed to mitigate their strengths.

Once technological advances in missile weapons, especially firearms and cannon, occurred, infantry gained the ascendancy over cavalry, which afterward were mostly used for reconnaissance and scouting, with occasional charges against exposed flanks. During the premodern era, artillery performed the long-range firepower function once the province of siege weapons and missile troops.

In the modern era, when horses were replaced by motorized and mechanized vehicles, cavalry of a sort again gained an ascendancy. But antitank guided missiles reasserted parity between the four major weapon systems.

Classifying weapon systems based on their strengths and weaknesses, as Jones does, assists staff officers in planning for their employment. Different units—land, sea, or air—have different characteristics that make them uniquely effective—or uniquely vulnerable—against others. It is the task of the operations staff to coordinate combinations of the various units available to take advantage of their strengths and to cover for their vulnerabilities. The term for this is "combined arms," and from Alexander the Great to today, militaries that successfully combine arms of different characteristics are superior to masses of like units. Combined arms seems simple, but it is easy to forget and exceedingly difficult for military forces to master. Even advanced and experienced militaries fail to coordinate arms effectively. When Chinese forces attacked the U.S., Republic of Korea, and U.N. forces in North Korea in 1950, achieving surprise was their key to success. American units that were deployed to maintain combined arms were better able to recover from that surprise. The U.S. X Corps, under Maj. Gen. Edward Almond, was so widely dispersed throughout the battlespace that units could not support each other. One of these, 1st Marine Division under Maj. Gen. O. P. Smith, stayed concentrated for mutual, combined-arms support. While the rest of X Corps collapsed under the Chinese assault, the 1st Marine Division was able to operate cohesively and fight its way out with the survivors.[6]

A THEORY OF OPERATIONS

Laying out the strengths and weaknesses of various military units across history would be a monumental task. The following concepts describe combinations in general that can assist operations planning to manage the time, space, and forces aspect of a campaign.

Clausewitz covered "assembly of forces in space" in book 3, chapter 11 of *On War* and "assembly of force in time" in the following chapter. He refers back to these concepts, along with the use of military forces, throughout the rest of his volume. This three-dimensional view of operations is remarkably flexible, covering the full range of ways to arrange tactical forces across time in a given space. In the chapter on time, he refers to "men, time, and space" as the "elements" of combat.[7] Milan Vego refers to these as operational factors.[8] However they are labeled, it is the job of the operations staff to coordinate them.

OPERATIONS AND SPACE

There are a number of theories on how combat forces should be employed and coordinated across time and space. None are inherently superior to any other; some are just more appropriate for the time and place, the friendly forces available, the opposing forces, and the constraints and restraints on the operations staff. The art of the discipline is assessing and deciding on a method that accounts for those factors. How the operations staff visualizes and conceptualizes the battlespace and the tactical situation can have a great effect on the outcome.

FORCE-TO-SPACE RATIO

Force-to-space ratios are intimately connected with the initiative. An inadequate force-to-space ratio permits the adversary to use space to both avoid battle and to find weak points such as flanks. Across history, a sufficient force-to-space ratio has usually been necessary to being an opponent to battle. The side with a better ratio for the terrain at hand can dictate the locale and pace of tactical engagements.[9] Conversely, if both sides have a high force-to-space ratio, then it can produce a stalemate, such as the western front of World War I. Analyzing this ratio for a given mission and the available terrain can yield insight into which tactics are supportable—and which are not.

Force-to-space ratios are a special concern for naval forces, as a commander will rarely have a favorable ratio, given the vastness of the oceans. The ability to first find the opponent and then force him to fight is a rare commodity for fleets. This is why maritime terrain such as chokepoints between land formations has been incredibly important to naval warfare: restricted waterways offer a chance to force an opponent to fight. Air operations feature high space-to-force ratios, as airspace can be contested, not controlled, and completely lacks for chokepoints or other intervening terrain.

ASYMMETRIC EMPLOYMENT: WEIGHTING THE MAIN EFFORT

A key goal for managing the time-space-forces aspect of a campaign is to generate opportunities for maneuver. Maneuver is facilitated by asymmetry, concentrating combat power at a place and time that is advantageous. Asymmetric employment is accomplished through the designation of a main effort and supporting efforts. The main effort, sometimes referred to as the commander's "bid for success," is the force designated to perform the decisive portion of the plan; it is usually "weighted" in some way, either by simply being larger than adjacent forces or receiving key enablers and priority for support. Supporting units have tasks that are no less important but instead facilitate the actions of the main effort, such as fixing an enemy force to prevent it from interfering with the main effort.

These roles are not static and can shift based on the situation. They are usually accompanied by the designation of a reserve force, units held back to deal with unforeseen circumstances or used to exploit the success of the main effort.

Another view of asymmetric employment is the indirect approach, made famous by Sir Basil Liddell Hart.[10] This method can be summed up as favoring flanking, enveloping, or otherwise unexpected lines of attack rather than more direct ones. This also involves maneuvering against an opponent's lines of communication to induce them to give up on their chosen defensive or offensive position, forcing them to relocate or to fight at a disadvantage. The campaign that exemplifies the approach is Major General William T. Sherman's effort to capture Atlanta in 1864 during the American Civil War. During this campaign, Sherman only gave battle where he wanted. Whenever his Confederate opponents established a defense, he dislocated it by maneuvering around it, making the position irrelevant rather than just trying to destroy it. This approach worked because Sherman had the time and space available to complete these maneuvers. At this same time in the eastern theater, where Major General George Meade faced General Robert E. Lee's Army of Northern Virginia, the terrain was much more restricted and the need for a decision, given the proximity of Washington, D.C., and Richmond, more immediate. Meade, at the direction of Lieutenant General Ulysses S. Grant, adopted a far more direct approach. Neither method was inherently superior to the other, just more appropriate to the time, space, force ratio, and circumstances of the theater.

Asymmetric maneuver is usually facilitated by an economy of force. While it is usually presented as a principle of war and almost always independently, it is, in fact, the converse of weighting the main effort. As a guide, it is committing just enough forces in nondecisive areas to permit the commitment of more forces in the decisive area. In order to achieve asymmetry by weighting a main effort, other supporting efforts must be completed with a minimum amount of forces, hence economizing the force. This is not to say, however, that supporting efforts should not have the resources required to complete their mission. Weighting the main effort is as subject to the law of diminishing returns as anything else.[11]

INTERIOR AND EXTERIOR LINES

Interior and exterior lines refer to the relationship between the arrayed combat forces and the lines of communication on which those forces can shift from one place to another. There is an element of time, based on sheer geometric principles, to this idea; the force with interior lines can generally shift forces to meet contingencies faster than an opponent operating on exterior lines. Conversely, the opponent operating on exterior lines usually has more space to maneuver, thus more options, than the opponent operating on interior lines.

Napoleon used this concept to great effect, but by no means did he invent it. Trusting his troops' fighting and marching ability, he would interpose his army between two opposing armies, concentrate his forces, and then turn on one opponent, then the other, preventing the two opposing forces from combining against him. This was not always successful: it notably failed at Waterloo, where the Prussian army under Field Marshal Gebhardt von Blücher managed to attack the French flank as Napoleon was arrayed against the British.

Antoine-Henri Jomini, a member of Napoleon's staff, defined interior lines as "those adopted by one or two armies to oppose several hostile bodies, and having such a direction that the general can concentrate the masses and maneuver with his whole force in a shorter period of time than it would require for the enemy to oppose to them a greater force." Exterior lines he described as those that "lead to the opposite result, and are those formed by an army which operates at the same time on both flanks of the enemy, or against several of his masses."[12]

While Napoleon was a master of using interior and exterior lines, earlier examples abound. In 207 BC, at the height of the Second Punic War, Hasdrubal Barca invaded Italy with a Carthaginian army and had a good chance of pinning the Roman army between him and his brother Hannibal, whom the Romans had besieged in the south. Appraised of his arrival, however, the Roman consul Gaius Claudius Nero exploited his interior position between the two Carthaginian forces to quickly turn on Hasdrubal's army and destroy it. He then returned to maintain the siege before Hannibal even realized the Roman army had shifted.[13] The Siege of Petersburg in 1865 is another example. General Grant has been criticized for pushing Meade into direct attacks on the rebel lines, but these attacks forced the Army of Northern Virginia to extend its forces to meet them. Although Lee's Confederates were operating on interior lines and could shift troops quickly, Grant knew that he had enough forces to maintain his strength throughout his exterior position and that Lee could not receive reinforcements to maintain his own throughout. The Union general created a situation where no matter what Lee did to maneuver, eventually the rebel general would simply run out of forces to hold his lines. Grant obviated Lee's greatest strength in his interior position, and the result was inevitable. Mass tends to enable the advantages of exterior lines, while maneuver tends to enable the advantages of interior lines.

OPERATIONS AND TIME

The primary concern of the operations staff when it comes to time is the culminating point. Every offensive campaign will either culminate or attenuate at some point, but it must not do so too early.[14] Just as the operations must conceptualize the battlespace, it must conceptualize the timing of the campaign to stave off culmination until the mission is accomplished and to synchronize the tactical actions of the forces available.

SEQUENCING

The most common method of controlling a campaign's timing is sequencing, organizing the tactical actions by phases. Phases should feed into the next—that is, establishing support bases that then supply the maneuver forces that then seize the objectives. Phases can be event driven or time driven. Jim Storr writes, "If an echelon force is to be committed, it should be triggered by events (tactical success) rather than by time. Programmed attacks planned in advance rarely maintain the momentum of the advance."[15]

Proper sequencing does not merely synchronize forces, it can assist the staff in avoiding the culminating point by ensuring that support reaches tactical units at the right time and can help commanders avoid committing forces piecemeal, or in a disjointed manner.

SIMULTANEITY

Simultaneity is a Russian concept for producing shock.[16] It seeks to employ all the available combat arms against the opponent at the same time—not necessarily at the same place—to induce paralysis, as the opponent cannot focus on one without making themselves vulnerable to others. The simultaneous application of all available forces was intended to achieve two things: first, to prevent the opponent from maneuvering against any one part of the Soviet forces, and second, to prevent the opponent's tactical withdrawal.[17]

Operations research supports the aim of simultaneity. Achieving shock is strongly associated with success, second only to achieving surprise. But it is not just connected with time, as in the Soviet concept. Simultaneity is also connected with maneuver, specifically rapid movement and changing circumstances.[18] Thus, there is a space component that the operations staff must balance with time to achieve shock.

PERSISTING AND RAIDING CAMPAIGNS

Historian Jones identifies two "strategies"—persisting strategies and raiding strategies—that are actually types of campaigning.[19] A raiding campaign is transitory, one intended to meet a certain objective and then end, either through withdrawal or some other means. A persisting campaign is long term, although not necessarily open ended. It may have a certain objective as well, but the force designated to achieve it is prepared to operate for a long period of time, perhaps indefinitely.

The staff must identify the type of campaign that is necessary to achieve the mission and the commander's intent and make arrangements to enable and sustain either a raiding or persisting—a short-term or a long-term—campaign.

SEQUENTIAL VERSUS CUMULATIVE CAMPAIGNS

Admiral J. C. Wylie divided strategies into either sequential or cumulative strategies, or to use his own term, "operational patterns." In a sequential campaign, each action or phase flows from the previous one and is dependent on its outcome. In a cumulative campaign, actions are independent (though not sequentially interdependent). Each tactical action may be aimed at the same goal, but each is an individual "plus or minus" toward that goal.[20]

OPERATIONS AND FORCES
ANNIHILATION VERSUS EXHAUSTION

Annihilation (*Niederwerfungsstrategie*) and exhaustion (*Ermattungsstrategie*) are two concepts expounded by the German military historian Hans Delbrück (1848–1929). German military thinkers of the time focused on annihilation: defeating enemy forces in fast, massive campaigns focused on inflicting attrition to the point that the opponent can no longer resist.

Delbrück's deep study of history, captured in his *History of the Art of War*, led him to identify another method: slowly wearing down the opponent over time rather than attempting to outfight him quickly and in mass. Delbrück believed that neither of these two forms were necessarily superior, but a commander may have to choose one or the other. Some military forces lack the resources or ability to seek annihilation and therefore must pursue exhaustion. The key difference is time, and the operations staff must balance the resources and missions to employ the form that is more appropriate for the problem at hand.[21]

THE INDIRECT APPROACH

Although already discussed, Liddell Hart's indirect approach is worth reiterating. In his influential book *Strategy*, he examined a number of campaigns throughout European history and found that commanders succeeded more often when they attacked their opponent indirectly—however that may be—than directly.[22] He was primarily thinking spatially:

a flanking or envelopment attack is always better than a frontal attack against a point where the enemy is ready to receive it. Liddell Hart subsequently built an entire theory of strategy around this simple observation.

A staff should assess the mission and situation at hand and try to ascertain an indirect way to approach it, which may be less likely to be recognized by the opponent, or exploit friendly advantages. But there is not always an indirect approach available; direct approaches are sometimes necessary. Both methods can and should be combined where possible.

MANEUVER WARFARE VERSUS ATTRITION WARFARE

The dichotomy between maneuver and attrition has been expressed many times, although the most influential version is that in the U.S. Marine Corps' foundational philosophy, MCDP 1, *Warfighting*. That doctrine defines attrition warfare as a philosophy that "seeks victory through the cumulative destruction of the enemy's material assets by superior firepower," then goes on to define maneuver warfare as a philosophy that seeks to attack "the enemy system—to incapacitate the system systematically."[23] Importantly, attrition and maneuver are depicted as poles on a spectrum, where attrition warfare tends to leverage centralized control along with the tactical tenets of mass and firepower, while maneuver warfare tends to leverage decentralized command and control, maneuver, tempo, and shock.

Warfighting portrays maneuver warfare as the superior philosophy for the Marine Corps based on its institutional strengths and weaknesses, constraints, and statutory missions.[24] Other military organizations may have different institutional characteristics so that it favors a different point on this spectrum. Staff officers should take institutional philosophies into account, along with the intended campaign goals, to achieve a good mix between attrition and maneuver, both of which may be more appropriate for the operational situation at different times and places and for the various units involved.

AIR OPERATIONS

Coordination is key for aviation units, the goal being to ensure that the right airframe is in the right airspace at the right time and that sufficient air assets are "on station" based on the limitations of technology. Aircraft must frequently land to rest aircrews, refuel, and rearm.

Matching particular airframes to the mission involves the management of time, space, and forces. Matching their strengths and weaknesses with the mission, the time it needs to occur, and the range from the point of departure to the target and back is a gargantuan task, demanding a professional staff able to do it well, quickly, and repeatedly.

NAVAL OPERATIONS

Naval fleets and task forces have always needed to combine ships of different classes to create flexible and resilient combinations. At sea, combined arms is simply inherent. The requirements and constraints of space and time can be taken for granted by land-focused observers, who see only wide open seas and ships that can carry a great deal of sustenance. Any mariner, however, will scoff at this: the ocean is not just space, and keeping ships at sea is no easy task.

Key terrain, always a concern for the soldier, is no less important for the sailor.[25] Restricted or open waters can magnify or mitigate the strengths and weaknesses of the vessels available. This has not changed as the primary weapon of warships has transitioned from the ram, to the cannon, and to aircraft and missiles. This includes the depths as well since the invention of the submarine.

CONCLUSION

Only three traditional operational factors—space, time, and forces—are covered here. More research and thought is necessary before potential factors such as cyber and outer space can be considered in full. In truth, a chapter on the operations discipline—the coordination of tactical forces in time and space—is insufficient. There are many books on the subject, and this discussion is simply an introduction to some concepts and philosophies about how it should be accomplished. It is included merely to illustrate how the discipline revolves around the management and conceptualization of space, time, and tactical forces.

We will revisit Clausewitz's offense and defense concepts, Jones' persisting and raiding concepts, and Delbrück's annihilation and exhaustion concepts as ways to evaluate space, time, and forces in a later chapter.

10 FIRE SUPPORT

A battery of field artillery is worth a thousand muskets.
—William Tecumseh Sherman

The use of firepower to support a campaign is not as simple as it sounds. While the tacticians involved in any individual engagement would surely rather just call in supporting firepower to annihilate the opposing forces, the staff must balance the awesome destructive effects of such weaponry with the need to husband it, protect it, and coordinate it with the other operational functions.[1]

The coordination, sustainment, and employment of a military force's long-range, large-caliber weapon systems is of vital concern to commanders. But this is so complex that they cannot manage it on their own; if they try, they risk becoming consumed by mere targeting rather than focusing on actual command. The logistics burden of fire support is high, but so is the payoff when properly employed. **Fire support enables tactics by applying the force's long-range, stand-off, and heavy weapons in support of its other components.** It is differentiated from other aspects of operational art because, while fire support is critical, it is not decisive in and of itself.

HISTORICAL SURVEY

Fire-support systems, the platforms built to deliver munitions, have drastically changed over time. Despite this, their function during campaigns has not. Since the earliest times of catapults and ballistae, such systems have been ideally suited to breaking up opposing maneuver forces, enabling friendly maneuver, and reducing fortifications.

As early as the Mongol invasion of Europe in 1241–42, a new function was added. The Mongols used gunpowder devices to create smoke and noise on the battlefield to obscure actions and confuse opponents.[2] Since then, it has been not just the actual destructive force of firepower that commanders and staffs must consider but also the effects of other types of munitions. Fire support tends to overlap with information, especially in modern times.

Fire support came into its own with the introduction of cannon artillery. Cannons may have existed in China as early as 1132, although gunpowder had been in use even earlier.[3] They were first employed in the West at Crecy in 1346. In that case, however, only a few weak pieces were present, and they were not decisive contributions to the English victory.[4] In 1380 the Venetians were the first to use cannon to breach fortress walls at Borondolo.[5]

By the beginning of the fifteenth century, cannons were ubiquitous throughout European armies and states, both for sieges and battles. This led to a division between siege artillery, generally much larger and very difficult, if not impossible, to move, and field artillery, which was small and mobile enough to accompany units on the march. Horse artillery was the smallest variant, so named because it was small and adroit enough to accompany and support cavalry.

Breech-loading artillery appeared around the turn of the twentieth century.[6] In 1897 the French army developed a breech-loading gun called the "75," or "French 75," which could fire thirty-four rounds a minute.[7] Not only was it faster than the typical muzzle-loading artillery of the time, since rounds were loaded from the rear of the piece, it remained steady during the firing process. The 75 could also project a round roughly five times farther than previous guns, upward of 8,500 meters.[8]

Initially, the 75s were still intended to be used against visible targets. Aiming cannon indirectly—without sighting in on the target itself—was developed as early as 1888.[9] Once guns were capable of firing at targets from many kilometers away, however, these methods were mastered and systematized. A battery commander, usually in charge of roughly six guns, would personally move forward to observe the target and communicate calculations back to his guns, well out of view.

During World War I, German artillery officer Colonel Georg Bruchmüller developed a system to coordinate artillery fire above the battery level using data on the guns location and atmospheric conditions to calculate where rounds would land before they were fired. This capability was a key component in the German spring offensive of 1918.[10] The French developed similar predictive-fire capabilities, borrowing methods from their coastal-artillery branch.[11] During the interwar period, centralized fire-direction centers were developed to perform these calculations.[12]

World War II saw the introduction of rocket artillery to perform many of the same functions as cannon artillery. Italians, Germans, and U.S. Marines pioneered the use of aircraft to provide fire support to ground forces before the war, but by 1945, close air support as understood today was developed by

Marines in the Pacific theater. Since then, all forms of fire support, along with mortar systems, have become more potent and precise. Although conducting fire support by calculation is still standard across major militaries, precision munitions with internal guidance systems are proliferating around the world.

THE FIRE SUPPORT DISCIPLINE

Fire support can be used simplistically, employed merely to destroy opposing forces. But it is more potent when coordinated with other actions. A common aphorism is that artillery conquers, infantry occupies. It is not as simple as that, but fire support that is planned and employed to facilitate maneuver—as well as combined with other arms—is truly valuable to the commander.

FIRE COMBAT VERSUS CLOSE COMBAT

In an early work on tactics, Clausewitz divided combat into two forms: fire combat and close combat. Close combat refers to the direct application of an infantry unit (or charging cavalry) against another, as in a bayonet charge. Every action leading up to and preparing the way for that assault, including artillery fire and the massed volleys of the infantry, is fire combat. Essentially, it is the use of supporting arms and, in modern militaries, crew-served weapons, prior to closing with enemy forces.

For Clausewitz, close combat is defined by its certainty. The only way to be certain that an enemy force is defeated is to force it off its position and seize that ground. It also creates an impression of certainty in the mind of the enemy combatants, generating greater fear and sense of danger than fire combat. Nothing accomplishes this feat like an infantry assault.[13]

The difference between fire combat and close combat comes down to the psychological effect each produces. Although supporting arms have much greater potential for destruction, that destruction is only ever probable. Even modern precision-guided munitions only have a high *probability* of successful destruction, never certainty. With fire combat, the target always hopes for escape. Close combat, however, carries with it the certainty that the opponent is right there, or about to be, and has come to kill you. While being subject to either of these forms of combat is unpleasant, the psychological effect is different, and close combat imposes its will more readily than fire combat.

While this is one of Clausewitz's ideas that needs to be viewed in a more modern context, the difference between close combat and fire combat neatly captures the role of fire support—enabling maneuver—and the role of infantry, armor, and other similar forces in the assault.

OBSERVATION, PROCESSING, AND DELIVERY

Fire support does not just require weapons platforms, it also requires observation. To hit a target, the target must be seen and tracked. In other words, weapons must be paired with sensors, even if that sensor is the human eye. The information gained through observation then must be processed in some manner (recall the information discipline and the difference between information and intelligence). Only once these are accomplished can fires be delivered.

When it comes to artillery, a scout or other unit that requests support performs the observation, a fire-direction center processes the information, and cannons finally fire. There are similar processes for close air support. But these aspects can also be applied to emerging forms of fire support, such as electronic attack and offensive cyberwarfare. A target must be identified, information must be processed (perhaps by an actual server), and then some form of targeted action must be delivered. Delivery is the actual application of the means, which falls in the realm of tactics.

TARGETING

When it comes to planning, preparing, sustaining, and coordinating the above means, no commander has been lucky enough to be able to employ an unlimited amount of fire support. The logistical burden of both the platform itself and the ammunition required is immense. (The same applies to the networks required for cyberwarfare, for example.) Staff officers thus face a pervasive question: what to target with fire support and what not to target?

The process by which those questions are answered is targeting. This must balance a number of factors but especially precision and accuracy. These two concepts are not the same. Precision is the ability to hit the intended target. Accuracy is a judgment on whether the desired target was hit.[14] Targeting is an operational-art process whereby staffs fuse and coordinate available information and capabilities, preparing for eventual combat by prioritizing where and when fire support will be applied. The actual application of those means against the chosen targets is the realm of tactics.

WEAPONEERING

Weaponeering is matching the munition with the target. Different munitions have different effects, and each is better at different fire support tasks than others. There is a science to it as well as an art.

The *science* of weaponeering is called "technical fire direction" for surface-to-surface fires. It is the mathematics, ballistics, and physics of getting the explosive from one point to another. The science tells the fire-support staff what is physically possible.

The *art* of weaponeering is called "tactical fire direction," and it relies not on physics but on the judgment of the staff officers responsible. It might be possible to hit a target, but what is the best munition to use against it? Is there a higher-priority target for that munition? Is it safe to hit the target, or are civilians or friendly forces too close?

These same questions apply equally to aviation fires, naval fires, and other supporting arms such as electronic warfare and cyberwarfare (where they have offensive capabilities). The answers to these questions depend on the effects desired.

EFFECTS

Beyond its destructive capabilities, fire support can support tactical units through a number of other effects. These include obscuration (preventing opposing forces from detecting friendly ones), signaling (through the use of flares and illumination rounds), and illumination. Emergent capabilities, such as cyberwarfare, have a range of other effects.

The problem for the staff is that if the available fire support is performing these tasks, they are not performing others, especially lethal fires. The assigned staff has to balance the risks and rewards of both lethal and nonlethal fire support, the weapons and ammunition available, and the effect of weather on availability and accuracy with the mission and the plan.

EMERGENT FIRE-SUPPORT CAPABILITIES

Based on the above principles and aspects of fire support, there are a number of emergent capabilities that fit into this category and can potentially be employed in similar manners. These are forms of information warfare, cyberwarfare, and other electronic attacks.

Although these capabilities are too technical to discuss in depth, the problems they present for the staff officer are the same: a target must be detected, the means to strike it must be identified (and available), other options must be evaluated and prioritized, and the desired effect must be coordinated with other actions. Many of these emergent capabilities thus can be employed like traditional fire-support platforms.

CONCLUSION

The importance of fire support has, perhaps obviously, increased as the firepower of the systems themselves has increased. The coordination of fire support became extremely complex with the advent of indirect fires, in which the gunners themselves cannot see the target and must trust others to verify the target's location, that it is hostile, and the accuracy of the fire itself. Making fire-support arrangements, validating them, and then executing them properly in combat consumes a great deal of a staff's energy.

11 LOGISTICS

History knows many more armies ruined by want and disorder than by the efforts of their enemies.

— **Cardinal Richelieu**

Nothing happens without logistics. Warfare is, at its core, organized violence, and the first aspect of that organization is the equipping and moving of military forces. The discipline of logistics encompasses not just moving forces but also sustaining them. Jomini's definition from *The Art of War* is, "The practical art of moving armies . . . , providing for the successive arrival of convoys of supplies . . . , [and] establishing and organizing lines of supplies." This encompasses moving combat forces, supplying them, and securing the lines of communication through which supplies and troops must transit. It is commonly referred to as "sustainment" on the lists of the warfighting functions, but this encompasses much more than just sustainment. The importance of logistics demands a more comprehensive understanding. The protostaffs that existed prior to Napoleon were almost all focused on logistics and finance. Modern staffs later grew from these logistics and finance staffs. The first recognizably modern staff officer was the quartermaster general, charged with moving ahead of armies and finding billets.[1]

There is also an aspect of "cold calculation" to logistics, which has led it to be understudied, although few deny its importance.[2] George Thorpe, author of *Pure Logistics*, likens the discipline to the stage management of a theater production: the audience is interested in actors and lines and props, but they do not care about the gritty details necessary to put on the play.[3] Because these gritty details are necessary for everything else in militaries, logistics is the foundation of operational art. In fact, some have argued that if there is a level between tactics and strategy, it is actually logistics. **Logistics enables tactics by facilitating the movement and sustainment of tactical forces.**

HISTORICAL SURVEY

For centuries, the primary focus of logistics was food, fodder, and water. Food could not be reliably stored for long nor easily prepped on the march, and the transportation of food via livestock required obtaining fodder, compounding the logistical problem.

Most armies were tied to reliance on local food sources, and then only during the right seasons of the year. Opposing armies competed with each other for this forage, as both had to live off the land when they were in close proximity. Scorched-earth tactics to deprive an opponent of sustainment were effective and common, though they could backfire too. Concentration of forces intensified the problems of supply even further. The arrival of an army, friendly or not, did not portend anything good for local populations.

The exception was naval logistics. Although ships were not able to reliably navigate and could not store enough water to sail for more than short periods of time, transporting food stocks via ships helped sustain large armies ashore, such as the massive Persian invasion of Greece in 480–479 BC. But naval logistics could become a vulnerability as well. In this effort, land battles did not defeat the Persians, but the Greeks achieved several naval victories, after which Xerxes could no longer logistically support his invading army.[4]

Alexander the Great was one of the first commanders to minimize baggage and camp followers, utilize planned lines of communication to sustain sieges, and plan army movements based on the availability of local supplies.[5] His fastest and most successful campaigns occurred in coastal regions, where he could be supplied from ships.[6] He also fought the Persian navy indirectly through its logistical needs, capturing Persian ports from the landward side and thus depriving the navy from sustainment.

After Alexander, the Romans became the masters of logistics in the ancient world. The famous Roman road network, still in use in some places today, was designed in part to solve military logistics problems. This extensive network provided the Romans the ability to communicate across the vast empire and to move and supply troops. Both improved roads and agricultural methods tended to increase the range and size of the imperial armies.

Military logistics is so profoundly influential that it shaped society itself in the wake of the collapse of the Roman Empire. After the disappearance of the professional legions, local rulers needed security but lacked the funds to pay for it outright, leading to a system whereby control of land and its inhabitants was delegated by rulers in exchange for military service. This became known as feudalism in the West.

These logistics methods and constraints pertained until the late medieval period, when a number of societal and technological improvements—including better division of labor and increased productivity—enabled the support of large armies without the need for the delegation of control of land. Access to more wealth also led to the use of mercenary armies. The technical duties of supply, handled by military professionals under the Romans, now became the responsibility of private contractors.[7]

Despite these improvements, along with the late medieval rise of merchant naval shipping, armies still had to rely on local sourcing for much of their sustenance. By the Thirty Years' War, commanders began to attempt making local purchasing arrangements due to the increased size of armies. Some commanders, such as the Bohemian count Mansfield, were successful. But looting and pillaging remained such a problem that armies had to contend not just with their battlefield opponents but also with local insurgents who fought back against looting troops, sometimes quite effectively.[8] The tactical plans of commanders were also, at times, limited by the necessities of logistical support.

It was during this period that formal logistics systems began to appear, especially in the form of magazines. Campaigns were limited by a number of restrictions, now including the necessity to keep moving, as military units looted everything available in an area, and the need to control and utilize rivers to move supplies. In 1640 the French appointed Michel Le Tellier as minister to improve the administration and logistics of the Army of Italy; he later rose to secretary of state for military affairs. Under Le Tellier, the military formalized the use of magazines for both domestic defensive operations (*places fortes du roi*) and expeditionary operations (*magasins généraux*).[9] While magazines could extend the range of armies and the campaign system, the system depended on reliable lines of communication, which meant that commanders now needed to defend their lines of supply but could also attack those of the opponent. These changes were part of a number of French army reforms that enabled more advanced campaigns by enhancing the military's capacity to sustain mass, maneuver, tempo, and firepower.[10]

In the nineteenth century, railroads began to influence operational logistics. They were first used to improve the mobility and sustainment of units during the American Civil War. Both sides used rail lines not just to supply but also to move troops, which quickly led to efforts, especially during Major General Sherman's 1865 campaign through the Carolinas, to destroy railroads in use by the opponent. Railroads also increased the size and mobility of armies in Europe. The Royal Prussian Army under Moltke the Elder was the first military to master their use, thanks to the general-staff system, which could handle the complex planning and timing necessary to exploit them.

Logistics reached an inflection point in the twentieth century. Up until around the 1870s, less than 1 percent of transported supplies consisted of ammunition, the rest dedicated to subsistence. By the opening years of World War I, this proportion had flipped. By the end of World War II, only 8–12 percent of transported logistics consisted of subsistence, the rest being parts, maintenance, fuel, oil, or ammunition.[11]

During World War I, motor transport began to augment horse-drawn logistics just as the supply requirements of the now-massive industrial armies needed it. The huge quantities of ammunition needed by the western-front armies is notorious, and failures in logistics determined failures in operations. The breakdown of German logistics systems in 1914 gave the French and English an opportunity to halt their enemy's advances at the Battle of the Marne. The battle occurred when 60 percent of the German motorized transport vehicles had broken down, decreasing their forces' ability to continue offensive maneuver.[12] German offensives in 1918, by which point the development of infiltration tactics enabled them to break fortified trench defensives, could not be adroitly supported and thus failed. Conversely, the French, British, and American forces were able to shift forces quickly enough to contain German efforts.[13]

By World War II, motor transport and aviation transport had matured, but the needs of armies—especially in terms of oil for producing both fuel and lubricants—had also increased. The pace of mechanized and motorized warfare frequently outpaced supply capacity.[14] Aircraft that could transport supplies and troops quickly and at great ranges also have logistics requirements and limitations of their own, such as the need for runways, airspace restrictions, and fuel requirements. Again, it was the Germans who struggled the most with logistics.

German strategy was both constrained and undermined by logistics. Their tactical skill in maneuver and tempo was underwritten by mechanized and motorized platforms: trucks, tanks, and aircraft. All of these platforms required oil for fuel and maintenance fluid that Germany lacked. This focus on logistics colored even strategic-level decisions. By 1942 the OKH was planning attacks against Soviet oil-producing territories, the logic being that the captured oil reserves would support future operations while denying the resource to Soviet forces, which would be unable to continue the war. It was a poor assumption but, in the event, was never tested; staunch Soviet resistance prevented Wehrmacht forces from achieving their goals, and it was the Germans who were unable to continue.[15]

This admittedly shallow historical survey, like the others, makes it seem like the military history of logistics can be compartmentalized into easily understood stages or phases. While it is helpful to do so to provide the necessary context for theory, reality is always messier. Martin Van Creveld's study of military logistics from the Thirty Years' War to World War II demonstrates the extent to which continuities and changes coexist.[16]

NAVAL LOGISTICS

Although the above section mentions the provision of logistics through naval means, the logistics of naval forces and campaigns themselves requires its own discussion. Due to the nature of naval combat, the mobility of ships has had significant effects, unsurprisingly, on the course of naval warfare and naval tactics.

Ancient naval logistics, and thus mobility and tactics, were constrained by the limitations of rowing for seagoing propulsion and sailing vessels better suited to coastal operations than to oceanic voyages. Ships had to land each evening to take on water; in any event, night sailing was exceedingly dangerous. Given the limitations of rowing and the almost complete lack of firepower on ancient ships, naval tactics of the age revolved around ramming and boarding.

It was not until the sixteenth century that sail locomotion mostly displaced rowing. The last battle where rowing was a major feature was the Battle of Lepanto in 1571. Advances in ship design allowed vessels to carry more cargo, increasing logistics capacity for navies and commercial viability for merchants. This led to the process of economic globalization that continues to today, a global economy resting on cargo shipping and the need for navies to protect it. Large-capacity ships that could sail for greater distances without resupply changed the importance of ports as well as fleets' interactions with force in time and space.[17]

In turn, sail locomotion was displaced by steam during the late nineteenth century. Logistically, the transition had both advantages and disadvantages. Far more supplies and troops could be transported via naval means and at greater speeds, increasing the viability of expeditionary warfare. Winds were also no longer a factor. But steam power required coaling stations ashore for fuel resupply. The importance of naval bases and stations ashore increased with oil-driven steam locomotion, then the advent of gasoline locomotion and naval aviation. Counterintuitively, as the efficiency of locomotion on ships themselves has increased, so has the importance of ports and bases, even though vessels can stay at sea now longer than ever.

THE LOGISTICS DISCIPLINE

LOGISTICS AS THE OPERATIONAL LEVEL?

In his magisterial study of logistics in the American military system, Rear Admiral Henry E. Eccles looked at the discipline from the perspective of commanders. In his words, "the command point of view is that logistics itself has no purpose other than to create and to support combat forces which are responsive to the needs of the command."[18] The purpose of logistics is to support tactical commanders, and since nothing can happen without it, it is of vital importance.

Eccles views logistics as performing the function similar to some views of the operational level of war: "Logistics is the bridge between our national economy and the actual operations of our combat forces in the field."[19] But the translation of strategic direction into tactics is logistics, not a level of war.[20] He also identifies an inflection point between Napoleon and industrial war that necessitated the rise of staffs to handle the planning and coordination of logistics.[21]

Another logistics-focused version of operational art is that of Michael R. Matheny. He attributes the creation of operational art not to Soviet thinkers, but to American military leaders during the interwar period.[22] In Matheny's view, "During the interwar years, America's military leaders developed a framework for operational art that allowed them to apply U.S. economic power to project, sustain, and conduct large-scale operations."[23]

Still, logistics as the operational level of war is as poor a fit as any other conception. The economic power of a nation clearly has strategic- and policy-level implications. Even if taken as sustainment, such an idea would only account for a portion of Milan Vego's "plan, prepare, synchronize, and sustain" version of operational art, thus ignoring the majority of warfighting functions, staff sections, and requirements placed on military forces. While logistics is certainly a necessary discipline when it comes to warfare, it is wholly insufficient. To return to Thorpe's analogy, stage management may be vital to putting on the play, but it is not the play itself.

LINES OF COMMUNICATION

If operational art is about linking tactics together, lines of communication are the arteries. Lines of communications refer to the connective routes through which logistics staff must move people and material. They may be roads, railroads, movement corridors, rivers, airspace, airports, sea routes and straits, canals, harbors, or any manner of transportation infrastructure, natural or manmade. They connect combat forces with any source of supply and sustenance as well as reinforcements and combat forces not yet or in the process of being deployed, and they provide the means for commanders in the field to communicate their needs back to logistics professionals along and at the terminus of supply lines. Most importantly, lines of communication need to be defended and controlled. They are always a target for the opponent, and the more dependent a military force is on lavish supplies, the more likely it is that the opponent will target them.

FUNCTIONS OF LOGISTICS

In essence, the logistics staff must perform a process of acquisition, distribution, sustainment, and disposition. Acquisition is simply the procurement of all manner of necessary supplies and commodities. Distribution is the movement thereof, either inter- or intratheater. Sustainment is the provision of those supplies to forces engaged in combat. Disposition is the use, return, or disposal of those items by the military units themselves.[24]

This is in addition to the transportation of the military forces themselves. The combination of this process and transportation applied to the lines of communication within and outside the theater of war establishes a distribution system, which must not just be used but also be protected. Essentially, logistics must sustain the humans and equipment that provide the raw materials of military forces and sustain the ability of those composite units to move as units.

Lastly, military logistics is different from logistics in any other context in important ways. In a commercial context, for example, logistics is almost entirely concerned with efficiency: transporting goods as quickly as possible, as cheaply as possible. Military logistics must also be concerned with efficiency, as a network that is too inefficient will not be sustainable or effective. But military logisticians must balance efficiency with effectiveness.[25] Just-in-time or just-enough philosophies of logistics work in predictable, stable environments. War is not such an environment.

For example, an amphibious ship loaded with military equipment and supplies in a strictly efficient manner will focus on saving space, packing in as much stuff as possible, regardless of what each individual item is. But the landing-force commander cannot solely be concerned with efficiency; he or she must be concerned also with the order in which those supplies are available on the beach. The most necessary items—ammunition, heavy weapons, and so on—must be available for offloading first, even if packing the ship in such a manner is less efficient. Managing this balance between efficiency and effectiveness is the essence of military logistics.

CONCLUSION

Logistics is not just about sustaining the physical capabilities of combat forces; it is also about sustaining their moral cohesion.[26] Military units in aggregate and combatants individually cease to function in a cohesive manner if their basic sustenance is at risk. Logistics sustains the other aspects of operational art, even information and command and control: digital logistics involving network infrastructure, bandwidth, processing power, and electricity is a key issue for modern staffs.[27] Admiral Eccles was right about its importance, especially the connection between the need for better systems as armies expanded and the rise of military staffs: logistics is one of a staff's primary responsibilities. As long as humans are engaged in warfare, they will need to be sustained through the science and art of logistics.

12 COMMAND AND CONTROL

> *We decentralize and capitalize on the capabilities of our individual people rather than centralize and make automatons of them. That builds that essential pride of service and sense of accomplishment.*
>
> —**Alfred Thayer Mahan**

The command-and-control discipline is intimately bound up with leadership: who will lead, who will follow, and the nature of that relationship.

Importantly, command and control is not communications, which is not to say that the two are not connected; communications are the means of command and control but not the ends. **Command and control enables tactics by establishing a feedback loop between the commanders and subordinate commanders and their staffs, providing direction down and awareness up.** Better communications enable better command and control in terms of both accuracy and speed.

COMMAND AND CONTROL IN HISTORY
ANCIENT
Ancient military organizations dealt with far more constraints when it came to command and control but overcame those challenges in clever ways. Flags, pennants, and other visual aids originated in the East and quickly spread to the West. Personal leadership of troops on the part of the general or sovereign was as celebrated then as it is today, but it was also essential. In some situations, the only way to provide direction to troops was to physically lead them.

Even helmets could be used for command and control. Greek helmets tended to have a vertical crest, running from forehead to neck. The reason for this was that their leaders commanded from within the ranks of the phalanx; hoplites to their left and right could identify the leader and follow his lead by keeping an eye on the crest. Later Roman helmets, however, had a horizontal crest—it ran from ear to ear. A centurion tended to lead a formation from the front. It was legionnaires behind him who needed to see the identifying crest.

As military forces professionalized and became more capable of complex articulation, they required subordinate leaders. The articulation of a Roman legion required intermediate leadership between the general and the soldier; this was the centurion. The cavalry arm, frequently operating at a distance from the main infantry formation, also had its own commander, the magister equitum (master of the horse). Centurions and other subordinate officers provided a link from the commander down to individual maniples and cohorts.

MEDIEVAL

During the Middle Ages, the banner was both a means of command and control (directing a unit where to go) and an aspect of unit and moral cohesion, just as Roman eagle standards were in ancient times.[1]

Providing troops with direction—the command portion of command and control—is not just about telling them what to do but also about keeping them situationally informed to prevent surprise, confusion, and deception. Failure to do this was decisive at the Battle of the Fei River in China in 383. The Qin commander, during prebattle communications with the opposing Jin, agreed to let that army cross the river before he attacked them, although fully intending to strike before the Jin completed the crossing. When he ordered his army back from the river to lay the trap, the Qin troops assumed it was a retreat, broke ranks, and ran. Others saw this and followed suit. The Qin state collapsed following the Jin campaign.[2]

Confusion of signals during battle was a common occurrence, especially before the advent of military staffs. At the Battle of Manzikert in 1071, a Byzantine heavy cavalry force was lured into an ambush by Seljuk Turk horse archers. The heavy cavalry held their own, no mean feat against horse archers, until the commander—Byzantine emperor Romanus—passed signals to change the array of his wings and center. The signals were confused and chaotic, allowing the Turks to dislocate the Byzantines into smaller chunks and overwhelm them, capturing Romanus and virtually wiping out his entire force.[3]

During the premodern era, militaries began to master the organization of armies composed of troops equipped with firearms. Maurice of Nassau reintroduced articulated units, which multiplied the command-and-control requirements, leading to a need for a junior-officer corps.[4] In order to command and control, leaders and subordinates at multiple levels need to communicate with each other.

By the modern age, set-piece, linear tactics declined and then disappeared because they were no longer effective. When command and control required a direct view of the battlefield, visual signals, and courier communications, all that could be utilized were linear, set-piece tactics. Modern communications have enabled command and control beyond line of sight, situational awareness via proxy (such as digital displays), and other enhancements. In short, better means of communication, facilitating command and control, have enabled an increased set of tactical options beyond the concentrated, set-piece battle.

Modern communications technology, enabling complex and capable command-and-control arrangements, is a force multiplier but also vulnerable in a way that flags and visual signals were not. Through electronic warfare, cyberwarfare, and other means discussed in previous chapters, the mere act of command and control can provide the adversary with information, even if unable to intercept the message itself. Command and control can also be directly targeted. Antiradiation missiles, for example, are able to seek out and destroy command-and-control nodes.

During both Operation Desert Storm in 1991 and Operation Iraqi Freedom in 2003, both fought in Kuwait and Iraq, the U.S. military virtually destroyed Iraqi command-and-control networks through both electronic and physical means. In 1991 Iraq's National Air Defense Center, controlling its air-defense network, was destroyed.[5] During Operation Enduring Freedom in Afghanistan, aircraft normally used to jam air-defense radars were instead used to jam ground communications between Taliban forces.[6]

THE COMMAND-AND-CONTROL DISCIPLINE

First, command and control should not be confused with communications, although it depends on the means of communication between elements of a military force.[7] Communications staff members ensure that commanders and the commanded can effectively contact one another. The duties of the communications staff revolve around ensuring the availability of the necessary means and pathways for the commander to command and the staff to control.

Command and control is the combination of two distinct concepts that, when combined, form a feedback loop. A commander directs subordinate elements, but effective leadership can only be facilitated by information provided by those subordinate elements to the commander. Most command decisions, however, create multifaceted operational art requirements. A decision on the part of the commander may be to attack at dawn. This tactical decision requires logistical preparation to ensure ammunition is in place, information analysis to determine where exactly the enemy is and when exactly dawn will be, fire support to prepare the target area, and administrative decisions such as coordinating with higher headquarters or adjacent units. It is up to the staff to ensure the transfer of communication up, down, and across chains of command fluidly without overloading the system while ensuring the attack occurs at dawn. In short, command is what the commander does; control is what the staff does.

CENTRALIZED VERSUS DECENTRALIZED COMMAND AND CONTROL

In recent years there has been an effort to replace the term "command and control" with the term "mission command." This is based on an erroneous understanding of command and control. Mission tactics (or mission command) is merely one method of command and control. Many view it as a superior method, but it is not always the most appropriate for every situation. Firstly, it requires a high level of professionalization and training. Secondly, it requires a high level of cohesion, trust, and familiarity between military personnel. Only when these requirements are met can this method be employed effectively.

The best command-and-control arrangement is the one that is most appropriate for the mission, situation, and forces available. The tighter the necessary coordination between tactical units, supporting arms, and logistics and the less experienced the troops and subordinate leaders are, the more centralized the command-and-control plan must be. Conversely, highly trained, cohesive troops led by experienced commanders who are well known to and trusted by subordinates and each other can operate in a more decentralized manner. Centralized command and control fosters adherence to the directives of the overall commander. Decentralized command and control fosters tempo and initiative, allowing tactical forces the freedom of action to act in a high-pace environment to seize opportunities. The right choice depends on these and a variety of other factors that must be evaluated and balanced by the staff.

Traditionally, navies have favored decentralized command and control. This has partly been by necessity; for centuries, a ship at sea was completely cut off from any higher headquarters. Air operations, however, tend to favor centralized command and control due to the need for deconfliction of aircraft in both space and time, high maintenance requirements, and the pervasive need to prioritize sorties to preserve capability.

CONCLUSION

Command and control, unsurprisingly perhaps, is intimately connected with tactics. The commander can only create and employ a tactical plan that can be communicated to subordinates. And it can only be modified in the face of unfolding circumstances if those events are communicated to the commander. Command and control thus accounts for the inherent unpredictability and chaos of combat.

13 CAMPAIGNS, BATTLES, AND DECISION

In every battle there comes a time when both sides consider themselves beaten, then he who continues the attack wins.
— ULYSSES S. GRANT

Thus far we have examined operational art through six disciplines, but we must now turn to how the staff as a whole can conceptualize their function of planning, preparing, conducting, and sustaining tactics over the course of a campaign or battle. This raises a few questions: What are campaigns? What are battles? However each are defined, they are all heuristics; even tactics and strategy are heuristics. The terms and their definitions are all simply ways to understand events. This book has eschewed the term "battle" because it is generally associated with a specific phenomenon: a high-concentration of tactical events in a single place and time involving a large number of participants. It has instead used the term "campaign." A campaign is a grouping of tactics united in purpose, not necessarily in time or space. A battle is simply a particular type of campaign, one that is generally meant to be united in time, space, and purpose.

Operational art is the planning, preparing, conducting, and sustaining of tactics aimed at accomplishing strategic effect. To properly understand operational art, we must examine what we mean by battles, campaigns, and decisiveness, then contextualize it within a framework of strategic theory and its relationship with tactics and strategy.

CATHAL NOLAN'S *THE ALLURE OF BATTLE*

Cathal Nolan's thesis in his book *The Allure of Battle: A History of How Wars Have Been Won and Lost* (2017) is that very few battles are decisive, especially when it comes to deciding a war. Rather, battles simply consume a vast amount of resources, in terms of both blood and treasure, and it is their depletion that produces a decision in war. Nolan is right, most wars are won by protracted attrition and resource expenditure. It should be noted that he refers to a strategic decision, the outcome of a war. Still, operational staffs must support and organize tactics over the long term, with an understanding of the strategic context.

But, it does not necessarily follow that attrition should be the strategic goal or even a tactical one. Killing large numbers of enemy troops may or may not be effective, given the strategic context and political ends of the belligerents. Hannibal was really good at killing Roman soldiers; in fact, he was the all-time best at it. But he lost his war and died alone and hunted as an outlaw. The Romans were tenacious, and while the massive numbers of casualties they sustained caused them a great deal of stress, it had little effect on their will to continue. In fact, in 146 BC, when the next generations of Romans stood outside the walls of Carthage, which they would soon tear down, the Battle of Cannae (216 BC) was not far from their thoughts. The Romans could handle attrition; the Carthaginians could not.

The Punic Wars are not the only example of conflicts that could not be won by attrition or where attrition was inefficient. World War I, as Nolan notes, was finally decided when Germany simply could no longer support combat operations.[1] Bringing it to that point cost roughly 4.8 million lives for the Allies alone. To be sure, they had no choice but to pursue a strategy of attrition, but that is not always the case with every war. In World War II during the Battle of Britain (1940), the Luftwaffe was sustaining 80 percent attrition during bombing raids over England but was willing to continue so long as the high command assumed that the raids were effective.[2] It was only when the Germans ascertained that the raids were ineffective that they ceased. The Royal Air Force was not seeking attrition for attrition's sake, even though British industrial capacity outpaced Germany's. Instead, they focused their defense on the bombing raids and largely ignored German fighter raids. Later in the war, Hitler continued to fight even as the Luftwaffe was practically wiped out and the Wehrmacht reduced to wreckage, German cities bombed out, and the German homeland invaded and pillaged. He only gave up when the SS troops started to waiver and could no longer be trusted.[3] In short, there was no amount of attrition in terms of people and material that Hitler was not willing to force the German population to endure. It was only when the cohesion of his supporters wavered that he gave in. Attrition in and of itself is not necessarily determinative.

So while attrition of military forces affects the will of those sustaining the continuing losses, it is not a direct relationship. Attrition could produce despair or determination, depending on the opponent and the goal. There is no set point where the destruction of a certain amount of blood and treasure will automatically win a war, just as there are no perfectly geometric maneuvers that will automatically win a battle.[4] Lastly, attrition is frequently a byproduct of one side or the other simply being better at fighting and using its forces more effectively.[5] The correlation between attrition and winning wars is not necessarily causation.

THE DRAW OF DECISIVENESS
Battles are also frequently described as decisive or indecisive. The idea of decisiveness is an attempt to impose an external order on warfare while simultaneously ignoring its own internal order. Describing an event or battle as inherently decisive ignores the strategic effect of the event—that is, its effect on relevant audiences, namely the political leaders, civilian populations, and military forces of both sides. It is generally a marker of an undue focus on the means—a dramatic, come-from-behind battlefield victory or a great sacrifice—instead of the aim of an engagement. Dramatic events frequently lead to exaggerated historical focus, but that does not necessarily mean that strategic theory should follow the historians' lead. One example is Thermopylae (480 BC). This battle has been written about for centuries and occupies a large place in the public consciousness of Western countries. But it had little to no strategic effects on the war. The naval battle of Artemisium—which took place simultaneously and had far greater strategic effect—is largely forgotten.

But even this is not always true. The Battle of Saratoga (1777) during the War for Independence is generally described as decisive, but this is accurate because of the strategic effect produced by the tactical American victory: it convinced France to back American independence. Colin S. Gray's notion of strategic effect should, in fact, be substituted for such an idea of decisiveness. Lastly, as we shall see, decisiveness is usually attributed to battles where a transition between two types of campaigns occurred.

THE AIM OF THE WAR
Whether attrition will be decisive in the outcome of war depends not just on the character of the strategic actors involved but also on the nature of the war itself. The most important aspect is the political aims of the combatants. Specifically, it must be ascertained whether the political aims are unlimited or limited, to what extent, and how much value each combatant places on their aim.

Evaluating wars by analyzing their political aims is a concept devised by Clausewitz, although it was not fully elucidated before his death.[6] Having reached this conclusion, he turned to integrating it into *On War* but probably only did so in book 1.[7] In a recent publication, Donald Stoker, an eminent Clausewitz scholar, takes the concept and applies it to contemporary U.S. wars using Julian Corbett's terminology of limited and unlimited wars.

An unlimited war is one in which a combatant seeks the destruction of the opponent's *political power* to resist. This usually, but not always, entails the destruction of the opponent's military means as well. The point is that, at the end of the war, only one side of the conflict retains political power and usually extends it over the opponent, either permanently or temporarily. A limited war is one in which a combatant does not seek the removal of the opponent's political power to resist but instead seeks to induce that combatant to use its political power differently. The Iraq War in 2003, for example, was an unlimited war: the United States sought the destruction of the Saddam Hussein regime and the removal of Hussein himself. Operation Desert Storm in 1991, however, was a limited war. The United States sought to induce Hussein to use his political power to withdraw from Kuwait. In both cases, the United States was successful. The problem was that in 2003 it was not prepared for the implications of an unlimited war and the ensuing power vacuum.

In addition, the character of a war will depend on the value each combatant places on their aims. Attrition may serve to convince an opponent to give up a peripheral, unimportant province or two. If the political aim is something of vast importance, however, the butcher's bill in terms of attrition may be quite high—even complete extinction may not be too great a cost. For example, when it came to the value they placed on their freedom, the Jews of Masada (AD 73–74) could not be bought by any amount of attrition.

OPERATIONAL ART AND STRATEGY

This diversion into contemporary debates about strategy is a useful starting point to contextualize operational art as it has been defined in this book. Terms like "battle" and "decision" are both too imprecise and carry too much baggage for strategic theory. Tactics, operational art, strategic effect, strategy, and policy are better anchors for thought and conception. This book, however, is about operational art.

The fact that most wars are won or lost based on the attrition of resources is a function of the fact that they are limited in aim. It is easier to put a price on limited aims, and by their very definition, their loss is easier to live with.

A strategic actor that loses an unlimited war may not live at all. Opponents that seek unlimited aims—modern terrorist organizations and their insurgent allies, for example—are very unlikely to be overcome by attrition.

Operational art must serve strategy, and strategy is impossible without understanding the nature of the war, whether it is limited or unlimited in aim; whether the strategic actors are sensitive to attrition, and to what degree; and the amount of value placed on the aim by those with political power. These are political questions, as strategy is inherently political.

Operational art cannot be performed well absent the strategic context. It requires talented staff officers to do so. The German General Staff system is proof of both: it supplied talented staff officers but never accounted for their need to operate within a strategic context. The result was tactical success and strategic failure. While we are forever fortunate that they failed, modern conceptions of the operational level of war as a politics-free zone interposed between tactics and strategy is a recipe for this same twisted fate.

CONCLUSION

Defeat is a decision, a decision that the cost of achieving the goal is too high. Campaigns and battles are not decisive in and of themselves. Both terms are simply heuristics to describe organized groupings of tactics. Again, tactics is the use of armed forces in engagements. Operational art is the planning, preparing, conducting, and sustaining of tactics aimed at accomplishing strategic effect. Tactics produce strategic effects, positive or negative. Strategy seeks to harness these effects to achieve the political aim. The meaning of tactical events—be they battles or campaigns, be it attrition or decision—cannot be found in and of themselves but only in the effect they produce for strategy.

Confusion about these terms arises from an undue focus on means rather than aims—or more accurately, logic. Attrition may well and usually does help convince an opponent to make that decision, though not always and rarely, if ever, by attrition alone. Theory must avoid and alleviate confusion. Conceptions of the operational level of war, lacking an independent logic of their own, contribute to a focus on means, which only introduces confusion. Referring to groupings of tactics as campaigns is imperfect but introduces less confusion than either operations or battles. The terms "battle" and "decisiveness" both have too much baggage to be useful in theory, and in any case, these are more historiographical concepts than theoretical ones. The theorist and the practitioners should be exceedingly wary of terms and concepts that have grown and ossified on the theory of war, seeking instead to prune them away.

14 CAMPAIGN TAXONOMY I

Military organizations generally classify campaigns by a combination of geography and climate, such as jungle warfare, arctic warfare, or urban warfare. The specific techniques and procedures for operating in those specific combat biomes are outside the scope of this work, and doctrinal publications are sound sources for the particulars.

As theory should be designed to help us think, and categories are a useful way of organizing thought, we should categorize campaigns without regard to their geographic venue, something that is largely lacking in doctrine. Lacking a clear and coherent method to categorize campaigns has led to the rise of a cottage industry of operational concepts, usually labeled by adding a stylish adjective in front of or behind either "operations" or "warfare." These concepts lack both external and internal logic and are usually designed to influence budgets, not to assist practitioners in understanding warfare.[1]

Campaigns should be categorized based on their own internal nature, not the externalities of geography, location, weapon system, tactical organization, or any number of other malleable aspects of warfare. As mentioned in chapter 9, campaigns—applicable throughout history—are attempts to coordinate tactical forces across time and space in relation to an opponent. The operational discipline of coordination, resident in the operations staff, is both the central and the synergizing point of campaigns. This is the nature of campaigns and operational art, and thus it is a solid foundation on which to categorize them.

Since the management of time, space, and forces is so central, we can use it to establish a taxonomy of campaigns. This is composed of Clausewitz's offense and defense concepts to categorize *space*, Archer Jones' persisting and raiding concepts to categorize *time*, and Hans Delbrück's annihilation- and exhaustive-strategy concepts to categorize *forces*.

SPACE, TIME, AND FORCES

Campaigns can be categorized in terms of space by evaluating them as either offensive or defensive. Offense and defense, in the Clausewitzian sense, are about either seizing space (offense) or holding space (defense). To be clear, every campaign will be a mixture of both offense and defense, as neither exists without the other. Nevertheless, one or the other will dominate. Offensive and defensive operations both exploit space, but each does so differently. The offense typically exploits space via maneuver, while the defense typically does so through mass.

As mentioned in chapter 10, Jones describes how a raiding campaign is transitory, intended to meet a certain objective and then end, either through withdrawal or some other means. A persisting campaign is long term, although not necessarily open ended.

These divisions have tactical implications as well. An actor pursuing a raiding campaign tends to eschew direct combat, focusing instead on hit-and-run attacks or looting. An actor pursuing a persisting campaign will necessarily take and hold ground, defending it as needed.

Delbrück's cumulative concepts of annihilation and exhaustion are predicated on what the tactical forces involved are doing: they are either trying to destroy their opponent outright or attempting to wear them down gradually, in either case at least to the point where the balance of forces changes enough to switch modes.

Importantly, these categories are not stark and impermeable; they all overlap in practice. Both offense and defense also interact with time: the offense is always on the clock, the defense is always waiting. A raiding campaign also requires space: if space is restricted enough to preclude maneuver, a persisting campaign is all that is left. It goes without saying that a cumulative campaign requires time.

The following table categorizes these concepts via time and forces.

	Annihilation (A)	Cumulative (C)
Persisting (P)	Persisting annihilation (PA)	Persisting cumulative (PC)
Raiding (R)	Raiding annihilation (RA)	Raiding cumulative (RC)

- Examples of persisting annihilation: "Total war," World Wars I and II, Napoleonic Wars.
- Examples of persisting cumulative: Guerrilla warfare and counterinsurgency, Hannibal's invasion of Italy, Sherman's Atlanta campaign.
- Examples of raiding annihilation: Punitive/preemptive warfare, Austro-Prussian War, Franco-Prussian War.

- Examples of raiding cumulative: *Chevauchée, guerre de course,* unrestricted submarine warfare, strategic bombing (and defense).

Space, time, and forces is one consideration, but offense and defense is another. The dynamics of offense and defense revolve around the gaining and maintaining the initiative, given the paradox between the superior strength of the defense and the ultimate necessity of the offense. With the initiative, a commander can dictate the tactical situation to gain an advantage over the opponent. While the tactician is oscillating between the offense or the defense, the operational artist must be able to support both. Over the course of the campaign, both offense and defense come into play; each force may be acting either offensively, defensively, or both simultaneously at different points or may alternate between offense and defense at different times.

With the addition of offense and defense, an operational taxonomy can be created:

	Offense (O)	**Defense (D)**
Persisting annihilation (PA)	Offensive persisting annihilation (OPA)	Defensive persisting annihilation (DPA)
Persisting cumulative (PC)	Offensive persisting cumulative (OPC)	Defensive persisting cumulative (DPC)
Raiding annihilation (RA)	Offensive raiding annihilation (ORA)	Defensive raiding annihilation (DRA)
Raiding cumulative (RC)	Offensive raiding cumulative (ORC)	Defensive raiding cumulative (DRC)

This taxonomy succinctly captures the operational stance of a military organization engaged in warfare and its relationship with the opponent. It also has implications for the design and structure of military forces. For example, the modern U.S. military is arguably designed for offensive, persisting, annihilation (OPA) campaigns: it is not designed for raiding campaigns whatsoever (although one can make the case that Special Operations forces are designed as such), nor is it postured to wage a defensive campaign in and around the United States. This simultaneously explains its strengths, such as high-end conflict against other professional militaries or near-peer competitors, and its weakness, namely waging offensive, raiding, cumulative (ORC) campaigns against nonstate actors.

Historical campaigns can also be analyzed using this taxonomy. Two of Napoleon's campaigns serve here as examples: Austerlitz, described by many as one of the most masterful campaigns of all time, and the 1812 invasion of Russia, surely one of the worst executed campaigns in history and definitely the worst in Napoleon's career.

The Austerlitz Campaign, from the point that Napoleon ordered the Grand Armée east, defeated Field Marshal Karl Mack, invaded Austria, and defeated Russia and Austria at Austerlitz, was an OPA campaign, as all of Napoleon's campaigns were. The Russians and Austrians attempted to defeat it with its direct defensive corollary, a defensive, persisting, annihilation (DPA) campaign. This was, of course, exactly what Napoleon wanted, as it played to his strengths rather than to the coalition's.

Napoleon again employed an OPA campaign in 1812 when he invaded Russia itself. This time, however, the Russians employed a defensive, raiding, cumulative (DPC) campaign. To be sure, it was not purely DPC, and they did not settle on it immediately, but the Russians chose to defend their country by raiding means, rarely persisting to hold ground (like they did at Borodino) and trusting that the cumulative effect of, first, their own tactical actions and environmental factors, which stretched Napoleon's supply lines, and then the Russian winter would win the day. Whereas a DPA campaign had failed against the emperor in 1805, the DPC campaign in 1812 worked, and worked well. Napoleon himself escaped with his life, but very few of his soldiers did, shattering the Grande Armée.

These examples reveal the utility of this campaign taxonomy: certain types of campaign are strong against certain other types but weak against certain others. A commander and his staff, by identifying the category of campaign they must pursue and the type of campaign the enemy is likely to conduct, have a solid basis on which to form their plans. This aspect of the campaign taxonomy is further explored in the next chapter.

15 CAMPAIGN TAXONOMY II

Quintus Fabius Maximus Verrucosus, a Roman general during the Second Punic War, is famous for having counseled avoiding direct confrontation with Carthaginian forces under Hannibal, which were at that time running rampant through Italy. During the War of Independence, General George Washington, who explicitly alluded to Fabius, spent years avoiding direct confrontation with British forces until the time was right to do so at Yorktown in 1781. Both men were criticized for these decisions. Fabius was given the name Cunctator ("the Delayer"), and his fellow Romans eventually ignored him, replacing him with a general who hastily went on the offense, leading to the crushing defeat at Cannae in 216 BC. And yet, both Fabius and Washington were right.

The genius of these two men was their diagnosis of the operational relationship between their forces and those of their opponent, and then their selection of tactics that flowed from that analysis. They both recognized that their opponent's offensive-persistent-annihilation (OPA) campaigns could not be effectively countered with the resources they had available. In other words, meeting an OPA campaign with a defensive-persistent-annihilation (DPA) campaign would not have worked. They instead selected defensive-raiding-cumulative (DRC) campaigns that bought time—time that worked against their opponents and led to the opportunity for renewing or beginning a DPA campaign in the future. Their tactical decisions flowed from these campaign structures. Of course, Washington knew well Fabius' story and followed his example. This does not detract from his brilliance. Keep in mind that even today Washington is not considered a great general by some. Despite the benefit of over two centuries of hindsight, it is difficult for observers to make as accurate an operational assessment of the Continental situation as Washington did.

The operational taxonomy presented in the previous chapter can help those of us who lack Washington's talents to think through such issues in our own time. Nor is applying such a method to historical examples simply an exercise in curiosity; evaluating past military campaigns is practice for the future, training and drill for the mind. This chapter briefly assesses some major historical campaigns within the taxonomy as a series of examples. They are chosen first for their demonstrative power relative to the concepts of operational taxonomy, then second for their familiarity to general readers. Favoring campaigns that are known to a wide variety of audiences, such as the Punic Wars and World War II, takes advantage of preexisting common knowledge without burdening the reader with the need to learn about an unfamiliar campaign.

OFFENSIVE, PERSISTING, ANNIHILATION (OPA) CAMPAIGNS

Offensive, persisting, annihilation campaigns are in some ways the most simplistic, although the amount of combat power necessary to carry them to completion is immense and complex. They tend to be used when aims are unlimited, although not always. They are commonly used in pursuit of maximalist strategies that require the seizure or destruction of territory. Combat tends to be focused on the acquisition of territory and the destruction of the opposing military forces. These units are susceptible to culmination, as the opponent is usually on the defensive and operating on friendly territory.

Ancient OPA campaigns are some of the most famous military campaigns in history: Both Persian invasions of Greece, all of Alexander the Great's campaigns, and a great deal of Rome's wars were all OPA campaigns. Perhaps the most famous, and almost an ideal type, was the Roman campaign during the Third Punic War (149–146 BC). Though it probably did not actually end with the sowing of salt in their fields, it did end with the complete destruction of the Carthaginians and Carthage itself in 146 BC.

Few medieval rulers in the West were capable of generating and sustaining the combat power required for OPA campaigns. The various Crusades, which saw only temporary success amid a great deal of failure, are typical. An exception, however, were the Mongols. Although theirs was a culture fond of raiding, between 1206 and 1405 the Mongols used a series of OPA campaigns to develop into the most expansive empire in history.

Strategic actors became much more capable of power projection and sustainment during the premodern period with the development of professional state navies that could better support force projection. This led to an increase in OPA campaigns, especially against vulnerable states that lacked naval power and professionalized military forces. OPA campaigns colonized and subjugated people all over the world. This continued into modern times. Those of the Axis Powers, especially Nazi Germany and Imperial Japan, required OPA campaigns to turn them back.

DEFENSIVE, PERSISTING, ANNIHILATION (DPA) CAMPAIGNS

Defensive, persisting, annihilation campaigns are similar in character to OPA campaigns with the added benefit, as mentioned earlier, of the strengths of the defense. DPA campaigns tend to be limited; the defenders simply want the invaders out. While the forces conducting an OPA campaign usually have the initiative in terms of where to focus their strength, DPA forces can seize it by selecting where and when to stand. Although OPA forces are usually focused on attrition, this tends to work in favor of DPA forces, typically operating on friendly territory with greater access to reinforcements than are their opponents. Moral forces also tend to accrue to the defender: the Soviet Union's situation on the eastern front during World War II is an exemplary case.

Such campaigns can also transition. The Red Army's defense of the Soviet Union during Operation Barbarossa (1941) was a DPA campaign right up until it became an OPA campaign. The surrender of the German Sixth Army at Stalingrad (1943) is generally ascribed as the point when that transition occurred.

OFFENSIVE, PERSISTING, CUMULATIVE (OPC) CAMPAIGNS

Offensive, persisting, cumulative campaigns are seemingly counterintuitive; if enough combat power can be generated, deployed, and sustained to be offensive and persisting, why then should they be cumulative? Such campaigns occur when annihilation is not possible because one side cannot generate enough military superiority to destroy the other. The typical OPC campaign is a third-party counterinsurgency effort. The policy is usually limited, only concerned with preserving some kind of status quo in the theater, although campaigns of conquest may fall into this category as well. Tactics are similarly focused on attrition, albeit cumulative attrition, although this is almost always ineffective without political efforts, which fall more into strategy.

Rome had a lot of success with OPC campaigns, not just marching into and conquering a territory but also transforming it at a societal level in order to ensure pacification. Caesar's conquests in Gaul are one example. The Crusades are another, albeit less successful, example.

OPC campaigns are commonly counterinsurgency efforts, although they can also be insurgency campaigns themselves. Ongoing counterinsurgency operations in Afghanistan, further discussed below, are an example of the former. An example of the latter is the campaigns of the Islamic State (ongoing since 2014).

DEFENSIVE, PERSISTING, CUMULATIVE (DPC) CAMPAIGNS

Insurgencies, however, are more commonly defensive, persisting, cumulative campaigns. Tactics tend to be hit and run, even though the campaign itself is permanent and not a raid. The policy tends to be limited in the sense that, as in most defensive campaigns, the point is to resist the policy of the offensive actor, and strategy follows suit. Many examples of guerrilla warfare, such as the Spanish resistance to Napoleon (when the term "guerrilla" was coined), fall into this category.

Perhaps the most successful practitioners of DPC campaigns in history are the Vietnamese. The North Vietnamese were victorious in DPC campaigns against France, the United States, and South Vietnam between 1946 and 1973, then defeated South Vietnam in an OPA campaign in 1973–75.

OFFENSIVE, RAIDING, ANNIHILATION (ORA) CAMPAIGNS

Offensive, raiding, annihilation campaigns are more temporary in character than OPA campaigns. The difference is the result of the nature of the policy aims, which are almost exclusively limited: the acquisition of provinces, the enforcement of ultimatums, or punitive aims meant to punish or coerce. The aim is not to destroy or unseat the opponent, but rather to convince them to take a new political direction or abandon an established one. Although a raiding campaign, the tactics tend to be more direct and attrition focused; the goal is annihilation, not exhaustion.

Hannibal's invasion of Italy in 218 BC is an excellent case of an ORA campaign. Carthage desired no territory in Italy, indeed its forces could not have held any even if they had acquired it. Hannibal invaded Italy not to conquer but to break the credibility and legitimacy of Rome in the eyes of its Italian allies by repeatedly defeating its forces in battle. Once that had been accomplished, the Carthaginian army probably would have extracted a favorable peace and left. In the event, however, Hannibal drastically miscalculated both the amount of attrition Rome was willing to absorb and the level of support it enjoyed among its allies (which he assumed was none).

Much has been made of Hannibal's decision not to attack Rome itself, and for centuries, it has been called a mistake. But it makes complete sense viewed as part of an ORA strategy. Capturing Rome was unlikely anyway and the point was not to destroy the city but to weaken Roman alliances. Hannibal had no reason to gamble his entire campaign on a risky siege. In fact, his campaigns in southern Italy away from Rome did accomplish his strategic goal, at least for a time. No matter how many Roman armies he annihilated, however, Hannibal never broke the Roman will or depleted its alliances enough to disarm them completely.

An ORA campaign typified the English campaigns against France during the Hundred Years' War. Although territory was more or less permanently acquired and fortified, some of the most famous battles occurred during campaigns in which the English marched an army through French territory, causing as much damage as possible, and then waited for the French to attack. The battles of Crecy (1346), Poitiers (1356), and Agincourt (1415) all follow this pattern.[1]

Napoleon preferred, and was at his best, when pursuing OPA campaigns; these literally enabled him to redraw Europe's borders, some of which remain in place today. One exception, though, was his ORA campaign into Russia in 1812. Napoleon was under no illusions that he could conquer that vast nation. His aim was always to extract concessions from Tsar Alexander. Where he failed, however, was to follow through on this conclusion and modify his campaign and tactics accordingly. Taking Moscow was useless—it did not fit the strategic context—but Napoleon let habit guide him into his most epic defeat.[2]

ORA occurs when aims are limited, the military means necessary to conduct an OPA campaign are lacking, or both. Moltke the Elder's campaigns in Austria and France, the Schlieffen Plan of World War I, and the German blitz campaign against Britain during World War II are examples. Pure air campaigns, such as the blitz, are of the "raiding" sort as aircraft are inherently nonpersistent.[3]

An example of an ORA campaign under an unlimited policy is Sherman's March to the Sea in 1864. Although Union forces would, of course, occupy the South, Sherman's Army of the Tennessee was not the force that would do that. Instead, his campaign was punitive and attrition focused (in terms of resources and infrastructure), even as the tactics he employed against what Confederate forces his troops encountered were focused on maneuver rather than attrition. Sherman's campaign was one of the best executed in history, and its unique nature flowed from Grant's strategy to end the war.[4]

DEFENSIVE, RAIDING, ANNIHILATION (DRA) CAMPAIGNS

Defensive, raiding, annihilation campaigns are rare. They occur under limited-aim policies. Despite their defensive nature, tactics tend to be offensive to meet the goal of annihilation. They tend to occur in response to an invasion by a materially stronger opponent. The Russian campaign against the Grande Armée in 1812 is an example of not just a DRA campaign—the Russians ceded a lot of ground and only gave battle when they wanted—but also a truly successful one. Napoleon himself escaped annihilation, but very few of his troops did.

Another example is the U.K. campaign during the Battle of Britain in World War II. Although the RAF was simultaneously conducting offensive bombing attacks on Germany, that was not its main effort. Its focus was the defense of Great Britain itself from German bomber sorties. The defense offered a great many benefits: British aircraft could stay on the ground until needed, pilots could parachute to safety if shot down and return to duty, and German fighters expended a great deal of their fuel just to get to the combat area, sometimes only having twenty minutes to complete a mission.[5]

OFFENSIVE, RAIDING, CUMULATIVE (ORC) CAMPAIGNS

Offensive, raiding, cumulative campaigns usually occur under limited policy aims; otherwise, they would be persistent. They are usually termed "punitive campaigns" or just "raids." Strategies tend to be directly coercive, but they can be used for resource acquisition. Tactics tend to focus on the attrition of opposing forces, resources, or civilians and civilian infrastructure.

These were common in the ancient world. The Athenians found some success with an ORC campaign against the Spartans that culminated in their victory at Sphacteria in 425 BC. The Romans subjected Germanic tribes to repeated ORC campaigns to stop their raids on Roman lands but did not seek to acquire more territory in that region. They themselves were later subjected to the ORC campaigns of various nomadic peoples, the most famous of which were led by Attila the Hun.

The Byzantine Empire was subjected to numerous ORC campaigns into its eastern and western territories from nomadic cultures in the Middle East and from Bulgars, among others, in Europe. ORC campaigns were common because military forces were becoming more cavalry-centric, thus having more of a logistics burden, and transportation networks were unable to sustain anything else. The use of castles and fortresses also necessitated ORC campaigns for those who could not sustain a siege or utilize siege weaponry. The development of the *chevauchée*, a long-range heavy cavalry raid, was one result. The exception, of course, was the Mongols, who managed to unite effective light cavalry but also sustain OPA campaigns.

In modern times, Germany's unrestricted submarine-warfare campaign in World War I and the Luftwaffe's Operation Eagle in World War II, both of which will be discussed in case studies later in the book, are examples of ORC campaigns.

DEFENSIVE, RAIDING, CUMULATIVE (DRC) CAMPAIGNS

Defensive, raiding, cumulative campaigns were discussed at the beginning of this chapter. Among other examples are the operations of the Byzantine Empire to defend their borders against the Sassanid Empire and then the Arab caliphates, and the British defense of their homeland against the Luftwaffe during World War II.

HYBRIDS AND INTERACTIONS

Hybrid campaigns are more common than pure forms of those types. For instance, the Romans, during the Second Punic War, executed a DPC campaign against Hannibal in Italy, an OPA campaign in Spain, and an OPA campaign against Carthage itself afterward. The greatest practitioner/theorist of hybrid campaigns was Mao Tse-Tung, whose conception of "people's war" is a hybrid of aspects of DPC, OPC, and OPA campaigns.[6]

The American-French Quasi-War (1798–1800) is a unique example of a like-versus-like conflict. Both sides pursued a maritime *guerre de course* against each other's naval commerce—in other words, ORC versus ORC.[7] The outcome was largely inconclusive.

Some of the great "turning point" battles in history can be attributed to transitions between types of campaigns. Gettysburg in 1863 marked the transition between the Army of Northern Virginia's ORA campaign to a DPC campaign and the transition between the Army of the Potomac's DPA campaign to an OPA campaign. As alluded to above, the Battle of Stalingrad is another of these transition points.

The previous chapter noted that Napoleon could not be defeated by the Third Coalition's DPA campaign at Austerlitz. That is actually a little too determinative, as that battle certainly could have gone the other way; Fortuna always has her say. But the later DPC executed by General Mikhail Kutuzov in Russia during Napoleon's 1812 invasion was clearly more effective. Indeed, it almost unhinged the emperor himself, who spent days in the ruins of Moscow clearly at a loss as to what to do.

This does not necessarily mean that DPC campaigns are inherently effective against OPA campaigns. Rather, it is probable that Kutuzov was successful because his design was based on Russia's strengths: plenty of space to trade for time, persistent armies, and supply lines that would be shorter as his forces fell back. Napoleon based his campaign design on his own strengths: climactic, decisive battle against an opponent willing to take on the Grand Armée in a straight up fight. Kutuzov's DPC campaign was the proper campaign design for the time, the place, and the opponent. Here it is enough to say that such a taxonomy can assist commanders and staff officers in evaluating their campaign designs against their opponents, not that it offers a direct guidance on which type to choose.

CONCLUSION

Whatever the campaign, whomever the combatants, and whenever the time period, the nature of campaigns is determined by the character of the strategy and the political aim. Understanding those factors is the first step a staff must take toward understanding how a campaign must be planned, prepared, synchronized, and sustained.

An operational staff must also understand the nature of a campaign as they plan, prepare, synchronize, and sustain the tactical forces that will execute it. Different types will call for different tactics, which will require the staff to support them differently, perhaps creatively. Copying the plan for one campaign in one context and transferring it to another is never effective; each campaign must be evaluated to divine its own nature.[8]

Lastly, lest the reader confuse this method of campaign design and analysis with an operational level of war, it must be noted that decisions regarding taking the offense into an opponent's territory, defending one's own ground (or seas or airspace), the time allotted to do so, the method by which one intends to achieve success, and even the funding and organizing of forces specific to one or another type of campaign *are all fundamentally political decisions*, whether made democratically or autocratically. They are in the realm of strategy.

16 OPERATIONAL ART ACTUALIZED THROUGH A MODERN STAFF SYSTEM

We have seen over the course of this book how major militaries attempted to cope with and conceptualize the changes in warfare wrought by the Napoleonic Revolution and the Industrial Revolution, whereupon military organizations and operations became more complex. We have seen how the operational level of war as a doctrinal solution has yielded, at best, little increased effectiveness on the battlefield and probably has had detrimental effects on the ability to arrange tactics to pursue strategy, even when married to limited institutional changes such as the adoption of a general staff. We have seen how the combination of institutional changes within the Scharnhorst Model gave the German army a measurable advantage on the battlefield—for a time—even as political trends in Prussia and Germany severed it from its moorings, with tragic consequences. We have explored the nature of operational art through the lens of the warfighting functions around which staffs have been organized for decades.

Yet the Napoleonic- and Prussian-style staff systems were products of their times. They were both built around the assumption of individual command. One man, sometimes a sovereign emperor, exercised command assisted by a staff. The Prussian system also assumed a military organization dominated by an aristocracy in which the commander may be in his position not because of any effective training, education, or ability but merely because of his social station. Scharnhorst's reforms were partly motivated by a desire to have at least some military professionals available to guide such men.

It is for these reasons that simply adopting such systems in the modern era would be foolish. Much has changed since the nineteenth century. But the lessons learned from the Scharnhorst Model especially should be integrated with emerging ideas of military command, specifically General Stanley McChrystal's "Team of Teams" concept and Anthony King's collective-command concept. An examination of the current U.S. staff system, such as it is, will precede a review of these emergent trends in operational-staff organization.

FLAWED BY DESIGN

First, the U.S. military does not have a true general-staff system, but rather what is known as the Joint Staff. The Joint Staff grew out of wartime expedients during World War II, not any concerted effort to create a system for the conduct and oversight of operational art.[1] Nor is there the equivalent human-resources-management system that underpinned the Scharnhorst Model. Except for the principal members, the Joint Chiefs of Staff, the Joint Staff is manned by military officers fulfilling a career requirement to do so, regardless of their individual suitability for the position. There is no mechanism in any of the services to identify talented staff officers; no dedicated career path or specific staff academy, even if prospects were to be identified; and no incentives for excellence beyond routine end-of-tour awards and personnel evaluations. Promotions are instead tied to successful command tours, the implied assumption being that a talented commander is automatically a talented staff officer and vice versa. Thus, staff tours throughout the services are viewed as a way to prepare for command billets, not as necessary and valuable work in and of themselves.

The Joint Staff does not have the authority to coordinate service efforts. An attempt was made to fix this problem after it was found that U.S. military forces could not even communicate with each other in combat operations. This led to the Goldwater-Nichols Department of Defense Reorganization Act of 1986. Decades later, joint coordination has improved, although to little end it seems, as the military has gone through a series of ineffective and directionless wars with little to no coordination between services, combatant commands, and the Joint Staff. U.S. units from different services are still routinely unable to communicate with each other.

The lack of central coordination is not accidental; the powers and mechanisms that would allow the Joint Staff to perform the function of a general staff were deliberately withheld for reasons good and bad, including the fear of repeating the mistakes of the German General Staff.[2] Other such bodies, like the National Security Council, have not filled this gap either, operating at too high a level to do so.

It must be stressed that this is not to say that the United States—or any other country—should adopt the Scharnhorst Model wholesale. It should not, for it too is flawed. The Prussians and Germans never properly developed the logistics discipline, for example, instead simply reinforcing German cultural biases against it. And while it was no driver of Nazism, the general staff was certainly no effective brake system either. Its resistance to Hitler was feckless and driven more by practical concerns than by moral, ethic, or professional ones. Its failures were legion.

TEAM OF TEAMS

As commander, Joint Special Operations Command, then–lieutenant general McChrystal restructured his staff and teams in Iraq "from the ground up on principles of extremely transparent information sharing (what we call[ed] 'shared consciousness') and decentralized decision-making authority ('empowered execution')."[3] McChrystal specifically tied this effort to breaking down "industrial age" forms of organization and adopting new ones.[4]

This restructuring created multiple staff teams weighted toward the operational disciplines of information and operations. It succeeded in reducing the time between the acquisition of information, the analysis thereof to produce intelligence, and the planning and execution of operations. The tight coupling of information and operations was exactly the kind of staff structure that McChrystal needed for his mission and for his subordinate units.

But this is not necessarily the ideal organization for every unit or for every mission. A campaign might call for such a reorganization to tightly couple operations and logistics, for example. Operations and fire support, to be effective, must be tightly coordinated, something reflected in most staffs, with fire-support officers part of the operations staff itself. The lesson of McChrystal's experience is that the adaptation of his staff to their mission and situation paid off since the traditional staff structure was inadequate for modern warfare.

COLLABORATIVE COMMAND

For his 2019 book, *Command: The Twenty-First-Century General*, British scholar Anthony King developed a series of case studies documenting the changes to division command from the early twentieth century until very recent operations in Iraq and Afghanistan, examining division commanders and their staffs from different nations and campaigns. King found, firstly, that command styles range from more individualistic to more collective. Secondly, he noticed a clear trend from the early twentieth century, when more individualistic commands predominated, to the early twenty-first century, when commands are commonly more collective in their planning, decision making, and execution.[5]

This is not to say that decisions are made by committee (although, at times, they certainly are). Rather, the function of staff officers has expanded even as the commander retains ultimate authority. In terms of leadership and management—the planning, preparing, synchronization, and sustainment of operations—the roles and responsibilities of a staff officer are at least equal to those of the commander in terms of importance, even as the latter retains sole purview only over the command-authority function. As King found, "Commanders can no longer command alone."[6] The personnel system and institutionalized officer career paths, however, still assume they can and do.

IMPLICATIONS

The strength of traditional staff systems, especially the Scharnhorst Model, was the development of personnel with deep knowledge in their discipline. The price paid for this was poor coordination and synchronization across staff disciplines as each staff function stayed within its own "silo." The commander was the one who had to coordinate and synchronize. Most of the Scharnhorst Model is now either outdated or, in the case of measures taken to ensure that politically appointed commanders would be surrounded by professionals, unnecessary for most military forces. The best part of this system, though, and the one still lacking in modern militaries, is a dedicated human-resources pipeline to identify, educate, and develop talented staff officers.

All staff systems are fundamentally information-processing organizations. The supported commands and sections do the heavy physical lifting, while staff officers receive, evaluate, analyze, and disseminate information to accomplish their planning function. Yet most staffs remain fundamentally linear information-processing organizations. Growing awareness of the inherent nonlinearity of warfare and the information-processing potential of networks should spur restructured staffs. This is essentially what McChrystal accomplished with his reorganization: turning a linear stovepipe staff into a nonlinear networked staff. Most, however, simply graft an ever-growing amount of digital networks onto a nonnetworked structure to compensate. This can yield some efficiencies, though not as much as organizing the staff for nonlinear information processing and then building a digital network to support that structure. A true leap in staff capacity can only be achieved by doing both.

McChrystal found that the synchronization and coordination across staff sections that did occur in the traditional organization was not fast enough, so he restructured the staff to foster a high tempo of planning and execution. King found that the amount of planning, preparing, synchronization, and sustainment required by a modern division necessitated a more collaborative style of staff leadership.

What is needed is a marriage of the best part of the Scharnhorst Model—the career pipeline—with a "base model" staff designed to be collaborative as well as the empowerment of commanders to modify their staff organization based on their mission and situation. This will require deep changes across the doctrine, organization, training and education, matériel, leadership, personnel, and facilities spectrum for most military organizations.

DOCTRINE

The structure of staffs is usually determined by set tables of organization, changes to which are slow and laborious. Instead, a basic staff format should be set by such means with the assumption that, in practice, the commander will task organize it. Military services should then promulgate a doctrinal publication containing principles of organization theory and bureaucratic administration with examples of staffs task organized for different situations. Doctrinal publications for specific types of geographic operations, such as urban or jungle, usually have a chapter for planning considerations. These should have an additional chapter on staff organization tailored to the publication's subject.

Doctrine itself should be reorganized around its audience, rather than trying to be one-size-fits-all manuals for different subjects. Doctrinal publications should be realigned along five levels: tactical doctrine for commanders, operational doctrine for staffs, and joint/combined doctrine for higher-level commanders and staff. Targeting doctrine to the specific audience will make it both more used and useful: foundational doctrine for institutional culture building, such as FMFM 1, *Warfighting*, and procedural manuals. Not all military actions can be left to the discretion of tacticians. Artillery procedures, for example, are necessary due to the nature of such operations being closely tied to ballistics. Procedural manuals should, and must, be prescriptive for the safe and effective employment of complex mechanical and digital systems. Such segregation is necessary to preserve the more artistic nature of tactics.

But doctrine always carries with it the danger of stultification. Once so enshrined, a tactic or practice is used regardless of the situation and location. This is magnified by the professionalization of staff officers and must be resisted. No less an authority than Clausewitz warned against the petrification and enforcement of doctrinal straitjackets.[7]

Finally, doctrine should not be written to be employed systematically, like an instruction manual for building a piece of furniture—in other words, like it is now. Rather, it should be written to provide examples of processes that have worked in the past but may need to be modified for local conditions.

ORGANIZATION

As noted above, General McChrystal's modification of his staff was beneficial, but constant modifications to staffs is impossible. The table of organization for a base staff should build in redundancies without restraining the commander by forcing certain arrangements. The teambuilding aspect should be assumed; commanders will typically build standing, semipermanent teams of staff officers by mission, subject, or issue. To do so, they will need a deep bench with multiple staff officers of each discipline to facilitate teambuilding.

TRAINING AND EDUCATION

Training and education establishments must be modified to support the human-resources pipeline necessary to complete such a reform of the staff system in two areas: curriculum and throughput.

Curriculum for professional military education should and usually does focus on command billets vice staff billets, but where it does focus on staff billets, it should do so less in the context of specific decision-making processes (which can be easily accomplished through training rather than taking up valuable educational time) and more in the study of staffs and organizational theory. Curriculum tends to focus on historical case studies through the perspective of commanders, but this should also be done from the perspective of staffs.

When it comes to throughput, officers and enlisted service members who have been identified as having the talent and proclivity for operational art should not be the only ones who attend professional military education. In other words, the current education pipelines should remain, but they should be augmented so that those identified by the staff human resources system get priority to attend residential educational programs *regardless of rank requirements*. This has a dual benefit: it provides talented operational artists this vital education earlier in their careers and provides their senior classmates access to the perspectives of junior officers and enlisted service members as they are preparing for command.

MATÉRIEL

Matériel is not normally associated with military staffs, but nevertheless a staff needs a significant amount of equipment in order to function, especially on contemporary battlefields. Computers, both personal and networked, to assist in planning, preparing, synchronizing, and other tasks are increasingly necessary, as are survivable and secure communications.

LEADERSHIP

When it comes to the success of military staffs, the most important factor is the commander. The second most important factor, however, is the chief of staff. Some staffs have an identified chief whose entire job is to run the staff on behalf of the commander. For others, the executive officer is expected to perform the role of chief of staff. In either case, there is usually little training or education on how to run a staff (professional military education focuses on how to be a member of a staff, not on how to run one). This could partly be fixed through the training and educational changes noted above and the existing human-resources systems. Directing trained and educated staff officers to chief-of-staff and executive-officer roles, similar to the German General Staff's Ia, will have numerous benefits for staffs and commanders.

PERSONNEL

As command becomes more task organized and collaborative, the current U.S. practice of using staffs as mere waiting rooms for officers until command billets open up is wholly negligent. Commanders will need and should expect their collaborative staffs to be filled with motivated, prepared, and diligent officers. Those people serve in a role at least as important as their commanders, one without which commanders could not function. They should be equally prepared and motivated. The U.S. Army has been experimenting with creating a competitive system through Assignment Interactive Module 2.0, by which commanders can "advertise" billets and soldiers can "apply" for them.[8] If this effort is successful, a similar system should be used to fill staff positions (although not necessarily command billets).

Creating a career path for talented staff officers is one part, encouraging them to take that path is another. Similar to the greater inducements for special-operations personnel, such incentives could include priority placement at resident professional-military-education schools, preference for high-level staffs, and even unique uniform items (Prussian General Staff officers wore a unique uniform highlighting that they had completed courses of studies above and beyond their peers).

FACILITIES

As noted in the more modern case studies—the Battle of the Atlantic (3), the Battle of Britain (4), and Operation Watchtower (5)—it is frequently staffs and organizations at the national level or otherwise far removed from the actual operating area that gain and ascertain information relevant to those staffs on the ground (or at sea). Yet relevant information is not always exploited because it does not always reach the staffs or the staff officer who needs it. Those stationed forward need to be able to connect with those elsewhere who may have relevant information or analysis. Today this is known as "reach back."

This obviously has doctrinal, matériel, and personnel implications as well, but the implications for facilities matters too. It takes significant infrastructure to complete a "reach back" capability loop reliably and securely. Secure communications infrastructure, as well as secure buildings and rooms, need to exist both forward and in the rear. Commanders and staff officers on the ground during an operation obviously have a better visceral feel for the situation, but those not in the immediate vicinity may have better access to data, analytical tools, subject-matter expertise, or other resources to assist tacticians through their operational disciplines. Successfully linking front and rear together can increase the effectiveness of units forward and reduce the amount of personnel who must be deployed and sustained there.

CONCLUSION

These conclusions point us to a realization that the complexity of modern warfare in our time can best be met by effectively institutionalizing operational art as performed by professionally trained staffs and aligning doctrine and other aspects of military organizations to the newly modernized structure. These changes—modernizing the staff, modernizing the personnel system, and aligning the doctrine—should not be executed concurrently. Instead, they should be accomplished sequentially. Modernizing the staff will guide the needs of the personnel system that will create the institutional capacity to align doctrine.

Military staffs were created to manage the increasing complexity of planning, preparing, synchronizing, and sustaining tactics due to technological, sociological, bureaucratic, and political changes resulting from the Enlightenment and the Industrial Revolution. As changes in those same areas accelerate along with the ongoing Information Revolution, actualizing operational art through these processes is a military necessity.

17 A NOTE ON FORCE PROTECTION

Force protection, also known as security, is a common warfighting function. U.S. joint doctrine defines it as "preventive measures taken to mitigate hostile actions against Department of Defense personnel (to include family members), resources, facilities, and critical information."[1] It is on most lists of warfighting functions in doctrine, regardless of institution. Its popularity, however, is not evidence of theoretical viability.

Force protection is generally used to describe anything a military organization does to preserve itself, the secrecy of its operations, and its personnel. Nothing it describes, however, is compelling enough to warrant its inclusion in this volume. Military-base and fixed-site security measures like trenches, walls, barriers, and gates—all manner of fortifications, actually—are not force protection, they are defensive operations. Military-deception plans and tight operational security are not force protection, they are defensive-information operations. Final protective fires are not force protection, they are defensive fire support. Staff officers must think about and plan for the defensive measures within their purview, just as commanders at every level must think about defense as well as offense. Segregating force protection in theory could lead to a similar segregation in practice, stovepiping defensive measures and preventing the vital integration of offensive and defensive measures. Force protection as its own discipline cannot be effective; the defense must employ aspects of the offense.

It does, perhaps, have some applicability to the garrison. Ensuring that troops take safety measures during physical training, are protected and kept orderly by military police on base, and screened to prevent prying eyes from observing garrison military activities are certainly necessary measures. But these internally focused, regulation-driven aspects of military organization are better left there.

CONCLUSION

> *The first business of every theory is to clear up conceptions and ideas which have been jumbled together, and, we may say, entangled and confused.*
>
> — CARL VON CLAUSEWITZ

The above is Clausewitz's test for theory.[1] Hopefully, this book has passed his test by amputating the operational level of war from operational art, grounding operational art in the activities of military staffs, and examining that concept through its six major disciplines. The practical application aspect of the test are the case studies that follow: if this vision of operational art and operational disciplines makes it easier to evaluate historical campaigns, then clarity has been achieved.

Prussian and German success in warfare was at least in large part tied to the development of a modern staff system. Yet Germany's eventual failure in war can also be tied to that development: the German General Staff was so powerful, so uninhibited by strategic and political concerns, that, absent a guiding strategic mind like Otto von Bismarck, it merely engineered the suicide of its country not once but twice. Herein we see the danger inherent in the transposition of an operational level of war between tactics and strategy—it severs the connection between the two. Doing this is akin to building an extensive nervous system for torso and limbs while severing the spinal nerve connecting them to the brain. A "purely military understanding of strategy" took over in Germany instead of a Clausewitzian understanding in which political and social forces dominate.[2] The operational level of war is a replication of that mistake.

This book has attempted to discuss a few subjects as a necessary connection between its predecessor, *On Tactics*, and strategy. First, it has endeavored to tell the story of how the operational level of war, a concept invented in part to allow Soviet officers to shirk the demands of Marxist-Leninist ideas about strategy, became a concept that has encouraged modern officers to shirk the demands of understanding the inherent political nature of war, strategy, and tactics. Second, it has endeavored to root the very real changes in warfare that coincided with the conception of the operational level of war instead in organizational changes, especially those exemplified in the Napoleonic Revolution and the measurable benefits provided by the development of a staff along the lines of the Scharnhorst Model. Third, this book has endeavored not to throw the operational-art baby out with the operational-level bathwater by instead examining operational art through the lens of the warfighting functions.

The case against the operational level of war can be restated thusly. The operational level of war was conceived by Red Army officers to provide a venue to discuss strategy without the risk of disagreeing with Marxist-Leninist doctrine, stripping strategy of its inherent political nature in the process. The concept was built on an extremely limited data set that completely ignored much of military history, many contemporary conflicts that did not conform to it, and naval and aerial warfare. Western militaries, especially the U.S. Army, misinterpreted the Soviet vision and transplanted it into their own doctrine, regarding it as the solution to both the greater scale and complexity of modern warfare and the disastrous outcome of the Vietnam War. In 1976 the concept gained credibility in part because Michael Howard and Peter Paret erroneously inserted the words "operations" and "operational" in their translation of Clausewitz's *On War*, when the Prussian officer himself never used those words.[3] Subsequently, ideas about the operational level of war wavered between more strategic definitions and more tactical definitions, never finding purchase in something unique.[4] This process led to the amputation of strategy from tactics, a conceptual problem shared across the U.S. armed forces.[5] The American military entered into numerous wars after the turn of the twenty-first century bearing with it this conceptual flaw. It now finds itself unable to translate tactical success to strategic effect, the false idea of an operational level of war as a necessary linkage between the two being shattered by contact with the reality of warfare.

The story of the operational level of war has thus far been one of tragedy and error, from Stalin's purges to mistranslation after mistranslation to the continual waste of American blood and treasure in directionless, ineffectual wars. It is a story that cannot end too soon.

OPERATIONAL ART AND OPERATIONAL ARTISTS

Commanders see themselves as tacticians, which they are. But few tacticians can do everything by themselves, and certainly not in the modern world. Commanders require a staff of professionals who have mastered or are in the process of mastering their particular function to offer advice and perform planning, coordination, and sustainment functions that are beyond any one person. These operational artists have received little respect in history, in fiction, and all too often in their own organizations. They are necessary, but they are never treated—or promoted—as such.

This book has examined what a staff actually does through the lens of warfighting functions—more properly named "disciplines," as the word "function" implies an aspect of mechanistic automation that may be a trait of some staffs, though not good ones. It has also reorganized them, moving intelligence under information to reflect the nature of intelligence as a product of processed information (and therefore a subset), dropping force protection, and adding administration. No military organization operates without some form of administration, even if it is as simple as counting the number of people available. It is time these professionals get the recognition in theory that they deserve.

The deconstruction of the operational level of war leads to another conclusion: there are no levels of war. At the very least, trying to conceptualize war in levels is not ideal. Neither tactics nor strategy are a level, but rather activities or functions that operate continuously and in parallel. Viewing strategy as a level is especially harmful as it allows practitioners to ignore it or at least minimize its importance. Recovering the significance of strategy is, perhaps, a book for another time.

For now, it is enough to prune the ossification of military theory where it can and should be pruned. This will always be an ongoing process as ideas are conceived, codified, and disseminated among theorists, academics, and practitioners, usually fading quickly, sometimes succeeding in edifying the community, and other times wearing out a welcome that should not have been offered in the first place. The operational level of war is one of the latter, and it is time for it to die.

CASE STUDY 1
THE AUSTERLITZ CAMPAIGN, 1805

The Austerlitz Campaign is almost certainly Napoleon Bonaparte's finest and in the running for the greatest land campaign in history. Napoleon redirected an army poised to invade England and sent it rocketing across Europe, aimed squarely at Austria. It consumed opposing armies and supplies as it went until finally exploding just west of Austerlitz, in what is now the Czech Republic, in a climactic battle on 2 December 1804. The entire War of the Third Coalition was simply the lead up to Austerlitz, or a supporting effort to it, the battle that decided the war in France's favor.

This case study looks at Austerlitz only from the perspective of the French to illuminate the disciplines of operational art during a land campaign; a full campaign study would require much more than a chapter. It showcases Napoleon's system—including the staff built by and for him—at the height of its powers. His was the first modern staff system, and his chief of staff, Louis-Alexandre Berthier, perhaps the first modern chief of staff. The campaign demonstrates the superiority of such a system, especially when it comes to information. Napoleon not only had a better idea of how the campaign was progressing but also adroitly deceived his opponents on numerous occasions. The superiority of his information system was decisive, even mitigating the failures of his logistics system (as will be seen). As was typical for him, Napoleon pursued an offensive, persisting, annihilation (OPA) campaign, while his opponents tried to meet it directly with a defensive, persisting, annihilation (DPA) campaign, just as he hoped. This case study uses the operational disciplines as tools to analyze the Austerlitz Campaign in an organized way.

HISTORICAL NARRATIVE
THE ROAD TO WAR
Napoleon did not want war with Austria. He wanted war with Britain. To that end, in June 1803 he ordered the formation of the Army of England.[1]

Formed in a series of training camps in Normandy, the Army of England spent two years preparing for a cross-channel invasion. It was not wholly formed of raw recruits, however, for a quarter of the troops were veterans of previous campaigns, men who were able to train and mentor the rest.[2] By the time it was rechristened as the Grand Armée, having absorbed other French units from various parts of the empire, and then redirected to invade Austria in 1805, it was the best-drilled, best-organized, and most-cohesive army in the world.

Britain, however, had no intention of sitting across the channel and waiting. While the Royal Navy lay in wait, the nation used its vast wealth and diplomatic clout to underwrite an anti-French alliance primarily composed of Austria, Russia, Sweden, and itself. Parliament, led by Prime Minister William Pitt, committed to pay the tsar 1.25 million pounds in golden guineas for every 100,000 Russian troops committed against France, with similar subsidies for the other allies.[3]

Although not all of these arrangements were public knowledge, tensions in Europe were high. As early as August 1805, Napoleon began gathering information for a Continental war by ordering maps of Austrian territory and sending spies to relevant areas.[4] On 25 August he deployed cavalry units to begin patrolling the stretch of the Rhine where he planned to cross with his army.[5] In fact, Napoleon had the entire movement from the channel coast to Vienna planned out by date, road, and division before the war officially began; he could even dictate it from memory.[6] At this point, he had probably already decided to give up on the invasion of Britain, now requiring those troops on the Continent.

On 26 August the Grande Armée received orders to march east on routes that indicated plans to invade the Danube Valley in Austria through the Black Forest.[7] By the twenty-eighth or twenty-ninth, his lead divisions were already on the move, following in the wake of staff officers assigned to arrange supply and bivouac points.[8] Despite these arrangements, the troops still suffered from a lack of supplies early on. The month-long march to the Rhine strained the supply system and the soldiers alike. On 27 September, by which date various units had consolidated along the Rhine, Napoleon had massed 184,000 troops. The emperor himself had arrived on the twenty-sixth and started shifting units across the Rhine toward Austrian field marshal Mack's force of 72,000 men. Mack believed that Napoleon's army numbered 70,000 troops.[9]

ULM

Mack's mission was to guard the Black Forest approach into the Danube Valley, of which Napoleon was already aware based on tracking the movements of the Austrian troops to Ulm, where Mack was based. Once he arrived, Napoleon ordered cavalry units under Marshal Joachim Murat to feint through the forest while the rest of the Grande Armée crossed the Rhine.[10] As his troops were moving and skirmishing with Austrians troops, Napoleon turned his attention to information. The emperor wrote the first of many public bulletins during this campaign, using printing presses with the army to communicate with local civilians, knowing full well that the Austrians would inevitably see them as well.[11] He also detailed troops to "desert" to the Austrians, reporting to them that many French units were on the verge of munity, and planted rumors that there had been a coup against his government in Paris.[12] These information efforts reinforced Mack's belief that Napoleon would move through the Black Forest—a common movement corridor—and that the French army was weak, convincing him to stay rather than withdraw.

Far to the north and east of Ulm, however, five of the Grande Armée's seven corps were crossing the Rhine in a sweeping envelopment maneuver to interpose themselves behind Mack and between him and his nearest reinforcements, farther east at Munich.[13] They met no serious resistance and by 13 October had encircled and trapped Mack, who remained unaware of his predicament.

Although the Grande Armée continued to struggle with supply issues, it defeated an Austrian attempt at a relief expedition at Trochttelfingen on 17 October.[14] Mack, still ignorant of his army's dire position, attended a conference with Napoleon at his own headquarters on the seventeenth. The emperor showed him a map of the French positions, which convinced the Austrian commander to surrender, which he did on the twentieth.[15]

VIENNA

The next day the Grande Armée was on the march eastward.[16] The Allies were consolidating their remaining troops under Field Marshal Kutuzov. The Russian commander was wilier than Mack, and while he contested Napoleon's advance where and when he could, his primary plan was to fall back on reinforcements so that he could mass as many troops as possible against the French. This was especially important after 23 October, when he learned of Mack's surrender. On the twenty-sixth the Grande Armée began crossing the Iser River; Kutuzov ordered a withdrawal. Although the French continued to experience supply shortfalls, the Allied pullback was so botched that Austrian stockpiles were left behind and captured.[17]

While all this was occurring, there was also action in the Italian theater of the campaign. On 30 October French troops under Marshal Andre Massena defeated an Austrian army at Caldiero, preventing it from moving north to defend Vienna.[18] The one bright spot for the Allies was the effective rearguard actions of troops under General Peter Bagration, who was able to slow down the French advance and protect Kutuzov's rear.[19]

Vienna itself was increasingly in a panic as the first French troops crossed the Danube on 6 November. About the eighth or the ninth, Kutuzov decided to abandon the Austrian capital and ordered another withdrawal. On the thirteenth the French captured the key Tabor Bridge over the Danube by spreading a rumor among the guarding troops that the war was over.[20] The next day they occupied Vienna in force.

Napoleon did not get bogged down by the occupation. Instead, his advance continued, inducing Kutuzov to order another withdrawal on 17 November.[21] On that same day, the emperor learned of the crushing defeat of the French navy at Trafalgar on 21 October.[22] He ordered the news kept secret from the troops, for obvious reasons, but his postponed invasion of England was now all but impossible.

On 19 November the French reached the town of Brunn, which the Allies had left two days earlier, and captured more supplies when the city officially surrendered the next day. The Allies, meanwhile, were consolidating their troops at Olmutz, completed by the twenty-second.[23] As the Grande Armée rested, Napoleon scouted ahead and reached the ground around Austerlitz, where he decided he would fight a battle. He ordered the fortification of supporting positions immediately.[24]

Tsar Alexander led an Allied council of war on 24 November. Although Kutuzov had ably preserved the main army and drawn Napoleon along ever-stretching supply lines, advisors convinced the tsar to override his general's desire to wait for the rest of the expected reinforcements and to begin advancing against the Grande Armée.[25] The next day a French envoy returned from the Allied camp and reported this new offensive mood to Napoleon. When a Russian envoy met with him on the twenty-seventh, Napoleon pretended to be nervous and acted like he needed an immediate armistice. This was, of course, a ruse. The envoy returned and reported to Tsar Alexander that the time to attack was now.[26]

On the twenty-seventh the Allies transitioned to the offense and moved west. Napoleon ordered his distant units to return to the area.[27] As Alexander's forces advanced, French units forward of Brunn began falling back to the positions previously identified by Napoleon. The Allies advanced slowly, not reaching the emperor's preselected area until 1 December. French troops on the Pratzen Heights, west of Austerlitz, observed these movements, at one point joined by Napoleon himself, who recognized the Allied intention to attack his right flank at Telnitz. The emperor made his final dispositions. He concentrated his troops on the left and center, intending to maneuver against the right flanks of the Allied army as it attacked his right, which would stall the attack but allow his forces to fall back if necessary. His own reinforcements were only a day's march away, able to arrive in time to participate in the coming battle. That afternoon the Allies made their final deployments in full view of the French. In the evening Napoleon toured his units as they prepared to move, instructing the troops to light their campfires, which the Allies interpreted as signaling a withdrawal.[28]

AUSTERLITZ

As 2 December dawned, the French positions were still shrouded in fog as Napoleon conducted a personal reconnaissance. At 0600 he met with his marshals and gave final orders. The emperor wrote a proclamation sent or read to all of the troops, outlining the basics of the plan. Around 0630, the Allied troop movements began, coming into contact with the French right at about 0700. They immediately encountered stiff resistance, although lead French units fell back as they fought according to Napoleon's plan to draw the Austrians away from the Pratzen Plateau to the north.[29] Although the Grande Armée was concentrated on its center and left flank, Napoleon could depend on his better-trained troops to fix the Allies on its right. Around Sokolnitz about 10,000 French troops under Marshal Louis Davout delayed and fixed 36,000 Allied troops through the morning.[30]

This was the essence of Napoleon's plan. Although the total numbers of troops were roughly even on both sides, his skillful deployments, driven by information efforts that allowed him to ascertain the Allied plan ahead of time, allowed the French to generate numerical superiority in space and time where it mattered and encourage the Allies to concentrate where it did not matter. The Russians and Austrians continually fed troops to their left (the French right) through the morning until about 1000, when Napoleon learned that the Pratzen Plateau at the center was empty of Allied forces.

(The report was inaccurate; it was not devoid of enemy troops, but there were very few holding the center.) At about that time, he ordered an attack across the heights against the Allied center. Around 24,000 French troops faced about 12,000 defenders.[31]

The result was predictable, with the Allied line collapsing about forty-five minutes after the order was sent. The hard-pressed troops hastily formed a second line, which held about fifteen minutes before also collapsing.[32] Both Kutuzov and Tsar Alexander were on the plateau; the general was slightly wounded by a bullet as soldiers retreated around him. The collapse in the center was finally stemmed in dramatic fashion by a charge on the part of the Russian Imperial Guard against the advancing French, but their success was quickly wiped out with a countercharge by the French Imperial Guard.

What saved the Allies from total encirclement was a staunch defense to the north. The French left also attacked that morning, and Napoleon intended to roll up the enemy line from the north and then fall upon the Allied concentration in the south. But the Allied right flank, under Bagration, managed to keep the French troops fixed, although doing so finally depended on a line of Russian artillery, behind which the Allied troops retreated.[33]

French success in the center, however, was more than enough to win the battle. Around 1400 Napoleon ordered his units in the center to turn south and attack where light troops were holding off the Russians in intense house-to-house fighting. They succeeded in cutting off a large number of the tsar's troops, whose commander had ignored Kutuzov's earlier orders. Other Allied troops collapsed here, too, breaking and running into a headlong retreat over the frozen Satschen Lake. French artillery fire, the weight of the retreating men and horses, or a combination broke the ice, and many Russian soldiers drowned.[34] Austrian cavalry were able to block further pursuit, but by 1600 the Allied army was defeated. The next day Austria sued for peace, ending the campaign and the war.

OPERATIONAL DISCIPLINES

ADMINISTRATION

Military administration began modernizing before Napoleon was even born. European states formed the modern bureaucratic systems necessary to manage ever larger armies, and ever larger budgets, as early as the sixteenth century. Still, Napoleon's concern for even the lowest-ranking soldiers and their needs extended the need for administration downward, which had real benefits on the battlefield.

Administration is as much a moral issue as it is a bureaucratic one. Detailed and effective management ties the soldier to his or her institution by ensuring that individual issues are tracked, communicated, and hopefully solved, engendering moral cohesion and loyalty. Napoleon expected detailed and concerned leadership on the part of his subordinate officers, and his care for the enlisted troops remains legendary today, as evidenced by instructions he sent to one of his marshals on administration:

> Pay great attention to the soldiers, and see about them in detail. The first time you arrive at the camp, line up the battalions, and spend eight hours at a stretch seeing the soldiers one by one; receive their complaints, inspect their weapons, and make sure they lack nothing. There are many advantages to making these reviews of seven to eight hours; the soldier becomes accustomed to being armed and on duty, it proves to him that the leader is paying attention to and taking complete care of him; which is a great confidence-inspiring motivation for the soldier.[35]

The feelings of loyalty and esprit de corps instilled in the French troops toward Napoleon's leadership clearly had an effect on the battlefield at Austerlitz. By comparison, the opposing Russian forced mostly comprised conscripted serfs, men who were little more than slaves—and knew it. This difference enabled Napoleon to depend on his troops in battle to both withstand punishment and withdraw in good order rather than collapsing. Since his plan at Austerlitz hinged on the troops on the right flank fighting and withdrawing while heavily outnumbered, his longstanding attention to their needs and the morale it engendered had a decisive effect.

Napoleon's need for administration was so great that his chief of staff, Berthier, had developed a mobile filing system on a specially designed wagon to organize administrative information (both for military needs and civil-governmental functions that Napoleon handled, initially as first consul and then as emperor).[36]

INFORMATION

Information was clearly a determining factor in this campaign. The Allies consistently made decisions based on inaccurate knowledge about their opponent, the circumstances of the campaign, and the capabilities of their own forces. Not all of this was due to Napoleon's effective deception. Although he adeptly reinforced Mack's assumption that the French would invade through the Black Forest, the Austrian commander at Ulm made no dispositions for security in the event that he was wrong. At Austerlitz, of course, the Allies chose the exact course of action that Napoleon wanted them to choose, failing to wait for more reinforcements to arrive before attacking the French right.

Spying and intelligence, ancient as it is, was already a common practice among the constantly vying nations of Europe. Neither side was a stranger to it, but Napoleon's spy system was at its best in 1805. In early October, before the emperor even arrived at the front, his spy chief, Charles Schulmeister, was behind Austrian lines and feeding information back to him.[37] Schulmeister was old friends with Mack's chief of intelligence, Hauptmann Wendt, who introduced him directly to the field marshal. He then proceeded to feed false information, even prepared false documents, directly to Mack.[38] After Ulm, Schulmeister was paid by the retreating Austrians for information, but he was actually feeding information back to Napoleon about their troop movements.[39] In Vienna he managed to get appointed commissioner general of the Viennese police and ran a spy network from the city, possibly with contacts in both the Austrian and Russian high commands.[40]

The information Napoleon received through these extensive efforts, among others, enabled both intelligence and deception. Information about Allied troop movements made it easy for him to predict their plans, right up until the morning of Austerlitz. His knowledge of their mood and plans also allowed Napoleon to consistently reinforce the assumptions of Allied commanders and exploit their subsequent decisions.

OPERATIONS

It is clear from the outline of the campaign above that Napoleon was extremely skillful at managing time and space. Mack positioned himself too far forward in space for reinforcements to reach him in time, allowing the Grande Armée to interpose between them. The sheer speed of the French troops, relative to their opponents, enabled more options when it came to maneuver; the complete encirclement of Mack at Ulm is an ideal case. Their reliability made other options possible, such as the weak right flank that Napoleon used at Austerlitz. The French troops at that position were heavily outnumbered and hard pressed by the Allies, but they not only held as long as they could, they withdrew in good order when necessary. Allied troops, in contrast, collapsed more often than not (the exception being the northern sector, where Bagration's troops, old hands at orderly withdrawals, stymied Napoleon's plan to envelop the entire Allied line).

Kutuzov, however, also managed time and space well. He stymied Napoleon's advance where possible and continually kept his main forces out of range of French maneuver, falling back on reinforcements as they deployed and formed. Had Mack also done so and fallen back toward the main Allied army, Napoleon would have been heavily outnumbered at Austerlitz or wherever the Allies made their stand. Furthermore, Kutuzov wanted to draw Napoleon even farther east than Austerlitz, potentially overburdening the French supply lines, further depleting the Grande Armée, and enhancing his own forces with even more reinforcements. Had the general not been overruled, the campaign may well have had a different result. In 1812, when Kutuzov had his way in Russia, it did.

Napoleon's encirclement of Mack at Ulm was his signature tactic, the *manoeuvre de derrière*. It cut off his opponent from reinforcements, withdrawal, and logistics by placing the Grande Armée in a central position between its opponent's forward and rear forces. It was brutally effective but depended on Napoleon's troops being able to swiftly confront the encircled forces before the arrival of a relief column (or confronting reinforcements before the encircled forces could react). Kutuzov was right to avoid falling victim to this tactic, which he successfully did again in Russia in 1812.

In addition to time and space, the forces available to Napoleon were better organized as well as better led. The key was his corps system. Although it had been used in experimentation previously, Napoleon institutionalized it.[41] A French army corps was not just a corps-sized unit (that is, three or four divisions), but a full combined-arms formation. In addition to its own cavalry and artillery, a corps had its own information service, supply, transportation, engineering, medical, pay, and commissary apparatuses.[42] This allowed each one to move and, if necessary, fight on its own while sustaining itself. Few Allied units or commanders—Bagration's rear guard being one such exception—were able to operate independent of the main army.

FIRE SUPPORT

Napoleon was an artillery officer by trade, so it should not be surprising that he was an innovator when it came to fire support. The Austerlitz Campaign does not capture this aspect of his career, however, as artillery played little role in his plans at Ulm or at Austerlitz. French artillery was, of course, in action all along the line at Austerlitz and played a role in the exploitation of the collapse of the Allied left in the afternoon, but the battle was dominated more by infantry and cavalry forces.

But the Allies really made artillery count at Austerlitz. Russian cannon were placed on high ground and well established on the northern flank, enabling Bagration to withdraw his troops to safety within their range and stop the momentum of the French assault. This, in turn, prevented the French left from rolling up the entire Allied front.

LOGISTICS

As mentioned above, Napoleon demanded detailed planning when it came to logistics and had a well-developed logistic system to include supply officers at many levels. Yet, despite such arrangements, the Grande Armée was chronically undersupplied. Napoleon's logistic system could not replace the traditional foraging methods of military forces, but that was probably impossible in 1805 anyway. Repeated capture of stocks that the withdrawing Allies had neglected to destroy was Napoleon's saving grace.

But supplies are just one component of logistics: the movement of troops is another. Napoleon, knowing that he had to depend at least in part on foraging and local-contracted supplies, moved his army corps on varied, roughly parallel roads, concentrating them only for action. This not only mitigated the risk of overloading the stocks on any one line of advance but also prevented bottlenecks and jams resulting from too many units marching down too few roads. The corps system, as mentioned above, enabled such movements. The risk of any individual corps being cut off and overwhelmed was mitigated by their combined-arms composition, which allowed them to at least hold off numerically superior forces long enough for other French units to react.

The speed at which the Grande Armée crossed much of the European continent on foot remains impressive. The distance between Rouen in Normandy and Brunn, the town where the Grande Armée paused just before Austerlitz (now Brno in the Czech Republic), is more than eight hundred miles.

COMMAND AND CONTROL

Allied command was so disjointed and confused, a common malady in coalition warfare, that their troops fought isolated, individual battles against an opponent who was unified by one vision, transmitted through an empowered and effective staff.[43] Kutuzov was overruled in major decisions and had to compete with other advisors to convince the tsar to adopt or reject courses of action. He also had to balance the advice and interests of the Austrians and other coalition members. Napoleon, of course, had to compete with no one.

Napoleon planned the battle essentially by himself, then communicated it not just to his principle subordinates but to the troops themselves. Although the emperor did not expect the soldiers to execute the plan themselves, his action represents part of the moral aspect to command and control. The men, confident as they were in Napoleon, were thus assured that there was a plan and empowered by the fact of being privy to it, even if only in a basic form. On the Allied side, soldiers were completely unaware of their commanders' battle plan or their role in it. Even high-ranking officers were kept in the dark. To them, the chaos and complexity of the combat must have been worse since there was no way for them to know that it had any purpose behind it.

Although French planning was highly centralized, the plan's execution was highly decentralized. Subordinate commanders could act and react based on the situation as it unfolded, while their opposite numbers were more dependent on information and guidance flowing from the Allied high command. Unifying a military force under a single overarching vision while still allowing subordinate commanders a measure of freedom of action to exploit opportunities, a command-and-control system that would be later known as mission command, is difficult for many modern military forces. Napoleon, however, was able to accomplish this during the Austerlitz Campaign.

CONCLUSION

Despite his success, Napoleon should be viewed with caution as a model for today's militaries. His highly centralized style of command is probably impossible in modern warfare. In fact, it is almost unbelievable that it even worked at the turn of the nineteenth century. That it did so must be attributed in part to the presence of a protostaff, designed by Napoleon for Napoleon and run (by Berthier) for Napoleon. To be fair, he also had a lot of help from his enemies. The Austrian supply system was wholly insufficient, as was the Russian system, and the pace at which both Austrian and Russian troops were forced to move to keep up with French troops was beyond their level of training.

Even as Napoleon conquered his way across Europe, eyes were upon him. The following year he would break another army, this time the Prussians at the twin battles of Jena and Auerstedt. The reform movement in Prussia that would grow out of that troubling defeat would institutionalize the personal staff of Napoleon and vastly improve upon it, producing an organization aimed at achieving Napoleonic success without the need for Napoleon himself.

CASE STUDY 2
THE KÖNIGGRÄTZ CAMPAIGN, 1866

The Austro-Prussian War of 1866 was really only one campaign, the Königgrätz Campaign. Although occurring in the same region as Austerlitz and featuring another defeat of the unfortunate Austrians, Königgrätz is a worthwhile case study of the Scharnhorst Model of a general staff in its realized form.

The Scharnhorst Model was developed to solve a specific problem: how to replicate Napoleon's success without depending on the emergence of genius of his caliber. The idea was to create a staff system that could provide the planning, coordination, information, and synthesis that Napoleon was able to perform himself to a commander of far less talent. The Königgrätz Campaign shows the Scharnhorst Model at the height of its powers, when the idea was fully institutionalized in the Royal Prussian Army but before it completed its slide into domination of it, severing the rechristened Imperial German Army from the demands of strategy.

Prussian success had a lot of assistance from their opponents. The Austrian staff system was a poor facsimile of the Prussian system, characterized by ineffective staff work and staff officers promoted because of who they were rather than what they could do.[1] It had the same form, but its spirit was the antithesis of the Prussian system. Still, Austria was a powerful, multinational empire and exerted a hegemonic influence over the various smaller German states, only one of which was Prussia. This was the two combatants' relative standing on the morning of 3 July 1866. By that evening, the Germanic world had changed.

HISTORICAL NARRATIVE
ROAD TO WAR
The march to the Austro-Prussian War began with another war, the Second Schleswig War of 1864. In that conflict, Prussia and Austria joined together to conquer Schleswig-Holstein, a small German state heretofore controlled by

Denmark. After successfully defeating the Danes, the two allies continually squabbled over how to administer the acquired state until tensions became high enough for each to mobilize troops in early 1866.

Austria was the first to move, mobilizing its troops on 21 April.[2] Prussia did not follow suit until 3 May, at which point a partial mobilization was issued, followed by a full mobilization on the twelfth.[3] One month later, on 12 June, Prussian troops went into action, occupying Holstein. On the sixteenth, after the German Diet had voted to mobilize all national armies against Prussia, more Prussian troops occupied Saxony, Kurresse, and Hesse.[4] These forces met serious resistance only in Hannover, which was invaded on the same day but avoided surrendering until 29 June.

By the time Prussia was gobbling up lesser German states, Austria was still mobilizing its forces and had yet to put them in action. The difference lay in the logistics planning and staff work conducted by the Prussian General Staff. Prussia had seen the value of railroads for mobilization and invested in them ahead of time. Its troops moved to their assigned positions for an invasion of the Austrian region of Bohemia over five different railroads. Austrian troops were moved via one.[5] This single rail line, through which both troops and supplies had to pass, virtually forced the Austrians to concentrate their forces in one area. This suited them fine: Austrian tactical theory focused on mass over everything else. But it also suited the Prussians.

PLANS

Helmuth von Moltke, chief of staff of the Prussian General Staff, newly granted near total authority over the Prussian army, would use the rail lines to converge on Bohemia, where the Austrian army was concentrating from multiple axes of advance. He planned to do so with four separate armies, but King William I allowed only three. Moltke's plan dubbed them the First Army, invading from the west; the Second Army, invading from the north; and the Army of the Elbe, a much smaller force that would also invade from the west on the First Army's southern flank.[6] Expecting the Austrian army to concentrate around Gitschin, he planned for these three armies to converge there, knowing that no matter how the Austrians were arrayed, at least one flank would be exposed to at least one of the Prussian armies.[7]

Although Moltke's name means something today, it did not then. Moltke was an unlikely choice to run an army. He was not particularly charismatic or high ranking in terms of nobility, and he had not commanded anything higher than a company in his entire career.[8]

Moltke's opponent was Field Marshal Ludwig von Benedek. He was beloved by his troops and had risen to high command following success after success in campaigns in Italy. When chosen for the command in Bohemia, Benedek protested because he knew nothing of the region and had never operated there.[9] Emperor Franz Joseph I pressed him to take the command, however, and he agreed. Benedek's general plan was to consolidate as many Austrian forces as possible into one army, advance west against the First Army, and defeat it.[10]

FIRST MOVES

The Austrian army began concentrating at Olmutz, just as the ill-fated Third Coalition had sixty-one years before. On 18 June it began slowly moving toward Josephstadt. Four days later Moltke ordered the three Prussian armies into Bohemia. Although they had moved to their starting positions via railroads, they would march into Austrian territory.

Supply problems began almost immediately. The Prussian (and later German) General Staff always focused more on the logistics of moving troops than on the logistics of supplying them. The German rail system was well developed, excellent for transporting troops and supplies up to a certain point. But the equipment necessary to move supplies from these railheads forward with the armies as they marched was totally insufficient.[11]

And the pace of advance Moltke had set was hard, so much so that army commanders asked to slacken it in order to rest their troops.[12] But not even skirmishes with advanced Austrian troops slowed the oncoming Prussians, as their advantage in modern weaponry was perfectly matched against outdated Austrian tactics that focused on direct massed assaults. Prussia had adopted the breach-loading needle gun and equipped all of its infantry units with it, while Austrian troops still carried muzzle-loading rifles. These initial clashes presaged the final confrontation: Austrians bravely charging Prussians, who calmly mowed them down.

The first major clashes occurred at the villages of Náchod and Trautenau on 27 June, both involving elements of the Second Army as it split up to pass through mountain passes on the border. At Náchod, Austrian forces repeatedly attacked an advance guard but were repulsed with heavy casualties. Austrian forces did better against the Prussians at Trautenau, pushing their advance forces back. Yet even here Austrian casualties were high.[13] The two forces clashed in separate engagements the next day at Soor and Skalitz. Both were Austrian defeats and far bloodier for the Austrians than the Prussians.[14]

The First Army, yet to fight any major Austrian forces, concentrated at Münchengrätz on 28 June after a small skirmish with Austrian forces holding the town. This concentration led to supply shortages as the Prussians struggled to feed so many troops in one small area.[15] The First Army's first major meeting with Austrian forces came the next day, at Gitschin. The Austrians held their own against Prussian forces attacking the town from multiple directions but received a withdrawal order from Benedek, who was completely unaware of the fighting there. The night withdrawal under fire was understandably chaotic and devolved into a panicked flight.[16]

Moltke had expected the Austrian army to consolidate around Gitschin, but it had not moved fast enough and so had not done so. On 1 July he ordered all three Prussian armies to move toward Königgrätz, although he did not know at this point that Benedek would make a stand between it and Sadowa.[17] The next day Moltke held a war council, during which the final form of the Prussian plan began to take shape. During the meeting, the king was pressed to unite the armies but sided with Moltke, who insisted that they be kept separated at least until it was ascertained where the Austrians were concentrated.[18] He would not have long to wait for this information.

While the Prussian high command was deliberating, First Army patrols had identified four Austrian corps concentrated between Königgrätz and Sadowa through both observation and interrogation of prisoners.[19] Prince Frederick Charles, who had thus far led the Second Army cautiously and slowly, decided to attack the next day, 3 July, with a portion of his command. Around 2100 that night, the Prussian plan was complete and promulgated, also being sent to the high command. Moltke was awakened and, after reviewing the intelligence and the plan, not only approved it but ordered the entire First Army, along with the Army of the Elbe and the Second Army, into the attack. He had ascertained that the Austrian army was in position to be attacked by all three armies at once, with the Second Army well positioned to hit the Austrian right flank from the north.[20]

THE CAMPAIGN

The Austrians were expertly arrayed in a strong defensive position. Their main line, facing west, was tied in to terrain features, including forests and hills that would canalize any enemy attacks, all arrayed along the Bistritz River, which the Prussians would have to cross. High points behind the lines bristled with the superior Austrian cannon, presighted and registered on likely avenues of approach.[21] This line curled around to the north and stretched back to the Elbe River. Benedek had placed the army in a position with its back to a river—always a dangerous move—but he had additional bridges and crossings in place should he need to escape. Both his western flank and his northern flank were arrayed right where the Prussian armies would have to attack them. Once the Prussians had broken themselves on his defenses, Benedek planned, his reserve would counterattack. The Austrians would also have the advantage of interior lines, able to shift forces quickly from one point of the line to other if needed. Far from being an advantage, however, the shifting of forces turned out to be the Austrians' downfall. Two units on the northern flank moved to more defensible ground the morning of 3 July, thereby opening up a gap and weakening the position.[22]

Both the First Army and the Army of the Elbe would attack the Austrian line from the west, crossing the Bistritz into the teeth of the defense, the First Army against the center and the Army of the Elbe against the Austrian right, with the hopes of turning it. Moltke's main bid for success, however, would be Second Army's attack on the northern flank—if it arrived in time.

The First Army was on the move at 0400, taking up its position for the attack. That assault finally started at 0700, with cavalry and horse artillery moving up to probe Austrian positions. Firing commenced with an artillery duel at 0730.[23] Moltke ordered the First Army to attack all along the line en masse; at 0830 Prussian infantry moved in. The artillery fire on both sides was intense; villages that had existed there for centuries were quickly ablaze.[24] By 1100, Prussian units became pinned down by the intense fire, and the attack began to stall.[25] Tiered, registered Austrian artillery on high points made any further advance murderous.

The Army of the Elbe was also in position by 0800. Austrian troops withdrew from its front after light skirmishing.[26] By late morning, though, a back-and-forth battle developed, with each side advancing, being pushed back, then advancing again. Far from being able to turn the Austrian flank, no progress was made on the right.

The hinge of the Austrian position, where the north-south main line turned to the west-east northern flank, was a forest called the Swiepwald. Strongly held by Austrian forces and covered by artillery, the heavy fire coming from the woods drew Prussian attention. At 0830 about six divisions of infantry rushed the position. At 0930 ten Austrian divisions withdrew from the forest with heavy losses, but they were far from finished. Immediately after this withdrawal, two other Austrian brigades were ordered to take back the Swiepwald. The difference in tactics between the two sides, however, began to tell. The Austrians moved and fired in formation over open ground, while the Prussians used the trees as cover and well-aimed, rapid fire to defend their positions. Despite the weight of Austrian numbers, the result was predictable. These two brigades were repulsed. Around 1100 two more fresh brigades took over the assault. But that also failed. Nineteen Prussian battalions had repulsed fifty Austrian battalions, but both sides suffered high casualties.[27]

The mauling of so many Austrian battalions in the Swiepwal had effects beyond just the casualties; the units sent into the forest were pulled from the northern flank of the Austrian army, precisely where the Second Army was rapidly approaching. Benedek, who was at this point planning a counterattack against the First Army, received a telegram around 1130 notifying him that the Second Army was about to arrive.[28] He immediately tried to move forces to the northern flank, but the only ones close enough to shift in time were those already bloodied by the fighting in the Swiepwald.[29] At about this same time, the Austrian attack on the Army of the Elbe also collapsed.[30]

The Prussian Second Army had left camp at 0800 and headed toward the Austrian army.[31] By 1000, two corps were up front, advancing on line by division. Moltke would have liked them to move faster, but wet weather and difficult terrain slowed their advance. At 1300 the attack hit the thinly held ridge known as Chlum. Fog still shrouded the low terrain so that, far from having to fight uphill against dug-in troops, the Prussian infantry seemed to materialize out of thin air right into the surprised and unprepared Austrian positions. Although Benedek and the Austrian General Staff had known for an hour and a half that the Prussian Second Army was coming, the troops that would actually have to fight them did not. The only Austrian forces ready were the artillery, which took the advancing Prussian divisions under fire. Prussian artillery, which was not originally planned to be as far forward until its commander insisted that very morning that the order be changed, fired on the Austrian batteries from exposed positions, drawing their fire away from the infantry.

The Austrians holding the village of Chlum, on the ridge of the same name, cracked quickly and retreated, although the house-to-house fighting was punishing for both sides. Prussian forces swarmed over the ridge to find two Austrian corps from the reserve arrayed in formation before them—both facing the wrong way. The Prussians simply kept the attack going. Some 25,000 Austrian troops, after witnessing this chaotic attack, simply left the battlefield entirely.[32]

For the First Army, the Second Army had arrived just in time. Around midday, fixing the Austrian main line in place had become enough of a strain that the commander wanted to commit his reserve, but this was vetoed by Moltke.[33] Around 1300, unit commanders considered withdrawing, whatever Moltke said.[34]

At 1500 Benedek realized that the northern line was lost, finally committing his reserve to a counterattack to preserve his withdrawal route.[35] Multiple Austrian assaults on the Prussians, now in possession of the high ground around Chlum, failed. They succeeded, however, in staving off further Prussian advances. At 1600 Moltke ordered the First Army into a general advance against the cracking Austrian lines.[36] Benedek, now focused on saving his army, largely succeeded, with fully 180,000 Austrian troops escaping the battlefield.[37] Even so, no units above the battalion level were remotely capable fighting or coordinating with each other. Many units completely lost their cohesion in their frantic flights for Königgrätz itself. Although many troops escaped Moltke's net, the Austrian army was broken. The last shots of the campaign were fired somewhere around 2100 as night fell on a new German order.[38]

OPERATIONAL DISCIPLINES

ADMINISTRATION

Even given the aforementioned weaknesses of Austria's general-staff system, its administration system was poor. The Austrian high command understood only the number of troops they had available on paper, not in actuality. Their available forces were generally 20–25 percent fewer than they thought them to be.[39]

Both combatants utilized conscription, but the opportunities to avoid service for people of means were far greater for the Austrians, ensuring that their troops were poorly educated and motivated when compared to their Prussian counterparts.[40] Prussian conscription was far from perfect, and influential aristocrats could certainly avoid service if they wished. But on the whole the Prussian system was better administered, and it made a marked difference on the battlefield.

The Austrian army also lacked standardization. An Italian brigade and an Austrian brigade and a Saxon brigade did not necessarily have the same amount of personnel or even like subordinate units. Their equipment could also be quite different. In addition, language barriers existed between all of these different units from the various nationalities composing the Austrian

Empire. Both administration and command and control faced internal friction due to the multitude of languages encountered.⁴¹

Prussian administration is rightly famous. The Royal Prussian Army had a regular and systematic system of conscription. And its units were organized in the same way during peace and war.⁴² The Austrians had to spend time during the Königgrätz Campaign organizing units and subunits. Prussian troops showed up ready.

INFORMATION

The Prussian system was weaker when it came to information. Moltke's cavalry was largely parceled out among infantry units, so it was inefficient when used for reconnaissance.⁴³ He had no forces available to conduct his own reconnaissance but had to rely on subordinate commanders. The First Army conspicuously failed to use its cavalry for reconnaissance and moved too slowly as a consequence, even though there were few Austrian forces along their route of march.⁴⁴ It even failed to detect Austrian withdrawals, leading to delays by planning and executing attacks on empty objectives.⁴⁵ The First Army got better at reconnaissance as the campaign continued; its cavalry patrols detected the Austrian concentration near Königgrätz.

Austrian information gathering was perhaps better, but their processing of it was worse. Information had to go all the way to Benedek himself for a decision, and it was often stale by then. The field marshal often failed to act on the information acquired. He was well aware of the Second Army's location and direction, if not perhaps the speed of their movement. But the Austrian commander did not act on that information until it was too late.

OPERATIONS

The Königgrätz Campaign can be framed as dueling conceptions of interior versus exterior lines. The conventional wisdom among European armies at the time was that gaining a position that offered interior lines was superior, as "proven" by Napoleon's preference for the central position. Benedek sought to achieve this and assumed that Moltke would concentrate both large armies on one flank before attacking. His nonchalance about the flanking threat presented by the Second Army can be traced to this belief.

Moltke, however, believed that the game had changed. The combination of using railroad transportation to move and supply armies operating on exterior lines and the increased firepower of the needle gun had made, in his mind, operating on exterior lines not only possible but also advantageous.⁴⁶

At Ulm Napoleon had to converge before fighting. At Königgrätz Moltke did not have to converge first—his armies converged on the Austrian army itself.

That convergence depended on Moltke's management of time and space. His armies would have to maneuver and fight independently while still being able to support each other if one was caught by itself. And in that case, it would have to hold out against the numerically superior Austrian forces to enable the flanking attack of the other.

The Austrian plan rested on the conventional wisdom of the time, much of it based on Napoleon's tactics despite changes in weaponry and technology. The Prussian plan rested on supposition, but supposition underpinned by detailed analysis and planning conducted by the general staff. The latter turned out to be right.

FIRE SUPPORT

The Austrians were clearly superior in terms of fire support, and the campaign showed this advantage. Their superiority was firstly technological. Austrian artillery was superior; Prussia had failed to fully move toward rifled guns and still retained far more smoothbore cannon. Austria fielded 736 rifled pieces and 58 smoothbores. Prussian forces fielded 492 rifled cannon and 306 smoothbores, all split between three armies. Prussia had only recently introduced the rifled pieces they did have, and thus the cannoneers had little experience with them.[47]

Many things went wrong for the Austrians during the battle itself, but not their artillery. It was the cannoneers, not the infantry, who fixed the First Army in place and held it there for the greater part of the day. If the Second Army had not arrived in time, the First Army may have collapsed. On the northern flank, the Austrian artillery could have stopped the Second Army's assault, not the depleted infantry screen. Had they not been engaged by the Prussian cannon and drawn into an artillery duel (one that the Prussians got the worst of in a calculated act of self-sacrifice on the part of their commander), instead continuing to fire on the Prussian infantry, the outcome of the battle may well have been different with the Austrian artillery the decisive factor.[48]

LOGISTICS

The logistics of the campaign have already been commented on extensively, but it is worth noting how a superior system gave Moltke far more options and flexibility than Benedek. Moltke knew the Austrians would concentrate all their forces in a single area in Bohemia because, given their logistics system, they *had* to. By contrast, the Prussians could move and sustain large forces over vast distances based on the detailed staff work on railroad transportation produced by the Prussian General Staff.[49]

As is so often the case when it comes to the Prussian and German armies, all of the focus went into the logistics of moving troops and never enough into the logistics of sustaining them. Supply issues were endemic on the Prussian side, and in the case of the First Army and the Army of the Elbe, these probably slowed them down.[50]

COMMAND AND CONTROL

Austrian command and control was a mess. Benedek had neither the ability to centralize command and control and personally direct the fight nor the ability to decentralize and let his unit commanders lead the fight. Initiative and subordinate decision making were actively discouraged in Austrian army.[51] The chief of staff in the Austrian army had ambiguous and weak authority over the rest of the army, leading to confusion and a lack of coordination. Nor could the general staff influence the selection of subordinate commanders.[52] On the day of the battle, there were three chiefs of staff in the Austrian headquarters, with questions then (that remain now) about which one of them, if any, was actually in control.[53]

By contrast, Prussian divisions were highly autonomous.[54] The corps level was done away with for ease of command and control, as division staffs were trusted and effective. The general staff commanded the armies, and the armies commanded their divisions. This simplification led to Prussian divisions that acted and reacted quickly and reduced burdens on higher-level staffs. Additionally, Moltke favored broad, flexible plans; subordinate commanders given little more than objectives were expected to fill in all details.[55] The Scharnhorst Model staff system made this possible, ensuring that staff officers at every level were trained, educated, and empowered. In any other military, simply dropping an entire level of the chain of command would produce chaos. With the Scharnhorst Model, it instead streamlined the chain of command.

This highly decentralized decision making led to the battle-winning decision: First Army commander Prince Frederick Charles' decision to attack at dawn, and Moltke's decision to not only allow it but also reinforce and exploit it.

The order issued by Moltke to the Second Army, which decided the campaign and the war in one of history's most decisive battles, was only fifty-seven words long (in English): "Your royal highness will at once make the arrangements necessary to be able to move with all your forces in support of the First Army against the right flank of the enemy's expected advance, and to come into action as soon as possible. The orders sent from here this afternoon under other conditions are no longer valid."[56] Few military orders in history have ever been written with more clarity and brevity.

Major, campaign-winning decisions were made by subordinate commanders on the spot in support of the overall plan. The lead units of the Second Army assaulted the ridge at Chlum immediately, before the Austrians could move troops to shore up the weak flank there and without waiting for input from Moltke. The Prussian artillery commander simply saw the attack as it began and fired on the Austrian artillery, drawing their fire against his own units rather than the assaulting infantrymen. It was impossible for Moltke at the high command to know the conditions on the northern front, analyze that information, and make such decisions for those subordinates. In a very real way, the tradition of *Aufragstaktik* won the battle for Prussia.

CONCLUSION

The Prussian General Staff, not particularly influential or credible up until 1866, was validated by the results of the Austro-Prussian War. Any remaining doubters would be silenced by the Franco-Prussian War four years later. Other nations intensified their efforts to replicate the Scharnhorst Model, and the prestige gained by the institution virtually guaranteed it would not be fully controlled by king, kaiser, führer, or legislature. Its strategic immunity quickly begat a strategic blind spot that led Germany down a dark path.

That remained in the future, however. The Königgrätz Campaign stands as an example of the importance of operational art and the staffs that conduct it. A force without a functional staff, such as the Austrian army, might have some advantages; their artillery and cavalry, for example, were far superior to their Prussian counterparts. Yet these advantages could not be coordinated, brought to bear where and when they were needed, or used to mitigate other vulnerabilities without a functional staff to do that work.

Austerlitz shows an example of a force with a protostaff facing one with no real staff. Königgrätz shows an example of a force with a high-functioning staff facing one with a dysfunctional staff. The remaining three case studies will examine more advanced, functional staffs in competition with each other.

CASE STUDY 3
THE ATLANTIC CAMPAIGN, 1914–18

This case focuses on the naval competition over the oceanic lines of communication in the Atlantic during World War I, sometimes called the Battle of the Atlantic. The passage of merchant ships was a vital source of supply for the United Kingdom, one that the Royal Navy sought to protect and the Imperial German Navy sought to cut.

In comparison to the first two case studies, it is an entirely maritime campaign, with limited amphibious and aerial actions, and featuring highly developed staffs on both sides. Where the two navies differed were in their domestic situations. Perhaps no navy in history has enjoyed as much prestige at home as the Royal Navy. In Germany, however, it was service in the army that was prestigious; the navy was a perennial underdog when it came to influencing policy, although Germany had been building it up for some time.

European militaries had adopted many advances in the operational disciplines since Königgrätz, especially in information and command and control. Both Napoleon and Moltke had to rely on human intelligence and physical reconnaissance to gain information about the enemy and the situation. By World War I, however, electronic and signals intelligence had brought about a profound change, allowing command and control to be accomplished through technological means. This was especially true for naval vessels, whose early radios could be powered by the ship itself.

HISTORICAL NARRATIVE
ROAD TO WAR

The complex web of alliances, fears, interests, and hatreds that created the conditions for instigating World War I, set off by Serbian Gavrilo Princip when he assassinated Archduke Franz Ferdinand of Austria-Hungary in Sarajevo on 28 June 1914, need not be recapitulated here. Instead, the two principal navies involved in the Atlantic Campaign will be examined.

The United Kingdom and Germany had been in a naval arms race well before the beginning of the war. During the decades around the turn of the twentieth century, German admiral Alfred von Tirpitz had pushed Kaiser Wilhelm II to expand Germany's naval forces, pushing to pass naval laws and to appropriate funds for shipbuilding.[1] Germany feared more than anything a blockade enforced by the larger Royal Navy in the event of war. In fact, the kaiser issued a directive on 3 December 1912 that the principal task of the Imperial German Navy was to defeat such a blockade.[2] Britain had responded in kind, intending to maintain numerical superiority over the German fleet, especially in terms of battleships.

The Royal Navy, of course, had centuries of institutional experience behind it and was one of the first military organizations to professionalize along modern lines, with a rank structure, detailed administration and doctrine, and a developed industrial base.[3]

PLANS

From the beginning, the Royal Navy planned a distant blockade against Germany. Rather than placing ships at German-controlled ports, patrols would attempt to seal off the exits of the North Sea. This blockade would be supported by battle-fleet sorties in the North Sea, but the main purpose was to prevent imports of goods, especially food, to Germany. The Royal Navy's Grand Fleet, under Admiral Sir John Jellicoe, was initially based at Scapa Flow, along with the Battle Cruiser Fleet (which was subordinate to the Grand Fleet), under Vice Admiral Sir David Beatty.[4]

Germany's naval leaders knew they were not likely to fare well in a direct confrontation with the Grand Fleet, although they would certainly prepare for one. Instead, they would focus on preventing the shipment of supplies to Britain. Rather than a distant blockade with surface vessels, Germany would have to use undersea warfare, supplemented by their cruiser force, which started the war outside the blockade, to sink as much merchant shipping as possible throughout the Atlantic sea lanes. This *Kleinkrieg* (small war) method resembled guerrilla warfare at sea. Indeed, German naval leaders said as much. Meanwhile, they would get their High Seas Fleet ready to break out of the Royal Navy's cordon.

OPENING GAMBITS—1914

The High Seas Fleet concentrated at Wilhelmshaven on the North Sea. Once the war began in August 1914 and the German army seized parts of Belgium, the navy gained access to ports on that coast. The German navy also operated cruiser forces around the globe, including the Atlantic. Specifically, the *Dresden* and the *Karlsruhe* were in the Caribbean Sea when the war broke out. Although the Royal Navy's battleships were the best in the world, its cruiser force was antiquated. Thus, the German cruisers posed a real threat to merchant shipping.[5]

Although both navies were husbanding their fleets of dreadnoughts, their lighter forces fought on 28 August at the First Battle of Heligoland Bight, a small island off the coast of Germany that acted as a protective barrier for the naval base at Wilhelmshaven. It was a clear British victory—three German cruisers were sunk—but it did little to change the situation. The Battle of Texel Island on 17 October was another bloody nose for the German navy that otherwise had little consequence. The submarines of both sides were immediately active as well, with the Germans focusing their efforts on merchant shipping.[6]

The German navy had more success with their surface units far from the North Sea, those in the Pacific and Atlantic Oceans. Although halfway around the world when the war began, the East Asian Squadron in the Pacific, under Vice Admiral Maximilian von Spee, raced to round Cape Horn at the southern tip of South America and break out into the Atlantic for commerce raiding. Spee was caught off the coast of Coronel, Chile, by a Royal Navy squadron under Rear Admiral Sir Christopher Cradock. But the German admiral had been concealing the size of his force by only transmitting radio traffic from one of his ships, the *Leipzig*, and keeping the others in radio silence. Cradock, in a poor position to fight and expecting to encounter only a single enemy warship, found himself heavily outgunned and outnumbered but decided to fight anyway. The Battle of Coronel was another lopsided victory, but this time for the Germans. The British lost two cruisers and 1,569 men, including Cradock, but the only injuries suffered by the Germans were two wounded sailors and slight damage to their ships.[7] Spee's way into the Atlantic Ocean was clear.

But the German commander would do little with the opportunity. On 8 December Spee's squadron approached Port Stanley in the Falkland Islands, intending to launch an amphibious raid on the radio-transmitting station there, a key command-and-control node for the Royal Navy in the South Atlantic. But the British used Spee's own trick against him, running their cruisers in radio silence to conceal a buildup at Port Stanley. The admiral expected little to no Royal Navy presence in the area but instead found himself overmatched. Spee wisely tried to make a break for it, but his squadron was run down. Only one German cruiser, the *Dresden*, escaped.[8]

In the end, the Royal Navy was well prepared to protect commerce in the Atlantic and indeed globally. The German surface navy, outside of the High Seas Fleet now confined to the North and Baltic Seas, was essentially neutralized by the end of 1914. What remained were the U-boats.[9]

RESTRICTED SUBMARINE WARFARE—1915

In 1915 the battle fleets of each side continued to spar in an attempt to find an advantage over the other. On 23 January at the Battle of Dogger Bank, the High Seas Fleet sought to ambush Royal Navy scouting squadrons. Alerted to this ahead of time through signals intelligence, British battle cruisers took position nearby and outgunned the Germany warships when they struck.[10]

By this time, the distant blockade was already causing food shortages in Germany. Since their cruisers were now out of the fight, the Germans had little choice but to intensify the U-boat campaign by making it fully unrestricted, that is, targeting neutral and Allied shipping alike.[11] On 4 February Vice Admiral Hugo von Pohl officially announced an "undersea blockade" of the British Isles.[12] Thereafter, the British lost between fifty and one hundred merchant ships per month in 1915. Despite this, the Allies' blockade of the Central Powers remained near total.[13]

The unrestricted U-boat campaign almost immediately led to tensions with neutral powers that Germany could ill afford, especially with the United States. In May the sinking of the *Lusitania* angered the American people and led to a series of diplomatic escalations. By September, restrictions on the activities of the U-boats were back in place after the sinking of another ship, the *Arabic*, had escalated the diplomatic breach with the United States.[14] The official end of the first campaign did not come until May 1916, after President Woodrow Wilson issued an ultimatum to Germany.[15]

BATTLE JOINED—1916

By that point, command of the High Seas Fleet had rotated to Vice Admiral Reinhard Scheer.[16] Scheer increased the rate of sorties and began bombarding the English coast again in an attempt to draw out the Grand Fleet.[17]

Although by that spring both fleets were spoiling for a fight, neither expected one when the Grand Fleet sallied on 30 May, followed the next day by the High Seas Fleet.[18] Both the predominantly dreadnought fleet under Jellicoe and the battlecruiser fleet under Beatty came into contact with the

High Seas Fleet at various times on 31 May and through the night to 1 June. The ensuing encounter the following day turned into a cataclysmic battle, with the High Seas Fleet dishing out more damage and sinking more British ships but sustaining significant damage itself, returning to Wilhelmshaven for months of repairs. In the end, the Battle of Jutland changed almost nothing.[19] The Royal Navy could afford the losses it suffered. The Imperial Germany Navy could not.

Britain's blockade was thus unaffected by the outcome of Jutland, no matter the High Seas Fleet's performance. Germany resumed its focus on submarine warfare, sinking neutral ships off the east coast of the United States in July. Britain largely kept its Grand Fleet confined to bases for fear of the U-boat threat, which its capital ships could not effectively counter.[20] As German submarine warfare began to ramp up, U-boats succeeded in sinking 231,573 tons in September, 341,363 tons in October, and 326,689 tons in November.[21]

By the end of 1916, the losses at Jutland no longer mattered. The Royal Navy had commissioned eight new capital ships, the German navy just two.[22] Jellicoe was promoted to First Sea Lord, turning over command of the Grand Fleet to Beatty.[23]

UNRESTRICTED SUBMARINE WARFARE RESUMES—1917

Having failed to break the distant blockade, Germany had to pin all of its hopes for the naval campaign on submarine warfare. On 1 February 1917 fully unrestricted submarine warfare was officially adopted by Germany.[24]

Once again the campaign was tactically successful. In February 520,410 tons of Allied shipping went to the bottom, 564,500 tons in March, and 860,330 tons in April.[25] But this tactical achievement was also strategically counterproductive: on 6 April the United States officially entered the war against Germany of the Central Powers.

American naval power had an almost immediate effect. Arriving far before any ground troops, U.S. naval officers, especially Admiral William S. Sims, contributed to the adoption of a convoy system to protect merchant vessels from the U-boat threat.[26] By June, there were already twenty-eight U.S. destroyers in the Atlantic theater alone. By the end of the year, four American dreadnoughts had joined the Grand Fleet.[27] U-boats sank 616,320 tons of Allied shipping in May and then 696,725 in June, but thereafter the numbers began to drop: U-boats claimed 555,510 tons in July, 472,370 in August, and 353,600 tons in October.[28]

Meanwhile, the High Seas Fleet, inactive for most of 1917, began experiencing mutinies due to inactivity, poor administration, food shortages, and the low morale these caused.[29] After their suppression, the High Seas Fleet began sorties late in the year.[30] There was one more confrontation between elements of the Grand Fleet and the High Seas Fleet at the Second Battle of Heligoland Bight on 17 November.[31] It was again inconclusive.

DENOUEMENT—1918

Despite increased losses due to convoy tactics and American reinforcements, Germany entered 1918 with 142 U-boats. The numbers of those actually at sea remained mostly stable.[32] The Royal Navy, now joined by the U.S. Navy, tightened the noose of the distant blockade ever more.[33] The Admiralty's intelligence section developed new methods of tracking German wireless signals, allowing them to better locate the U-boats.[34] The amount of shipping sunk per month continued to drop except for a spike in August, when U-boats sank 310,180 tons.[35] In October 1918, the last full month of the war, they claimed just 116,240 tons.[36]

Although it ultimately failed, the German navy's campaign against Allied shipping was the most successful in history by sheer amount of tonnage sunk. Neither the Kriegsmarine nor the U.S. Navy of World War II matched it.[37] The U-boat campaign did cause food rationing in Britain, but this was nowhere near the levels of privation endured by the German populace due to the distant blockade.

This is not to say that the Imperial German Navy was irrelevant to World War I—far from it. Had the Royal Navy not won this Battle of the Atlantic or not been as capable as it was, a combined cruiser/U-boat campaign against Allied shipping may well have been decisive. And the German navy had other victories to speak of that fall outside this campaign against Britain, namely the large-scale amphibious campaign Operation Albion against Russia in October 1917.

OPERATIONAL DISCIPLINES

ADMINISTRATION

Both sides tried new administrative arrangements late in the war, although it is unclear what effect these had beyond setting precedents, especially for the British and Americans, that would reappear during World War II.[38] The administration of the Royal Navy had roots going back centuries, and that it so quickly integrated U.S. Navy personnel is a testament to its efficiency. No

Royal Navy mutinies occurred during the war, although there was a minor one in 1919.

By contrast, poor administration contributed to naval mutinies in the Imperial German Navy, although probably not as much as the blockade itself and the inactivity of the High Seas Fleet.[39] Sailors and soldiers will generally put up with maladministration, inactivity, and at times even privation. All three at once, however, is a recipe for disaster.

Late in the war, Germany created the Naval High Command alongside a raft of reforms known as the Scheer Program. These contributed to the reassignment of a large number of skilled naval officers either to staff duty ashore or to the U-boat fleet, depriving the surface units of effective leadership.[40]

INFORMATION

Neither navy had sufficient reconnaissance forces, demonstrated by the fact that the Grand Fleet and the High Seas Fleet essentially blundered into each other at Jutland. Those units the Royal Navy did have—old cruisers and battlecruisers—were misused to engage in battle instead of scouting, with sometimes bloody results.[41]

While both sides employed signals and electromagnetic-spectrum intelligence, the British far outpaced their opponents. The Admiralty had cracked German naval codes early in the war, but the Germans remain convinced, even after the war, that their codes were unbreakable. Even when the Admiralty could not read every transmission, they could still use their radio-direction-finding network to essentially "see" where German ships were.

Early in the war, both sides pioneered the smart use of signals to deceive their opponents and prevent them from effectively understanding the situation, with decisive effects in battle. First Spee at the Battle of Coronel and then Vice Admiral Sir Doveton Sturdee at the Battle of the Falkland Islands used transmission signals to deceive their opponent.

OPERATIONS

The management of time and space is always difficult in naval campaigns for a specific reason: the lack of permanence. Ships and sailors can only stay at sea for so long. That combined with the sheer vastness of the world's oceans makes naval presence in any given area sporadic for even the largest navies. This is why key maritime terrain, such as ports, islands, straits, and the like, are so vital to naval campaigns, offering a semblance of permanence on an ever-changing field of competition.

The British had a large and well-developed global network of stations at key maritime terrain and centuries of experience running a global navy. The Germans also had such a network, but it was far smaller and had only recently developed a global navy. Their stations and colonies in the Pacific were quickly seized by Japanese and Australian forces early in the war. The U-boat quickly became the only way the Germany navy could operate outside of European waters.

Because of this, the German side of the Atlantic Campaign was almost purely focused on attrition, as their ability to maneuver was severely restricted. The numbers of Allied ships sunk show that they successfully achieved this. But that attrition did not translate to strategic effect, and it remains unclear if it ever would have.

The key coordination measure of the campaign was the development of the convoy system. Rather than allowing merchant ships to sail when, where, and how each captain decided, the British mandated convoys, in which a large number of ships would sail together under the protection of Royal Navy and U.S. Navy ships. This concentration of forces (both in merchant ships and accompanying warships) in time and space enabled the Allies to defend them easier and seize the initiative from the U-boats by choosing where and when to defend.

FIRE SUPPORT

Naval aviation was not yet developed enough to play a large role in fire support during World War I. Scheer did attempt to use zeppelins to bombard British shore positions but was stymied by the weather. Zeppelin bombing runs that did manage to occur did little damage.

Instead, fire support at sea revolved around the guns of the ships themselves as well as torpedoes, then still in their infancy. There is considerable debate about which side's gunnery was superior during World War I. There is some indication that superior German optics increased their forces' accuracy and reaction times.[42] Although gunnery is frequently decisive in naval operations, neither side had an overwhelming advantage here.

LOGISTICS

When it comes to logistics, the global naval network built and maintained by the Royal Navy again provided a key advantage. The German navy had few coaling stations and instead had to rely on neutral ports to extend the reach of its ships. Of course, these vessels were barred from ports controlled by their opponents. The Germans primarily and successfully used collier trains to extend the reach of their cruisers—until they were all lost.[43]

COMMAND AND CONTROL

Naval command and control had recently undergone a transformation. For centuries, a ship at sea was largely on its own, having presumably received guidance before its voyage and being able to report back only at its conclusion. Ship-to-ship communication was accomplished with semaphore flags.

The latter were still in use—as they are today—but by 1914 ships could use radio transmission to communicate with each other and headquarters staffs at home. Naval officers were still mastering the management of the massive amount of information, both incoming and outgoing, affecting naval vessels. This problem would be magnified during World War II with the introduction of the radar, which led to the development of combat information centers.

CONCLUSION

Successful naval campaigns are some of the most historically significant. Their success depends in large part on the sea power of a nation, only one component of which is the military naval dimension. In the Atlantic Campaign, the Royal Navy, designed as a global instrument of the United Kingdom's seapower, was more than a match for the more naval-battle-focused Imperial German Navy.

The Atlantic Campaign is largely overshadowed by the events on the western front during World War I, especially the gargantuan loss of life for both sides. Yet life at sea was no less dangerous for the sailor, with entire squadrons consumed by naval gunfire and going to the bottom of the ocean. And this high-seas campaign offers an excellent view into naval operational art and the importance of naval staffs, both at sea and on shore.

CASE STUDY 4
THE BATTLE OF BRITAIN, 1940

In the darkest part of World War II, the United Kingdom stood alone against a Nazi Germany that seemed unstoppable. Over the course of the summer of 1940, the only things that stood between Great Britain and 130 Wehrmacht divisions was the English Channel. If the Luftwaffe could protect their transports from the Royal Navy, then not even that would have stopped them. The war became, for a time, a campaign to establish that air supremacy, and in winning it the Royal Air Force (RAF) stopped the Nazi war machine in its tracks.

This case study focuses on the confrontation between the RAF and the Luftwaffe to highlight the operational art of an air campaign. Although technology matters a great deal in campaigns conducted entirely via aerial machines and their pilots, the campaign is also an example of the command-and-control operational discipline being decisive. The RAF's command-and-control system enabled its fighters to stay in the air and in the fight, despite relatively poor tactics and inexperienced pilots, until their greater production capacity could kick in. Few would have guessed that Nazi Germany could be defeated so decisively when the campaign began, but, as will be seen, the outcome was never as close as many would have guessed.

HISTORICAL NARRATIVE
ROAD TO WAR

France and Britain declared war on Germany on 3 September 1939. There followed a period of limited actions and economic warfare, sometimes called the Phony War, which then exploded with the German invasion of Belgium, the Netherlands, and Luxembourg on 10 May 1940 en route to France. Forty-six days later, France surrendered, and the United Kingdom was essentially alone against Germany.

After the amphibious withdrawal at Dunkirk, Britain itself was defended on the ground only by the survivors of the British Expeditionary Force, a total of thirteen or fourteen divisions with little heavy equipment.[1] And while the Royal Navy was, as per usual, well funded and well respected, it had global commitments to protect and defend in addition to the home islands. But what Britain also had for its defense was a new air force, the first independent air service in the world. The British government had been paying special attention to building up its air force and the infrastructure necessary for it to operate since 1937; by 1940, it had become an international force. Although 80 percent of the RAF was British, 10 percent of its members came from Commonwealth nations, while a good portion of the other 10 percent came from nations occupied by the Nazis.[2]

At first following the conquest of France, the Germans did nothing, spending June and most of July simply relishing their victory and assuming Britain would soon surrender. Any planning for an amphibious invasion of England was amateurish.[3] The German High Command assumed that, if the Luftwaffe could establish air supremacy over the English Channel and thus protect the transports, the invasion of Great Britain would be simple. In reality, the Royal Navy had more than enough surface ships to destroy any invasion force on the water.[4] Historians tend to scoff at Germany's chances of successfully invading England, but they have the benefit of hindsight and full access to German deliberations. At the time, however, this was a threat that the British had to take very seriously. The Wehrmacht had fully 130 rested and experienced divisions available; they just needed to move them.[5]

For once, Adolf Hitler was less enthusiastic about an invasion than his staff, but he also believed that Britain would simply bow to German success on the Continent and that the destruction of the RAF in particular would lead to an end of the war. On 21 May, he discussed the invasion with his generals and made air supremacy a prerequisite.[6]

The weapon he assigned to this mission was the Luftwaffe (literally "air weapon," or "air arm"). It was the most experienced air force in the world at the time, having participated in invasions of Poland, Norway, Denmark, Belgium, the Netherlands, and France, in addition to its active role during the Spanish Civil War (1936–39). These frequent campaigns allowed the Luftwaffe to continually refine its tactics and provide its aircrews with experience. Its basic tactical unit was the *Gruppe* (Group), which would be equipped with bombers, fighters, or other aircraft.[7] Its equipment was also technically advanced, especially regarding dive bombers and bombsights.[8]

While its tactics were advanced, the Luftwaffe's focus was usually on close air support or strategic bombing, not air-to-air combat. In addition, the training pipeline and its supply infrastructure was poor.[9] It had also suffered a significant amount of casualties in both pilots and aircraft during the fighting in France.[10] The Luftwaffe's other major problem was its leadership. The service was led by Herman Göring, who had some military experience as a pilot but was a political crony of Hitler. His leadership was not only poor, but he also fostered political infighting and competition among the senior air leaders.[11] Lastly, the Luftwaffe was designed to perform well in such short, sharp operations described above, as it had. But it was ill equipped to conduct a sustained, long-term air campaign.[12]

PLANS

The German amphibious invasion of Britain was called Operation Sealion. Thirty-nine divisions (around 500,000 troops) would be protected by the Kriegsmarine and the Luftwaffe as they crossed the English Channel in transports. But first, the Germans would have to achieve air superiority over the channel.

The Luftwaffe had three aims for this air campaign, dubbed Operation Eagle: first, to establish air superiority over the southeast of England; second, to weaken the RAF to the point that most of Britain would be vulnerable to strategic bombing; and third, to weaken the industrial capacity required for warfare.[13] Hitler allowed five weeks to achieve this, from 8 August to 15 September 1940.[14]

The two principle organizations within the RAF that would carry out the island's defense were Fighter Command and Bomber Command. Fighter Command's principle target would be the incoming German bombers, but they would also have to duel their fighter escorts. Bomber Command would fly missions against the Luftwaffe's airfields and aircraft and supporting factories in France, Belgium, and Germany itself.

But the real strength of the RAF was the Dowding System, named for its designer, Air Chief Marshal Hugh Dowding. This system consisted of a command-and-control network that covered the entire United Kingdom. Radar stations, strategically placed at regular intervals, detected Luftwaffe aircraft as soon as they took off in France; estimated their route, elevation, and composition; and then transmitted that information to a central point. Once processed, Fighter Command would dispatch squadrons to intercept them.

In such a campaign, it would seem that the Luftwaffe held the initiative. The Germans were on the offense and could decide on what targets to hit and when. But the RAF seized it back in a clever way: by declining to engage

Luftwaffe fighter sorties unless they were escorting bombers. Key RAF leaders, including Dowding and 11 Fighter Group commander Air Vice Marshal Keith Park (responsible for southern England), knew that the Luftwaffe wanted to eliminate Fighter Command specifically. But the only real threat to Britain was Luftwaffe bombers, not German fighters. So, Dowding, Park, and other fighter-group commanders usually only sent their squadrons against suspected bombing sorties, preserving their fighter force as much as possible. German fighter sorties flew over England unmolested, but they contributed nothing to the campaign. This recognition of how to maintain the initiative while on the defense was the key.[15]

Dowding contributed not only the advanced command-and-control system that allowed the RAF to adroitly outfight the Luftwaffe but also the overall plan of the campaign. Recognizing that only the enemy bombers were a threat, he focused on defending against them. The prime goal, however, was to maintain the RAF as an "airfleet in being." As long as the RAF existed, the Germans could never achieve untrammeled access to the air over Britain or the English Channel. The other key part of Dowding's defense was his ability to keep a reserve. Dowding rotated squadrons and pilots from the south to the defense of northern England, a quieter and slower sector, regularly. This allowed them the rest and relaxation necessary to stay sharp once they rotated back to southern England. The Germans, being perennially short on trained pilots, had no such policy, and their aircrews became mentally spent before the end of the campaign.[16]

FIRST PHASE—JULY AND AUGUST

During the first phase of the Battle of Britain, the Luftwaffe intended to lure Fighter Command forces into combat over the English Channel.[17] This was advantageous airspace for the Germans: any pilots forced to bail out over the channel or over France could be recovered and then return to duty; if they did this over Britain, however, they would become prisoners of war. The "lure" was Luftwaffe bombing sorties against English shipping in the channel and the ports and docks, factories, oil facilities, and airstrips in southern England, along with reconnaissance flights to identify targets and assess damage.[18]

This phase came to a head on 10 July. Eight British convoys were in the channel that day, and a Luftwaffe Dornier light bomber spotted one of them. RAF Spitfire fighters managed to damage the enemy aircraft and two of its escorts, driving them off.[19] Then the Dowding System detected a large incoming Luftwaffe raid of more than sixty aircraft over Calais. Three Fighter Command squadrons, in addition to the one already in the air, scrambled to intercept. The massive dogfight that resulted was a clear British victory. Only four RAF fighters were lost, and only one of the downed pilots. The German aircraft dropped about 150 bombs, but only one hit—the bombers simultaneously trying to avoid the British fighters—sinking one vessel. The Luftwaffe lost three bombers (Dornier Do 17s), three fighter-bombers (Bf 110s), and one fighter (Bf 109). Additionally, two Do 17s, two Bf 110s, and two Bf 109s were damaged.[20] In a theme that would continue throughout this campaign, the German assessment of this engagement was poor: the Luftwaffe thought that the RAF had lost over thirty aircraft.[21]

Although there were flights nearly every day, save for poor weather, larger raids like the one on 10 July occurred intermittently. The greatest German success of the month came on the nineteenth, when the RAF's 141 Squadron, an inexperienced unit equipped with the inferior Defiant interceptors, was attacked by a flight of German fighters, losing five aircraft before a squadron of Spitfires arrived. In total, the RAF lost ten aircraft to the Luftwaffe's four that day.[22] Between 10 July and 11 August, German pilots claimed 381 British aircraft destroyed. The actual total was 178.[23]

Although Luftwaffe leadership had no understanding of the Dowding System, they did know that radio towers were key infrastructure. On 12 August Erprobungsgruppe 210 (a fighter-bomber squadron) succeeded in destroying two of them, bringing the system down in that area. The window of opportunity was both short and uneventful as the Germans remained unaware of their chance. All stations were back in operation by the next day.[24]

SECOND PHASE—EAGLE DAY

The German attempt to bring the fight over the English Channel continued into August until the thirteenth, when the Luftwaffe planned a massive, concentrated bombing campaign against RAF bases in southern England. Casualties on both sides were high. The RAF also stopped flying missions over France just as Germany was focusing its attention more on the English airbases. This shift in tactics marked the beginning of the second phase of the campaign. The day was known as Eagle Day.[25]

This shift did not go well from the start. Ineffective German command and control led to poorly coordinated flights, including fighter squadrons failing to lift off to escort bombers that then flew on to their targets unprotected, as well as at least one friendly fire event.[26] The Luftwaffe did not lose many fighters, but the casualties among its bombers were high, while RAF operations were not significantly disrupted.[27]

Two days later the Luftwaffe again tried a massive, concentrated effort on a single day, trying to stretch the RAF's defenses to the breaking point. This time they had better luck getting bombers through and hitting their targets, but the losses were so heavy that the day became known in the Luftwaffe as "Black Thursday."[28] During this period, German losses were particularly high for the excellent (but slow) Stuka dive-bomber, leading Göring to ban their further use in the campaign on 17 August. This left very few aircraft available that could do precision bombing.[29]

Field Marshal Albert Kesselring, commander of the Luftwaffe units conducting the campaign, shifted tactics again on 24 August. This time, bombing raids were focused solely on Fighter Command targets, especially its airfields. Again, the bombers got through and many airfields were hit, but they were frequently repaired overnight. At no point did Kesselring attack the critical nodes of the Dowding System—the control rooms and sector stations that actually ran the radar network. The reason why he did not is simple: Kesselring did not know they existed.[30]

The most dangerous German tactic was one based on deception. At times, Bf 110 fighter-bombers and Bf 109 fighters would fly similar routes and patterns as bombers to imitate an unescorted raid. RAF fighters pounced on the seemingly unprotected bomber formation only to be ambushed. The trick only worked a few times, however. By the end of August, the operators and analysts of the Dowding System could recognize the deception and stopped taking the bait.[31]

THE FINAL PHASE—THE BLITZ

From 28 August to 5 September, Kesselring pushed the pilots and aircraft of the Luftwaffe to the limit in attempting to destroy Fighter Command, continuing to focus on its airfields.[32] The bombing was extensive enough to disrupt the system, but while strained, the RAF weathered the storm. On the night of 30 August, however, Bomber Command hit Berlin itself, inducing Hitler to change his policy about bombing London. It was no longer off limits.[33]

The Blitz of London, as it was known, began on 7 September. Bombing raids on city itself were planned for the entire day. The RAF, by now used to defending its airfields, was slow to react at first. Luftwaffe fighters succeeded in protecting the bombers, but this came at a high cost once Fighter Command reacted. This was the first of fifty-seven days and nights of bombing raids over London in addition to those still targeting RAF ground stations.[34]

By 15 September, when the Luftwaffe scheduled another large strike against London, the RAF had adapted again. Fighter Command succeeded in stripping the incoming bombers of their escorts and then focused on striking the vulnerable raiders while they were over London itself, slowing down to turn around and head back to their home airfields. The bombing raids were successful, but the cost in aircraft and crews was much higher for the Luftwaffe than for the RAF.[35]

By this time, Luftwaffe morale was beginning to strain. German pilots were not given rest or rotated out to quieter sectors like the opposing RAF pilots. Often, they were sortied multiple times a day until they were shot down.[36] On 17 September Hitler postponed Operation Sealion indefinitely, effectively canceling it. By this point, the Germans had assembled 1,700 barges and 200 ships, a fleet capable of transporting half a million troops and their equipment across the channel. But without the Luftwaffe having air supremacy over the area, they never would have made it. The troops earmarked for the invasion of Britain now shifted east, away from English Channel.[37]

The Luftwaffe settled into a rhythm of bombing London at night (to avoid RAF fighters, which could only operate in daylight) and conducting fighter sweeps of British airspace during the day. In late September the Germans did shift some bombing raids to target aircraft production, which might have worked earlier in the campaign but at this stage was too late. The Luftwaffe had shot its bolt.[38]

Bombing raids and fighter sweeps continued into September and October. But German leaders, including Hitler, realized that the aerial campaign at this point was at best a longshot hope that the United Kingdom might surrender based entirely on this blitz. The Luftwaffe may have already lost, but the RAF was the last to know. The last daylight raid on 7 October did little damage, and as usual the Germans lost more aircraft than the RAF. Fighting then trickled off throughout October, the official end date of the Battle of Britain later determined to be 31 October 1940.

AFTERMATH

The RAF had won. Air supremacy would eventually be achieved over the English Channel, but this would be in support of Operation Overlord in 1944, not Operation Sealion in 1940. The stalwart British defense of the air was the first defeat for Nazi Germany and, indeed, kept the defense of the free world going. Britain would not stand alone for long, with the Soviet Union switching sides after being invaded in June 1941 and the United States joining the war that December after Pearl Harbor. The strategic-bombing campaigns on both sides would continue, Germany's until attrition of bombers and pilots simply made hitting London untenable, and Britain's until the very end of the war, with the additional weight of the United States joining in.

OPERATIONAL DISCIPLINES

Military staffs by 1941 were, of course, highly developed institutions, but both the RAF and the Luftwaffe—as independent air services—were relatively new organizations. In the case of the RAF, it was the first independent air force in the world. Staff officers on both sides had to figure out how to plan, prepare, conduct, synchronize, and sustain air tactics with very little historical data to guide them. Although most of the key leaders on both sides were veteran aviators during World War I or (for the Germans) the Spanish Civil War, the rate of change in aviation technology was so rapid that it could not have been clear to them how to apply that experience.

ADMINISTRATION

The British had a distinct advantage when it came to administration. Roles and responsibilities for personnel and vis-à-vis the U.K. government were clear and simple.[39] As a newer organization, the administration of the RAF had perhaps not had time to calcify into a stifling nest of regulations and bureaucratic maneuvering. This may have facilitated key innovations such as the Dowding System.

In contrast, the Luftwaffe was a confused and competitive organization, an environment fostered by its incompetent chief, Hermann Göring, appointed more for his political loyalty to Hitler than for his qualifications. Senior leaders and pilots alike were highly individualistic, lacking the unit cohesion of RAF squadrons. These men rarely coordinated with each other prior to operations and, more frequently, undermined each other on purpose. This translated to a practical advantage for the RAF.[40]

INFORMATION

By World War II, radio detection of opposing forces was more advanced, and both sides used it effectively during the Battle of Britain. Both sides also used relatively new radar sets at sea and on land for the detection of aircraft (airborne radar had not yet been developed). The British, however, consistently applied radar technology better than the Germans, who used it more for the detection of enemy shipping at sea. The British also augmented this technology with the human eyes provided by the Royal Observer Corps, an organization of air sentries also tied into the Dowding System.[41] Luftwaffe intelligence never ascertained that there even was such an early detection system in place. Even if they had, many of its critical components would have been difficult to identify. For example, one sector's operations room was located in a butcher shop in the village of Caterham.

As mentioned above, Luftwaffe estimates of the situation were extremely poor. Nazi Germany had multiple, competing intelligence agencies, including two within the Luftwaffe itself. None of them cooperated or coordinated. This allowed planners to pick and choose the information that suited their own biases and preferences, rather than using information to better inform their plans.[42] When it came to battle-damage assessments, the Germans relied completely on the claims of pilots for enemy losses. The British cross-checked their pilots' claims with signals intelligence, providing them a much more accurate picture of how the campaign was progressing.[43]

OPERATIONS

The air campaign was highly attritional in nature. Military aircraft and highly trained pilots are not easily replaced, and both sides knew it. Despite the attritional nature of the campaign, the RAF better directed their efforts in this regard. Air Vice Marshal Park's decision to focus his interceptors on shooting down Luftwaffe bombers, not the fighters, was an insightful one and possibly the key to the entire campaign. It certainly led Göring to pull the valuable Stuka dive bombers from the theater. In order to succeed after that point, the twenty to thirty precision bombers the Luftwaffe had remaining for their effort would have to hit each radar station of the Dowding System once or twice a day, every day.[44] This was simply impossible with the technology available at the time. Conversely, Field Marshal Kesselring focused on destroying RAF fighters to establish air supremacy for Operation Sealion. Attrition only has strategic meaning if it is connected with such purposes, when it is pursued as a means to an end and not the end itself. Attrition as an end state is just astrategic slaughter.

Throughout the campaign, the Germans tried multiple time-space-force dispositions. Kesselring got the RAF used to seeing up to three waves a day, with hours of calm in between. On 30–31 August he filled the skies and hours with multiple, smaller fighter sorties in order to create enough confusion for bomber runs to slip through. This had some success and did result in knocking out some of the radar posts. But this high level of activity could not be sustained.[45] The range of German aircraft, however, both fighters and bombers, limited Kesselring's options.

FIRE SUPPORT

Defensive campaigns, to be successful, still must imbue the defense with elements of the offense. The RAF did this through Bomber Command and Coastal Command, targeting key infrastructure that supported Luftwaffe operations.[46]

The Battle of Britain also saw the debut of fighter-bombers, aircraft that could perform either role as needed, sometimes both in the same mission. The Luftwaffe created experimental squadrons, such as Erprobungsgruppe 210, specifically for this campaign, and the concept performed well.[47] As mentioned above, these aircraft seemed like fighters on radar and, since the RAF ignored flights of fighters, initially were not confronted, thus their bombing missions were often successful.[48]

LOGISTICS

No less than in ground operations, logistics always plays a key role in air campaigns. The availability of aircraft, pilots, parts, airfields, and viable airspace all limit or enable tactical options. As already mentioned, fuel limitations for the Luftwaffe restricted their options and the range of their aircraft.[49]

In the end, though, production was the major logistical factor. Both sides had their own aircraft industries and produced their own aircraft. The high rate of production by the British, though, was as decisive as any action in the air. At no point did the Luftwaffe come close to destroying enough RAF planes to outpace British production. At the end of July, for example, the RAF had twice as many warplanes as it had when the month began.[50] Of course, due to their poor intelligence, the Luftwaffe had no idea that this was the case.

COMMAND AND CONTROL

While the Germans focused on tactics and technology, their command and control of air operations languished. Junior Luftwaffe officers who proposed basic command-and-control improvements, such as installing radios in the aircraft, were not just refused but also ridiculed by higher officers. Pilot-to-pilot communication in the air was accomplished by "waggling" the wings of the aircraft.⁵¹ When higher officers did communicate, they more often fought with each other than coordinated actions in time or space.⁵²

By contrast, RAF aircraft not only had VHF radios to communicate with both other pilots and ground stations but also were sortied through the most advanced command-and-control system in the world at the time, the Dowding System. This network linked radar stations, radio towers, radar and radio analysts, and senior officers with squadron bases all over England. This allowed the RAF to rapidly detect, analyze, and respond to every move the Luftwaffe made. German raids were detected as they lifted off from their airfields on the Continent. Fighter Command headquarters was a processing center, which then let groups make tactical decisions. When radar stations were taken out of action by bombing raids, neighboring ones simply filled in for its role in the network. Since the damage could usually be repaired in a matter of hours, this did not overly stress the operators and analysts.⁵³

CONCLUSION

We know now that the Luftwaffe's goal of establishing air supremacy over southern England was well-nigh impossible, but no one could have known that at the time. It would definitely have been possible were it not for the stalwart RAF pilots from Britain and other nations who rose to the challenge and stopped them.

The Battle of Britain, as an almost entirely air-focused campaign, demonstrates the importance in air operations of command and control. Air operations are inherently transient; aircraft and pilots can only stay airborne for so long. Therefore, getting the right pilot in the right aircraft at the right place at the right time is critical.

It is also an example of an offensive, raiding, cumulative (ORC) campaign (on the German side) and a defensive, raiding, cumulative (DRC) campaign (on the British side). This perhaps explains, along with the Germans' intelligence incompetence, why neither side knew how well they were doing but simply had to keep going until one of them faltered. The British had no idea when Operation Sealion was canceled, a move that ensured their victory. The Germans never even knew when they had disrupted or taken down the Dowding System, at least in part. Since the theory of victory was cumulative attrition of aircraft, and neither side knew just how many planes and pilots the other was willing to lose, neither side could see how far or near victory was for them at any given time.

CASE STUDY 5
OPERATION WATCHTOWER, 1942

Operation Watchtower, the American amphibious campaign to seize and hold the island of Guadalcanal from Imperial Japanese control in 1942, offers an excellent case study. This campaign became a logistics competition, with each side striving to generate enough combat power on the island to overcome the other, while also demonstrating the integration of land, air, and sea combat.

This study focuses on the operations of 1st Marine Division and its associated units, including what became known as the Cactus Air Force, and the naval task forces involved in the fight to maintain sea control around Guadalcanal. Operation Watchtower was a complex and lengthy campaign and cannot be comprehensively covered in a chapter, however long. Each component tactical action of the campaign is covered below in only cursory fashion. The point here, as in the previous case studies, is not to delve into tactics but rather to examine the overall operational art that underpinned and supported tactical actions, the results of which accrued to a strategic effect, namely the U.S. acquisition of Guadalcanal and the withdrawal of Imperial Japanese forces.

Logistics became the key to this campaign, the logistics of both moving troops and supplying them. As discussed in chapter 13, logistics has the strongest claim to being a level of war between tactics and strategy; Operation Watchtower demonstrates why. Therefore, as each major event of the campaign is discussed, logistics will be a special focus. Guadalcanal featured constant skirmishes and clashes between patrols on land, at sea, and in the air, but a chapter-length examination must necessarily focus on major events.

HISTORICAL NARRATIVE
THE PLANS
Prior planning for contesting Guadalcanal in 1942 only occurred on the American side, which dubbed it Operation Watchtower; for some time, the Japanese were not certain that a major operation was even happening there.

The Imperial Japanese Navy was still recovering from its major defeat at Midway in June. The Imperial Japanese Army, still unaware of just how bad the defeat at Midway was, had conquered numerous locations in the South Pacific the previous year and was still consolidating and fending off attacks and raids from General Douglas MacArthur's forces. While the Japanese had constructed an airfield on Guadalcanal, it was lightly defended, and most of the personnel on the island were construction workers and engineers.

The four principal U.S. commanders for Operation Watchtower were: Vice Admiral Frank Fletcher, Rear Admiral Richmond Kelly Turner, Rear Admiral Leigh Noyes, and Major General Alexander Vandegrift. Admiral Fletcher was in charge of Task Force (TF) 61 and overall commander of the expeditionary force. He then split TF 61 into two task groups: the Amphibious Force under Admiral Turner and the Air Support Force under Admiral Noyes. General Vandegrift commanded the landing force, principally consisting of 1st Marine Division but including all units ashore as well as the aircraft that would operate from the airfield, soon to be named Henderson Field, home of the Cactus Air Force.[1]

But while the Marine Corps and the Navy had the luxury of planning, it did not go well. Not all of 1st Marine Division's units were available, and not all of those available were in the same location. Both maps and aerial photographs of the objective, dubbed Cactus, were poor. Lastly, the division's equipment and supplies could not all be loaded by priority and would have to be sorted out once ashore on Guadalcanal itself. The logistics of amphibious operations are unique and have an outsized effect on their success. Troops can only fight and equipment can only be used if it is ashore, so the landing force is highly dependent on the throughput from ship to shore. The goal is to get everything ashore as fast as possible. The Marines would not get the chance to do so on Guadalcanal.

THE LANDING

Turner and Vandegrift split the available landing forces in two groups. The largest group would land on Guadalcanal and establish a defensive position, which included and encompassed Henderson Field. The other, smaller force would land on the nearby islands of Gavutu and Tulagi, both of which had Japanese garrisons. The Marines on these smaller islands faced resistance but secured them by 9 August.

The main event on 7 August was the landing on Guadalcanal itself. Eight months to the day after Pearl Harbor, the first American troops landed on

Axis territory as 1st Battalion, 5th Marines scrambled out of the landing craft at 0910 in the morning. They were quickly followed by 3rd Battalion, 5th Marines and 1st Marines, formed up as a regiment to march inland to their objectives. There was no opposition, but Vandegrift was not taking any chances with possible enemy troops, and every available infantryman moved out to establish the perimeter. This led to a bottleneck on the landing beach, where equipment and supplies were being offloaded by disorganized support troops who lacked the manpower to do so quickly.[2]

The first Japanese response came in the form of large air raids that slipped through Navy air patrols and struck the landing site. A flight of Zero fighters and Betty medium bombers hit in the early afternoon, attacking the beachhead itself, then a flight of nine Val dive bombers attacked the shipping in the late afternoon. The air combat was costly for both sides, but while the Japanese bombers succeeded in dropping their payloads, minimal damage was done, and the landing was not significantly disrupted.[3]

General Vandegrift came ashore that afternoon and established his headquarters, making plans for further movement toward the airfield the next day. On 8 August Japanese planes searching for the American aircraft carriers instead attacked Turner's transports, doing little damage but suffering heavy losses. After moving out in the morning, Marines occupied the airfield at 1600. As the Marines, still spoiling for a fight, consolidated their lines on Guadalcanal, a fight was coming—but it was coming for the Navy first.

THE BATTLE OF SAVO ISLAND

Vice Admiral Gunichi Mikawa, commander of the Eighth Fleet at the Japanese stronghold of Rabaul, may have missed the U.S. operation until Marines were already on Guadalcanal, but he had no intention of letting the Americans rest. He quickly assembled a surface task force from his available ships and set course for the island. This flotilla included five heavy cruisers, two light cruisers, and a destroyer.[4]

On the night of 8 August, Mikawa's force slipped around Savo Island, a small island off Guadalcanal's north shore. The Japanese came across Turner's western screening ships, Task Group (TG) 62.6. TG 62.6 was a combined Australian/American force comprising six destroyers and six cruisers. While it outnumbered Mikawa, the Allies were not ready for a fight. The group's commander was not present due to a meeting on the afternoon of 8 August, and there was a great deal of confusion about who was actually in charge in his absence. Each ship of the task group would fight its own battle in the darkness.

The Japanese navy's experience in night combat began to tell immediately. Lookouts spotted the Allied ships first and therefore struck first, launching their superior torpedoes, then following up with gunfire. Mikawa's ships did not stop to slug it out with their opponents, but rather hit hard and fast and left. Worried about being caught in the open by American carrier aircraft in daylight, Mikawa withdrew before morning, with only light damage to his ships, leaving behind the wreckage of four Allied vessels, two more heavily damaged, and 1,077 sailors and Marines killed.[5]

The Battle of Savo Island, although a clear defeat for the Americans, could have been worse if Mikawa had found his intended target: the troop transports. Admiral Fletcher, after covering the initial landing with his carrier forces, withdrew for refueling and to keep his carriers safe and available to attack any Japanese carriers that arrived. After the withdrawal of so much air support, Admiral Turner decided to withdraw the supply ships and transports as well.[6] This decision has been heavily disputed and criticized ever since for leaving the Marines on Guadalcanal unsupported, but if Mikawa's ships came back, caught Turner's transports and supply ships, and destroyed a significant portion of them, Vandegrift's hold on the island probably would have been untenable. That the Japanese admiral had missed them and instead hit the screen was fortunate, but it was just the Japanese navy's opening gambit. Turner's sailors and Vandegrift's Marines frantically offloaded everything they could by the afternoon of 9 August before the transports withdrew. Everything else would have to arrive by convoy.[7]

THE BATTLE OF THE TENARU RIVER

The absence of the Navy support ships, except for quick supply runs, made the Marines ashore uncomfortable, but it would take ground troops to dislodge them from Guadalcanal. The first Imperial Japanese Army troops to arrive were elements of the 28th Infantry Regiment, led by Colonel Kiyoano Ichiki.

Ichiki was not well served by the navy and army staffs that sent him to Guadalcanal. Poor information gathering on the part of the army and intentionally dishonest intelligence estimates on the part of the navy together led to artificially low estimates of U.S. strength on the island. The Seventeenth Army was assigned the mission of destroying the Americans. Ichiki's regiment was available quickest and had experience with amphibious operations. His objective would be the airfield.[8]

Six destroyers landed Ichiki and his first troops, 917 men in total, at night on 19 August. These soldiers, still believing that they faced a small, remnant force after the withdrawal of the American transports, carried ashore only seven days' worth of food and 250 rounds of ammunition.[9] Heavy equipment such as artillery was left far behind because of the need to use destroyers as transports.

A skirmish occurred on 12 August between a Marine patrol and one of the Japanese patrols as Ichiki's troops moved toward the Marine positions around the airfield, Vandegrift's first indication that new Japanese forces had arrived. On 17 August Vandegrift received intelligence that a major landing of Japanese troops had occurred, but their current location was unclear.[10]

The general did not have to wonder long. On the night of 20 August, Ichiki launched a simplistic attack on Marine positions along Alligator Creek east of Henderson Field. Without reconnaissance or preparation, the colonel sent his troops across both the crocodile-infested creek and open beaches without cover right into the prepared positions of 2nd Battalion, 1st Marines. Ichiki only used what heavy weapons he did have after this first attack faltered.[11] On the twenty-first, 1st Battalion, 1st Marines maneuvered behind Ichiki's positions and pinned the Japanese troops against Alligator Creek, surrounding them. Forty-four Marines were killed and roughly seventy wounded in vicious fighting against Ichiki and his men, who in the end were almost completely destroyed. Only one Japanese soldier surrendered, and thirteen more were captured. The rest, including Ichiki, were killed or committed suicide.[12]

THE BATTLE OF THE EASTERN SOLOMONS

Although Allied naval forces were no longer concentrated around Guadalcanal itself and Turner was using convoys to transport troops and supplies to Vandegrift when possible, the Navy was not inactive. While both the U.S. Navy and the Imperial Japanese Navy were supporting the Guadalcanal Campaign, they each had another objective: destroy their adversary's carriers.

Admiral Fletcher found his target first. American planes spotted the *Ryūjō*, a light carrier, on the morning of 24 August. Fletcher waited until radar picked up aircraft launching from the *Ryūjō* toward Guadalcanal before launching strike planes from his flagship, the *Saratoga*. That afternoon the Japanese also spotted Fletcher's two groups of ships: the *Enterprise* and its screening forces, and the *Saratoga* and its screening escorts. Japanese aircraft from the carriers *Zuikaku* and *Shōkaku* launched their own attacks against the American vessels.

The battle was then in the hands of individual pilots and sailors on both sides. The *Shōkaku* was slightly damaged by aircraft from the *Enterprise* around 1500. But at 1600, planes from both of Fletcher's carriers converged on the *Ryūjō* and left it aflame, adrift, and about to sink. The *Enterprise* took the brunt of the Japanese attack. Seventy-four of its crew were killed and more were wounded, while the ship itself was heavily damaged, losing steering for a time before withdrawing to Pearl Harbor for repairs.[13]

The next day a large Japanese reinforcement convoy heading toward Guadalcanal was spotted and attacked by American planes both from the Cactus Air Force at Henderson Field and from the *Enterprise*. The aircraft strafed the transports and their naval escorts, sinking a destroyer and a transport and heavily damaging a cruiser. The commander of the convoy, wounded in the attack, ordered a withdrawal.[14]

The Battle of the Eastern Solomons cost the Japanese navy another aircraft carrier, but it also had a key effect for the Guadalcanal Campaign: the U.S. Navy achieved adequate control of the sea around the island to force the Japanese to stop using transports to move in fresh troops and supplies. That the navy could not protect the transports thus had a significant effect on the logistics aspect of the campaign. Rather than give up contesting Guadalcanal, though, the Japanese adapted.[15]

THE TOKYO EXPRESS

Instead of using transports, the Japanese navy now would cram troops on destroyers, which could quickly move through the Solomon Islands, defend themselves from surface attack, and then deposit the soldiers on Guadalcanal. Each destroyer could only carry about 150 men (in addition to its crew) and limited amounts of heavy equipment, but they could consistently avoid American air attack.[16] Since Vandegrift did not have nearly enough troops to defend the whole island, and the destroyers were more difficult targets than slow troop transports for carrier- and land-based aircraft, the Japanese could conceivably build up enough forces on the island to overwhelm the Marines around Henderson Field. The Americans dubbed this logistic effort the Tokyo Express; the Japanese navy termed it "rat transportation."[17] The effort was aided by the departure of the *Saratoga*, torpedoed by a Japanese submarine on 31 August and damaged enough to require extensive repairs in port.[18]

By the end of August, the Japanese navy began a buildup of airpower at Rabaul, and the army began a serious effort to increase ground troops on Guadalcanal itself, both with the aim of retaking the island. This combined effort, carried out under Admiral Isoroku Yamamoto's cognizance, was dubbed Operation KA. Destroyers ferried in fresh troops in small groups during the last days of August and, on the thirty-first, landed Major General Kiyotake Kawaguchi, who would command the ground fight against 1st Marine Division.

THE BATTLE OF EDSON'S RIDGE

By 5 September, Kawaguchi had roughly 6,200 troops ashore or on the way to Guadalcanal, including survivors of the previous fights and the rest of Ichiki's units. The general was confident enough to reject an additional battalion offered by the Seventeenth Army. But he also could not concentrate the forces he had: 1,000 troops were west of the American perimeter, while the rest were to the east. Vigorous Marine patrolling and fire support from 5th Battalion, 11th Marines and the Cactus Air Force prevented a linkup. Kawaguchi further split his forces in the east to attack the perimeter from the south, southeast, and west simultaneously. The assault from the south was the strongest, his main effort aimed at breaking through and seizing Henderson Field.[19]

But events began to stack up against Kawaguchi. He planned to attack on 12 September, but the navy ships that would bombard the Marine position in support were told of this mission only on the eleventh. On 8 September 1st Raider Battalion executed an amphibious raid out of the perimeter against Kawaguchi's base area. The Raiders fended off attacks from Japanese rear guards to capture and destroy supplies, ammunition, field guns, and Kawaguchi's main radio station. Then the general's main maneuver units became lost and entangled in the approach to their assault points. Finally, the last Japanese reinforcements scheduled to arrive were unable to move quickly by barge because of Cactus Air Force attacks, instead moving out across the island by foot; they did not arrive in time.[20]

On 11 September 1st Raider Battalion, already back from its amphibious raid, and 1st Parachute Battalion were ordered to defensive positions on a ridge south of Henderson Field, right in the path of Kawaguchi's main attack. Both units were under the command of Lieutenant Colonel Merritt "Red Mike" Edson, commanding officer of 1st Raider Battalion. The following evening, just after 2130, Kawaguchi's roughly 5,200-strong main attack hit Edson's battalions straight on. But the Japanese found the terrain so difficult and the fire from Marine lines so intense that the general pulled back, rescheduling his attack again, this time for the night of the thirteenth.

In the interval, Edson pulled his lines back about two hundred meters to even better terrain and dug in a series of platoon strong points rather than a continuous line. The second attack began earlier in the evening, around 1830, and lasted all night, the Marines and Japanese troops fighting at bayonet and sword range in the dark. In the morning pilots from Henderson Field worked over the Japanese positions with cannon and machine guns from the air, but Kawaguchi managed to concentrate roughly 1,700 soldiers for a mass attack on 1st Raider Battalion. This final assault was broken too, but barely. Sporadic fighting and ambushes continued throughout the fourteenth, but Kawaguchi's main force was broken. His other assaulting forces, on the west and southeast, struck late and were likewise repulsed. At 2100 on the fifteenth, the general ordered his ragged and hungry troops (their food had run out on the fourteenth) to withdraw.[21]

THE BATTLE OF CAPE ESPERANCE

In October a Tokyo Express run under Rear Admiral Aritomo Goto was formed with a dual mission: bombard Henderson Field and other Marine positions ashore and deliver troops and supplies to Guadalcanal. Goto divided his vessels into two groups, one for each task. His Bombardment Force consisted of three heavy cruisers and two destroyers, while the Reinforcement Group numbered two seaplane tenders and five destroyers loaded down with troops and supplies. This was the opening move of a massive navy and army counteroffensive planned by Admiral Yamamoto for later in the month.[22]

Goto's force would meet TF 64 under Rear Admiral Norman Scott, commander, Night Screening and Attack Force. Scott's entire mission was to intercept Tokyo Express runs with his two cruisers, two light cruisers, and five destroyers. On the night of 11 October, he found his quarry.[23]

This time it was the Americans who got the drop on the Japanese. Scott's vessels spotted and tracked Goto's force throughout the eleventh. When the Japanese arrived west of Savo Island in the evening, Scott was positioned to execute a textbook "crossing of the T," whereby all of his guns could fire on the lead elements of the opposing force, which could respond only with its forward guns. The Americans did not quite pull off the maneuver in execution, but they still started the battle with an advantage.[24]

Goto's flagship, the cruiser *Aoba*, was struck first, and the admiral apparently thought it was being hit by friendly fire. Regardless, the ship was burning and had suffered massive casualties among its crew in the first twenty minutes of the battle. Goto himself was mortally wounded.[25] After the initial salvos, many Japanese ships were aflame and now easily targeted in the darkness.

The battle did not get any better for the bombardment force from there, although the Americans had significant command-and-control issues that led to confusion and to at least one U.S. ship, the destroyer *Farenholt*, being hit by friendly fire as well as hostile fire. But in the end, the remnants of Goto's Bombardment Force slunk away from the battle.

The result was a partial American victory. The Bombardment Force was defeated with heavy losses, including one heavy cruiser and three destroyers, suffered between the night battle and other losses thereafter.[26]

THE BATTLE OF HENDERSON FIELD

While the Japanese succeeded in reinforcing their troops on Guadalcanal, TF 64's success also facilitated an American convoy that brought the U.S. Army's 164th Infantry Regiment (Americal Division) to Guadalcanal to augment Vandegrift's command.[27] Turner's convoy landed on 13 October and also included Marine replacements, the First Marine Air Wing to help run Henderson Field, and supplies and vehicles. But another strong Tokyo Express run was on the way.

On 14 October Japanese warships bombarded Henderson Field, causing heavy damage and destroying a stock of aviation fuel, temporarily limiting the number of sorties available to hunt down Tokyo Express runs. The following night two Japanese reinforcement convoys unloaded without interference until daylight, when an air battle between covering Japanese planes and the Cactus Air Force developed as the latter attacked Japanese beach-landing crews as offloading continued.[28] By mid-October, the number of Japanese troops on Guadalcanal was roughly 15,000 men. Although the American soldiers, sailors, and Marines outnumbered them, not all of these were ground troops.[29] Additionally, over 4,000 Americans were holding nearby Tulagi, although Vandegrift wisely used the requirement to garrison that island as a way both to create a reserve force and to give frontline units a rest.

The Japanese Seventeenth Army, now headquartered on Guadalcanal itself, planned a massive assault on the American lines for late October, coordinated with both air and sea offensives. The plan for the army itself was twofold. A strong concentration of artillery, infantry, and a few light tanks would execute a feint at the Matinakau River, where the far right of the

American perimeter met the sea. This would be preceded by days of artillery fire to give the impression that the main attack would occur there. In the meantime, the Japanese 2nd Division would infiltrate through the thick jungle of the island and attack the perimeter from the south, where they erroneously thought it was undefended. Lastly, a regiment's worth of troops would make an amphibious landing inside the American perimeter.[30]

It was a complicated plan, but the Seventeenth Army largely managed to execute it. First Marine Division did shift troops and artillery to the eastward portion of its line to meet the feint attack at the Matinakau. The Cactus Air Force was almost constantly in action against the air offensive, which probably contributed to the fact that 2nd Division's long approach march went undetected. And the Japanese navy concentrated surface combatants in the waters around Guadalcanal to control the sea. First Marine Division was essentially surrounded. The Seventeenth Army achieved surprise and a nine-to-one numerical superiority at the point of attack.[31]

But the grueling march through driving rains with disassembled artillery and other heavy equipment left the Japanese troops spent before they even reached their attack positions; navigation errors led some units to veer off course and miss their attacks entirely. Where they did assault, the Japanese found not undefended gaps in the line, but crack units—Lieutenant Colonel Lewis "Chesty" Puller's 1st Battalion, 7th Marines and Lieutenant Colonel Herman H. Hannekan's 2nd Battalion, 7th Marines—on strong defensive ground. Puller's unit took the brunt of the attack—successive night assaults by an entire Japanese regiment—and was reinforced by 3rd Battalion, 164th Infantry.[32]

After two days and nights of fighting, the Seventeenth Army called off the operation before the final landing. The first well-coordinated land, sea, and air counteroffensive against the American force had failed. Final casualties on both sides are still not clear, but the Americans lost roughly ninety men killed. The Japanese likely lost more than 2,200 soldiers from both combat and the strenuous march.[33]

THE NAVAL BATTLE OF GUADALCANAL

The U.S. Navy was not idle during this time. On 26 October a carrier battle developed between TF 64, including the carriers *Enterprise* and *Hornet*, and Imperial Japanese Navy forces, including the carriers *Jun'yō*, *Shōkaku*, *Zuikaku*, and *Zuihō*. The Japanese got the better of the battle, sinking the *Hornet*, but lost additional aircraft and experienced pilots and suffered heavy damage to their fleet.³⁴ Three of the carriers would have to leave the theater for replenishment and repair, hindering Japanese naval aviation in the coming months. In the wake of the Japanese defeat on Guadalcanal itself and the American defeat at sea, both sides shifted to reinforcement in preparation for future operations. Admiral Yamamoto committed to reinforcing and resupplying the tenuous Seventeenth Army positions on the island, while Vice Admiral William "Bull" Halsey, now the South Pacific theater commander, promised Vandegrift additional forces, including the establishment of an additional beachhead.

By now, as new squadrons, pilots, and planes flowed into Guadalcanal to join the Cactus Air Force, the American position featured, not one, but three airstrips—the original Henderson Field and two smaller airstrips scratched out of the soil, Fighter One and Fighter Two.³⁵ Pilots from the Marine Corps, Navy, and Army Air Corps all used these facilities.

But Vandegrift allowed no lull as he waited for reinforcements. First Marine Division went on the offensive in early November to push the Japanese away from the perimeter, even as Tokyo Express runs continued.³⁶ On the American side, 8th Marines and 2nd Raider Battalion arrived and joined these efforts.

By 8 November American cryptanalysts deciphered Yamamoto's planned reinforcement offensive and its date: 13 November. This prompted Vandegrift to pull his forces back in expectation.³⁷ Japanese air forces would cover a large convoy of transports to augment Tokyo Express runs, while their naval forces would bombard Henderson Field on two successive nights to neutralize the Cactus Air Force long enough to land troops and supplies.

On the night of 12 November, a Japanese task force under Rear Admiral Hiroaki Abe entered Iron Bottom Sound to shell Henderson Field. Abe commanded the Volunteer Attack Force, consisting of two battleships escorted by light cruisers and destroyers. They were intercepted by U.S. ships under Rear Admiral Daniel J. Callaghan, the eight destroyers, three light cruisers, and two cruisers of TG 67.4.³⁸ In a vicious night battle at extremely close range, the stronger Japanese force pounded the American ships, causing massive casualties, including Admiral Callaghan and Admiral Scott, the victor of the Battle of Cape Esperance, who was with the task force but not in command. While the Japanese got the better of the fight, sinking four destroyers and a light cruiser while only losing two destroyers and a battleship, it caused Abe to abandon his mission of bombarding Henderson Field.³⁹

On 14 November, thanks to the reprieve from bombardment resulting from the sacrifice of TG 67.4, the Cactus Air Force sank seven of eleven inbound Japanese transports.[40] That night the naval force for the second planned bombardment of Henderson Field approached, accompanied by transports loaded with troops and supplies that would land as well. This task force, under Vice Admiral Nobutake Kondo, was mostly destroyers and cruisers but included the battleship *Kirishima*. His warships were caught by a numerically much smaller American task force under Rear Admiral Willis Lee, but Lee had two battleships along with four destroyers.[41] Another furious, close-range night battle developed, but this time it was the U.S. Navy that won, thanks to Lee's more effective command and control and his use of advanced radars. The *Kirishima* went to the bottom, and Admiral Kondo had to abandon his plans to bombard Henderson Field.[42]

Between air and naval actions in mid-November during Yamamoto's strongest effort at reinforcement yet, Japanese losses in terms of ships, sailors, aircraft, and pilots outweighed American losses, although the Japanese won more than one of the individual tactical actions.[43]

Yamamoto had planned to land 12,000 soldiers on Guadalcanal in mid-November, but only about 2,000 made it ashore. The entire Japanese force on the island ended up with only about four days' worth of food. Meanwhile, Admiral Turner was responsible for landing 5,500 additional American troops. Every single one made it ashore.[44] But the price of successful reinforcement was high. For every Marine and soldier who was killed in action ashore on Guadalcanal, three sailors made the ultimate sacrifice.[45]

THE BATTLE OF TASSAFARONGA

The Naval Battle of Guadalcanal largely determined the outcome of the campaign; the Japanese did not, and now could not, get enough combat power on the island itself to overcome Vandegrift's forces. Moreover, although the Japanese navy could get some reinforcements through, they could not sustain them or the rest of their army. Not for nothing did the Japanese soldiers refer to Guadalcanal as "Starvation Island." The more Japanese soldiers who landed, the less food they ate.

By the end of November, Admiral Halsey had reorganized the naval forces and formed TF 67 under Rear Admiral Carleton H. Wright, whose mission was to prevent any further landings by the Japanese. On the night of 30 November, Wright caught the last major run of the Tokyo Express just as it began landing operations. His task force, composed of heavy and light cruisers and four destroyers, caught a Japanese force of eight destroyers under Rear Admiral Raizo Tanaka, who aborted the landing and turned to face TF 67. The American force heavily outgunned the Japanese force in naval guns—but not in torpedoes.[46]

Once again, the Japanese navy's skill at night fighting and its far-superior Long Lance torpedoes made a difference. Unbeknownst to the Navy at the time but discovered later, American naval guns had faulty aiming technology, which contributed to the outcome of the fighting. Tassafaronga is generally considered another combat defeat for the U.S. Navy, but Wright accomplished his mission; Tanaka abandoned his landing efforts, and no supplies reached the Seventeenth Army.[47]

THE JAPANESE DECISION AND OPERATION KE

Throughout December, the Japanese tried increasingly desperate measures to supply their troops on Guadalcanal. Tokyo Express runs now switched to towing barrels full of supplies and releasing them in the waters west of Marine lines, but interference from the Cactus Air Force and U.S. Navy PT boats, which waited at ambush points close to shore, made these efforts almost worthless as very few barrels made it ashore. Attempts to load patrol boats with supplies and beach them inside Japanese lines and even air drop supplies met with little success. Only submarines could consistently complete supply runs, but they could embark only a limited amount of supplies. Japanese troops on the island wasted away. Of roughly 6,000 present at this time, only about 250 could fight. Those too starving to walk were propped up in defensive positions to man a weapon as long as possible.[48]

Meanwhile, U.S. reinforcements were flowing in. Most of the exhausted 1st Marine Division pulled out as it was replaced by 2nd Marine Division and the rest of the Americal Division. General Vandegrift turned over command of the combined Army/Marine force to Army major general Alexander M. Patch on 8 December.[49]

Imperial General Headquarters spent December analyzing various plans for Guadalcanal, including various ways to reinforce and renew offensive operations. In the end, however, the only one that seemed feasible was withdrawal. On 31 December the army and navy chiefs presented, and Emperor Hirohito approved, Operation KE, the amphibious withdrawal of the remaining Japanese forces on Guadalcanal.[50]

Operation KE involved a buildup of air and naval forces to affect the withdrawal. This buildup and the transition between operations was detected by American intelligence, but based on the information available, it was indistinguishable from preparations for a renewed offensive. Commanders from Admiral Nimitz on down expected and prepared for another Japanese offensive.[51]

General Patch used the lull to improve his position. He planned an offensive operation southeast of the U.S. position at Lunga Point to capture Mount Austen, from which the Japanese could observe everything that happened in the American perimeter. In the process, 132nd Infantry was stymied by one of the last strong Japanese defensive positions on the island. In a preview of later Japanese tactics in the Pacific, the Seventeenth Army had created a honeycomb of pillboxes and obstacle belts tied in with strong terrain and vegetation. Termed the Gifu by the Japanese, the position was undetectable by air and by ground until its defenders fired. Repeated assaults by 132nd Infantry soldiers surrounded but could not carry the Gifu.[52]

On 2 January 1943 General Patch activated XIV Corps headquarters at Lunga Point, the corps comprising the Americal Division, the newly arrived 25th Infantry Division, 2nd Marine Division, and the independent 147th Infantry Regiment. The Seventeenth Army had about 14,000–16,000 soldiers left on the island, not all of whom were healthy enough to perform duties of any kind, let alone combat duties. Nor did the Japanese have much firepower available. By this point, they were down to roughly ten artillery pieces with very little ammunition. Conversely, combined Marine and Army artillery pieces on the ground amounted to 167 cannon—from 75-mm up to 155-mm in caliber—all of which had deep stocks of ammunition.[53]

Patch did not intend to wait for an offensive but instead to use these forces to clear Guadalcanal entirely. Twenty-Fifth Infantry Division attacked south and southeast toward the Gifu and other key hills around Mount Austen, eventually clearing the Gifu itself on 23 January.[54] Second Marine Division attacked west along the coast with 27th Infantry Regiment, while the Americal Division stood in reserve around Henderson Field.[55]

On 15 January the withdrawal order reached Seventeenth Army headquarters on Guadalcanal, much to the consternation of the Japanese soldiers, who had sacrificed greatly to maintain their hold on the island.[56] During the night of 1–2 February, the first Tokyo Express run of Operation KE arrived, disembarking fresh troops to act as a rear guard and protect the withdrawal. The destroyers left Guadalcanal with 4,935 exhausted and starving troops.[57] Orders went out to the Japanese troops on the island to either withdraw to the embarkation point, make a final stand, or commit suicide. The second

Tokyo Express run also went smoothly, carrying off 3,921 soldiers.[58] The last run, on 8 February, sailed from Guadalcanal with 1,972 soldiers aboard, the last to escape.[59] Those remaining behind starved, surrendered, or were hunted down by Patch's forces.[60] The last Japanese soldier to surrender on Guadalcanal did so in October 1947.[61]

OPERATIONAL DISCIPLINES

Unlike the previous case studies, Guadalcanal was "triphibious," Winston Churchill's term for all Pacific warfare. The story of Operation Watchtower demonstrates the interaction of the operational disciplines in a joint, or multidomain, campaign. The air campaign, viewed in isolation, was largely attritional, as it revolved around the destruction of each side's aircraft and aircrews. Viewed in terms of the entire campaign, however, air power matters a great deal for the sea and ground fights and vice versa. The ability to sortie fighters and control or contest airspace, even temporarily, created space and freedom of action for naval and ground forces. The exploitation of air control materially assisted ground forces; Vandegrift's Marines used close air support at multiple points to defeat Japanese army offensives. The Cactus Air Force contributed a great deal to defeating Japanese efforts at reinforcement and resupply, as did the U.S. Navy. Finally, the interaction of air forces with the ground domain matters a great deal. The ability of 1st Marine Division to seize and hold Henderson Field enhanced American air operations as Marine, Navy, and Army Air Force warplanes were all based there at different points. The distance between Guadalcanal and Rabaul, the main Japanese air base, limited the ability to employ air support for the Seventeenth Army. Japanese attempts to shorten this distance by seizing Buna failed, but had it succeeded, it would have been a dire problem for the Americans. Lastly, it may seem strange that the U.S. Navy, Army, and Marine Corps all had aircraft of their own, flown by their own personnel. But rather than producing confusion, this provided a diversification in airframes and pilot expertise that was an advantage. Whether air forces were required to attack naval targets, air targets, or ground targets or to support naval, air, or ground operations, suitable squadrons were available.

The Guadalcanal Campaign occurred because both sides knew the value of seizing ground for a naval campaign. The Marine position at Lunga Point performed both air control and denial as well as sea control and denial functions. Although the seizure of the airfield and the stalwart defense thereof usually garners the most attention, Navy PT boats operated in its vicinity and contested control of the water with the Japanese warships, with assistance from both Marine and Army coastal guns that eventually made it to the island. Lastly, the Japanese lack of combat engineers able to quickly construct airfields in the Solomon Islands, not just on Guadalcanal, was a significant limitation on their operations.[62] By contrast, U.S. Marines and Navy Seabees not only materially improved Henderson Field after American forces captured it but produced two supplementary airstrips as well.

Naval warfare made the campaign possible in the first place, and neither the ground forces nor the air forces on Guadalcanal could have been sustained without the U.S. Navy. Indeed, it was largely the failure of the Imperial Japanese Navy to both simultaneously contest sea space and sustain ground and air forces (and the U.S. Navy's success in doing so) that determined the outcome of the campaign. No matter how much Vandegrift and the Marines outfought the Japanese army, without the U.S. Navy, they just would have starved to death as victors. This is not to say that Vandergrift's units were lavishly supplied. Indeed, at one point only captured Japanese food stood between 1st Marine Division and defeat by malnutrition. It was the U.S. Navy reestablishing a supply chain that truly staved off starvation, while the Japanese navy's failure to do so condemned many Japanese soldiers to agonizing deaths.

Although all six operational disciplines were necessary for such a complex and massive campaign, two stand out for this case study: information and logistics. Administration during this campaign was covered in chapter 7. Due to the length considerations, only information and logistics will be covered.

U.S. forces gained and maintained information superiority over the Japanese early in the campaign. Famously, a large part of this was the American ability to decrypt and read high-level Japanese transmissions, including to and from Admiral Yamamoto himself. This information coup, however, merely provided occasional windows through which American forces could ascertain exactly what opposing commanders were saying as the Japanese codes were periodically replaced. The real information coup was less technological: the Coast Watchers. The Coast Watchers comprised local civilians and auxiliary military personnel organized under the Royal Australian Navy. Placed or recruited on various South Pacific islands, these people merely watched the comings and goings of Japanese forces and reported them to the Allies. They routinely warned of incoming air strikes against Henderson Field forty to forty-five minutes prior to their arrival, in addition to reliably reporting the movements of Japanese naval forces. There is no indication that the Japanese ever figured out that the Coast Watchers network existed during the campaign. Conversely, Japanese information about the size and disposition of U.S. forces on Guadalcanal was consistently wrong. In addition, the navy frequently deliberately deceived the army about their capabilities and forces.[63]

Historian Richard Frank has described Operation Watchtower/Operation KA as a state of "mutual siege." The Americans dominated the sea by day, the Japanese did so by night. Thus, each side was able to prevent the other from supplying and reinforcing their forces at will.[64] The campaign then became a competition to transport troops and supplies to Guadalcanal, with the air and naval forces of both sides active in this effort. Viewed in total as a campaign, the actual ground fighting almost becomes a side show, such that while American victories certainly contributed to the challenges faced by the Japanese on the island, they would not have mattered had Admiral Turner been unable to sustain the forces ashore. Even getting troops to Guadalcanal would not have mattered were they not sustained, as the Japanese experience shows. The Japanese navy succeeded in putting multiple divisions ashore to mount major offensives during times when Vandegrift did not have enough Marines to even form a full perimeter around Henderson Field. In other words, the Japanese probably managed to put enough soldiers on Guadalcanal to win. But, since they ended up starving so many of them and wasting so many lives in piecemeal attacks, they could not.

Lastly, there were a few key innovations that occurred on the ground at Guadalcanal that had deep implications for later U.S. ground operations and thus should be mentioned. These were the creation of the first modern American sniper units, the first use of special forces, and the first formal use of infantry squads as a unit below the platoon level. Vandegrift, realizing the difficulty of land navigation and patrolling in Guadalcanal's deep jungle using inaccurate maps, recruited Marines from across the division who showed talent at navigation, fieldcraft, and marksmanship. Dubbed Scout-Snipers, these Marines, operating alone or in teams, infiltrated deep into the jungle to identify Japanese positions, then acted as pathfinders to lead maneuver units to them.[65] The two battalions of Raiders, created at the same time as similar Army units, were the first in action. Each Raider battalion was organized along different lines according to the desires of its commander. Edson's 1st Raider Battalion was organized along more traditional infantry battalion lines, but Evan Carlson's 2nd Raider Battalion was organized with squads as the lowest tactical unit, an idea that Carlson had learned from his time as an observer embedded with Chinese communist guerrillas. This was the first introduction of the squad to U.S. forces, and the practice spread from Carlson's Raiders to the rest of the Marine Corps and on to the Army from there.

CONCLUSION

This admittedly cursory look at Operation Watchtower is included as a means of demonstrating the interaction both of the operational disciplines and of multiple services and multiple domains (air, land, and sea). The domains are as discreet as the tactics that occur in them. The operational disciplines, however, permeate across domains and across services. Ground, naval, and air forces, operating on land, at sea, and in the air, were united by the operational disciplines that cut across them all: administration, information, operations, fire support, logistics, and command and control. This permeation of operational art is enabled by staff officers of similar disciplines interacting across service and domain lines, for it is necessary to plan, prepare, synchronize, and sustain tactics across a campaign. This is sometimes quite literal, as a fire-support officer on the ground may direct the attack of an air force officer from the air or a sailor may depend on coastal-artillery officers to attack opposing ships in key maritime terrain. What is today termed multidomain operations is, in a sense, merely good staff work.

NOTES

INTRODUCTION

1. Howard, *War in European History*, 100.
2. The term "staff officer," as used in this book, is inclusive of all members of a military staff, both military and civilian. Commissioned officers, warrant officers, noncommissioned officers, staff noncommissioned officers, and civilian advisors are all integral members of a military staff. The term is not intended to mean only the commissioned officers so assigned.
3. Lenin, "War and Revolution."
4. Freedman, *Strategy*, 202.
5. Storr, *Hall of Mirrors*, xi.
6. Storr, 55, 82.
7. Storr, 89.
8. As we shall see, the conventional wisdom that the operational level was developed by the Germans, the Russians, or both is a myth.
9. Epstein, *Napoleon's Last Victory*, 11.
10. The other major originator, Russian historian James J. Schneider, a professor at the U.S. Army School of Advanced Military Studies, gets closer to the mark and is discussed in chapter 5.
11. Beyerchen, "Clausewitz, Nonlinearity, and the Unpredictability of War," 59–90.
12. Winton, "Imperfect Jewel," 853–77.
13. Vego, *Joint Operational Warfare*, I-4.
14. Naveh, *In Pursuit of Military Excellence*, 9–10.
15. Clausewitz, *On War* (2004), 70.
16. Kelly and Brennan, *Alien*, 93.
17. Owen, "Operational Level of War Does Not Exist," 17.
18. Owen, 18.
19. Strachan, "Strategy or Alibi," 157–82.
20. Strachan, 177.
21. Viggers, "Policy, Strategy, and Tactics," 49.
22. Gray, *Strategy Bridge*, 18.
23. Gray, 21.
24. Gray, 32.
25. Schroden, *Why Special Operations?*, 19.
26. Clausewitz, *On War* (2004), 71.
27. Clausewitz, 66.

28. For more on tactics, see Friedman, *On Tactics*. For more on strategic effect, see Gray, *Strategy Bridge*, chap. 5.

CHAPTER 1. OPERATIONS AND THE NAPOLEONIC REVOLUTION

1. Arsht, "Napoleon Was the Best General Ever."
2. Pichichero, *Military Enlightenment*.
3. See Gray, *Postmodern War*, 111.
4. It is fashionable these days to say that war is more complex. War does not change, warfare does.
5. Bell, *First Total War*, 82.
6. Pichichero, *Military Enlightenment*, 66.
7. Pichichero, 74.
8. Bell, *First Total War*, 115.
9. Howard, *War in European History*, 49.
10. Bell, *First Total War*, 73.
11. Roberts, *Napoleon*, 85.
12. Jones, *Art of War in the Western World*, 272.
13. Pichichero, *Military Enlightenment*, 60.
14. Howard, *War in European History*, 54.
15. King, *Command*, 39.
16. Rothenberg, *Art of Warfare in the Age of Napoleon*, 61.
17. Rothenberg, 113.
18. Howard, *War in European History*, 77–78.
19. Rothenberg, *Art of Warfare in the Age of Napoleon*, 138.
20. Rothenberg, 75.
21. Rothenberg, 74.
22. Howard, *War in European History*, 76–77.
23. Howard, 79.
24. Rothenberg, *Art of Warfare in the Age of Napoleon*, 139.
25. Howard, *War in European History*, 64.
26. Rothenberg, *Art of Warfare in the Age of Napoleon*, 110.
27. The Napoleonic Revolution is distinct from the Military Revolution that some historians place in Europe roughly in the period 1470–1660 (the dates are hotly contested). See Jeremy Black, "A Military Revolution? Military Change and European Society," in Rogers, *Military Revolution Debate*, 95–114.
28. Camus, *The Rebel*, 106.
29. Quimby, *Background of Napoleonic Warfare*, 344.
30. See Clifford J. Rogers, "Military Revolutions of the Hundred Years War," in Rogers, *Military Revolution Debate*, 76–77.
31. Bell, *First Total War*, 215.
32. Bell, 269.
33. Engberg-Pederson, *Empire of Chance*, 4.

34. Roberts, *Napoleon*, 49–50.
35. Rothenberg, *Art of Warfare in the Age of Napoleon*, 128.
36. Rothenberg, 128.
37. Rothenberg, 128.
38. Rothenberg, 130.
39. Bell, *First Total War*, 198.
40. Roberts, *Napoleon*, 61.
41. Rothenberg, *Art of Warfare in the Age of Napoleon*, 208.
42. Rothenberg, 209.
43. Quimby, *Background of Napoleonic Warfare*, 175–76.
44. Quimby, 86.
45. Rothenberg, 209.
46. Roberts, 80.
47. Rothenberg, 209–10.
48. Rothenberg, 209–10.
49. Roberts, xxxvi.
50. Roberts, 109.
51. Rothenberg, *Art of Warfare in the Age of Napoleon*, 129.
52. King, *Command*, 93.
53. Kott, "Future of War Technology."
54. See Bell, *First Total War*, 44; and Whitman, *Verdict of Battle*.

CHAPTER 2. GERMAN OPERATIONAL THOUGHT

1. Paret, *Clausewitz and the State*, 45.
2. Van Creveld, *Command in War*, 29.
3. Van Creveld, 30.
4. Van Creveld, 31.
5. Van Creveld, 33.
6. Van Creveld, 34.
7. Van Creveld, 35.
8. Van Creveld, 37.
9. Dupuy, *Genius for War*, 20.
10. Dupuy, 22.
11. See especially Bellinger, "Introducing Scharnhorst."
12. Dupuy, *Genius for War*, 25.
13. White, *Enlightened Soldier*, 65.
14. These reforms included opening the officer corps to anyone based on merit, examination systems, a modern military-justice system, a military-academy system, the establishment of a war ministry, and other improvements to tie the military to the people rather than to just the monarchy. The focus here, however, is on the general staff. For these reforms in context, see especially Bellinger, "Introducing Scharnhorst."

15. Dupuy, *Genius for War*, 38.
16. White, *Enlightened Soldier*, 138.
17. White, 39.
18. See King, *Command*, 95–96.
19. Citino, *German Way of War*, 131.
20. Dupuy, *Genius for War*, 24.
21. Dupuy, 303.
22. Wilkinson, *Brain of an Army*, 97.
23. Jones, *Art of War in the Western World*, 392.
24. Hone, *Learning War*, 3.
25. Goerlitz, *History of the German General Staff*, Location 2021.
26. Goerlitz, Location 2053.
27. Goerlitz, Location 2310.
28. Goerlitz, Location 2253.
29. Citino, *German Way of War*, 172.
30. Citino, 188–89.
31. Matheny, *Carrying the War to the Enemy*, 13.
32. Similar tactics were also developed by the Union army during the American Civil War, specifically by Emory Upton, and the British Army during World War I but were never executed at scale.
33. Storr, *Hall of Mirrors*, 91–92.
34. Naveh, *In Pursuit of Military Excellence*, 119.
35. Gross, *Myth and Reality of German Warfare*, 181–82.
36. Gross, 8.
37. Citino, *German Way of War*, xiv.
38. Citino, 51.
39. Citino, 82.
40. See Naveh, *In Pursuit of Military Excellence*, chap. 4. An English translation of *Truppenführung* (HD-300) produced by the U.S. Army can be accessed at https://upload.wikimedia.org/wikipedia/commons/0/02/Truppenf%C3%BChrung_translation_by_United_States_Army.pdf.
41. Van Creveld, *Supplying War*, 79.
42. Van Creveld, 117.

CHAPTER 3. SOVIET OPERATIONAL THOUGHT

1. Stoecker, *Forging Stalin's Army*, 10.
2. Stoecker, 18.
3. Jonsson, *Russian Understanding of War*, 3.
4. *Marxism-Leninism on War and Army* (Moscow, 1957; translation by U.S. Air Force, Washington, DC: Government Printing Office, 1972), 294–95. The book does not mention an operational level of war.
5. Schneider, *Structure of Strategic Revolution*, 112–13.

6. Svechin, *Strategy*, 69.
7. Svechin, 73 (emphasis added).
8. Svechin, 260.
9. Svechin, 69.
10. Schneider, *Structure of Strategic Revolution*, 179.
11. Schneider, 185.
12. Stoecker, *Forging Stalin's Army*, 135.
13. Storr, *Hall of Mirrors*, 89.
14. Glantz, *Soviet Military Operational Art*, 20.
15. Glantz, 22.
16. Naveh, *In Pursuit of Military Excellence*, 16.
17. Naveh, 17.
18. Stoecker, *Forging Stalin's Army*, 143.
19. Stoecker, 17.
20. Stoecker, 142.
21. Glantz, *Soviet Military Operational Art*, 10.
22. Glantz, 21.
23. Glantz, 43.
24. Glantz, 43.
25. Roberts, *Stalin's General*, 38.
26. Glantz, *Soviet Military Operational Art*, 10–11.
27. Glantz, 13.
28. Glantz, 24.
29. Rice, "Making of Soviet Strategy," 664.
30. Glantz, *Soviet Military Operational Art*, 25.
31. Glantz, 28.
32. Glantz, 29.
33. Glantz, 30–31.
34. Glantz, 33–34.
35. Glantz, 36.
36. Glantz, 41–42.
37. Naveh, *In Pursuit of Military Excellence*, 167.
38. National Technical Information Service, *Dictionary of Basic Military Terms*, 143.
39. National Technical Information Service, 145.
40. Reznichenko, *Tactics*, 3 (emphasis added).
41. Reznichenko, 3.
42. Kelly and Brennan, *Alien*, 47.

CHAPTER 4. AMERICAN OPERATIONAL THOUGHT
1. Blythe, "History of Operational Art," 37.
2. Trauschweizer, *Cold War U.S. Army*, 199.
3. Trauschweizer, 200–201.

4. Trauschweizer, 206.
5. Trauschweizer, 207.
6. Trauschweizer, 210.
7. Strachan, *Clausewitz's* On War, 109.
8. Blythe, "History of Operational Art," 44; Trauschweizer, *Cold War U.S. Army*, 218.
9. Blythe, "History of Operational Art," 44.
10. Blythe, 45. For the lack of an operational level in Soviet doctrine, which may have led to the writing team's reluctance to include it, see chapter 3. General Otis' insistence on including it anyway is questionable, to say the least.
11. Luttwak, "Operational Level of War," 61–79.
12. For Starry's collected works, see Sorley, *Press On!* The conflation of the tactical and operational levels is pervasive throughout his body of work.
13. Sorley, 1061, 1093, 1152.
14. Trauschweizer, *Cold War U.S. Army*, 222.
15. Blythe, "History of Operational Art," 2–3.
16. Blythe, 2–3.
17. Trauschweizer, *Cold War U.S. Army*, 235.
18. Blythe, "History of Operational Art," 10.
19. Blythe, 10.
20. Department of the Army, FM 100-5, *Operations*, 6-2.
21. Department of the Army, 6-2.
22. Department of the Navy, MCDP 1-1, *Campaigning*, 11.
23. J. F. Schmitt, personal communication with the author, 26 April 2020. Schmitt was the principal author of both publications.
24. Department of the Air Force, Air Force Manual 1-1, *Basic Aerospace Doctrine* (1992), and Department of the Air Force, Air Force Manual 1-1, *Basic Aerospace Doctrine* (1984).
25. Department of the Air Force, Air Force Manual 1-1, *Basic Aerospace Doctrine* (1992), 10.
26. See Hughes, "Naval Operations," and Department of the Navy, NDP 1, *Naval Warfare*.
27. Matheny, *Carrying the War to the Enemy*, 15.
28. Schneider, "Loose Marble," 85–99.
29. Schneider, *Structure of Strategic Revolution*, 51.
30. Department of the Army, ADP 3-0, *Unified Land Operations* (2011), 9.
31. Department of the Army, ADP 3-0, *Operations* (2019), 3-5, 3-6.
32. Eikmeier, "Operational Art and the Operational Level of War."
33. Doane, "It's Just Tactics."
34. Kuehn, *America's First General Staff*, 2.
35. See Hone, *Learning War*, 3.
36. Howarth, *To Shining Sea*, 294.
37. Wass de Czege, "Thinking and Acting like an Early Explorer."

CHAPTER 5. THE OPERATIONAL LEVEL AND THE CIVIL-MILITARY RELATIONSHIP

1. Paret and Moran, *Carl von Clausewitz*, 21–24.
2. Garard, *Carl von Clausewitz's Guide to Tactics*.
3. Craig, *Politics of the Prussian Army*, 193.
4. Craig, 195–96.
5. Craig, 204–5.
6. Craig, 218.
7. While Leo Tolstoy's depiction of staff officers during 1812 probably held a grain of truth, it is more likely that he was basing it on his own experience as an artillery officer in the Russian army during the Crimean War (1853–56).
8. Mahoney, *Role of the Soviet General Staff*, iii.
9. This collection of reforms is named for Minister of War Count Dmitry Alekseyevich Miliutin.
10. Mayzel, "Formation of the Russian General Staff," 298.
11. Mayzel, 300.
12. Mahoney, *Role of the Soviet General Staff*, iii–iv.
13. Hastings, *Vietnam*, 198.
14. Krepinevich, *The Army and Vietnam*, 262.
15. Freedman, *Strategy*, 207.
16. Brooks, "Paradoxes of Professionalism," 7–44.
17. For the Iraq surge, see Ricks, *The Gamble*. For the Afghanistan surge, see Woodward, *Obama's Wars*.
18. Ricks, *The Gamble*, 124.
19. Schulman, "Washington Is Never Quite Sure Where It Is at War."
20. Golby, "Danger of Military Partisanship."

CHAPTER 6. A THEORY OF OPERATIONAL ART

1. Garard, "The Interface: Reestablishing the Relationship between Politics and Tactics."
2. Clausewitz, *On War* (2004), 66.
3. Clausewitz, 66.
4. Paret and Moran, *Carl von Clausewitz*, 21 (emphasis in original).
5. Cormier, *War as Paradox*, 201.
6. The presence of so many contradictions in *On War* has led many a student of war, unfamiliar with dialectical logic, astray. The contradictory statements are not necessarily mistakes or oversights but integral components of the logical system.
7. Stoker, *Why America Loses Wars*, 5.
8. Bruscino, "Theory of Operational Art and Unified Land Operations," 6.
9. Beyerchen, "Clausewitz, Nonlinearity, and the Unpredictability of War," 59–90.
10. Kornberger and Engberg-Pederson, "Reading Clausewitz," 6.
11. Vego, *Joint Operational Warfare*, I-4.

12. Friedman, *On Tactics*, 16.
13. Gray, *Strategy Bridge*, 18.
14. Department of the Army, ADP 3-0, *Operations* (2019), 5-2.
15. *Army Doctrine Update #1*, 24 February 2007.

CHAPTER 7. ADMINISTRATION

1. "What Is Human Resource?," HumanResourcesEDU, https://www.humanresourcesedu.org/what-is-human-resources/.
2. Lylall, "The Strongest Military Is an Inclusive One."
3. Howard, *War in Military European History*, 63.
4. Pichichero, *Military Enlightenment*, 30.
5. Pichichero, 33.
6. See Venable, *How the Few Became the Proud*.
7. Gaudi, *African Kaiser*, 84–85.
8. Armstrong, *21st Century Mahan*, 15.
9. Armstrong, 16.
10. Armstrong, 15.
11. Van Creveld, *Supplying War*, 21.
12. King, *Command*, 344.
13. Garard, "Clausewitz on Alliances."
14. Sterne, Review of *One More Time*.
15. Potter, *Nimitz*, 197.
16. Frank, *Guadalcanal*, 351.
17. Frank, 263.
18. Frank, 556.
19. Frank, 570.
20. Spector, *Eagle against the Sun*, 540.
21. Tuchman, *Stilwell and the American Experience in China*, 519.

CHAPTER 8. INFORMATION

1. Luttwak, *Strategy*, 106.
2. Taylor, *Munitions of the Mind*, 21.
3. Taylor, 23.
4. Keegan, *Intelligence in War*, 9.
5. Keegan, 9.
6. Jones, *The Art of War in the Western World*, 70.
7. Keegan, *Intelligence in War*, 11.
8. Keegan, 13.
9. Maalouf, *Crusades through Arab Eyes*, 181.
10. Taylor, *Munitions of the Mind*, 96.
11. Taylor, 97.
12. Taylor, 99.

13. Taylor, 116.
14. Quoted in Taylor, 117–18.
15. Roberts, *Napoleon*, 171–72.
16. Roberts, 196–97.
17. Keegan, *Intelligence in War*, 78.
18. Keegan, 78.
19. Keegan, 82.
20. Keegan, 89.
21. Rhodes, "Thinking in Space," 90–108.
22. Rhodes, 144.
23. Rhodes, 119.
24. Rhodes, 120.
25. Rhodes, 121.
26. Rhodes, 123.
27. Rhodes, 124.
28. Rhodes, 126.
29. Keegan, *Intelligence in War*, 204.
30. Elkus, "Continuing Relevance," 21–24.
31. Armistead, *Information Operations*, 203.
32. Clausewitz, *On War* (2004), 56. Many English translations have modified this chapter and replaced the word "information" with "intelligence," which erroneously changes the scope of the chapter.
33. Clausewitz, *Principles of War*.
34. Bolt, *Violent Image*, 261.
35. The four subcomponents of information warfare are intelligence, political/psychological warfare, network/cyberwarfare, and electronic warfare. See Peter Mattis, "Modernizing Military Intelligence: The PLA Plays Catchup," in McReynolds, *China's Evolving Military Strategy*, 317.
36. See especially Denning, *Information Warfare and Security*, chap. 2.
37. See especially David and McKeldin, *Ideas as Weapons*, chaps. 15–16.
38. See Johnson, *Taliban Narratives*, and Stern and Berger, *ISIS*.
39. Ledwidge, *Aerial Warfare*, 73.
40. Ledwidge, 109.
41. Ledwidge, 110.
42. Friedman, *On Tactics*, chap. 7.
43. Elkus, "Continuing Relevance," 21–24.
44. Johnson, *Taliban Narratives*.
45. King, *Command*, 223.

CHAPTER 9. OPERATIONS

1. For a deeper discussion of maneuver, see Friedman, *On Tactics*, chap. 3.
2. Friedman, 26.

3. Clausewitz, *On War* (2004), 27.
4. Jones, *Art of War in the Western World*, 39.
5. Oman, *Art of War in the Middle Ages*, 76.
6. Citino, *Blitzkrieg to Desert Storm*, 140. General Smith was one of the few senior leaders on the ground who saw the Chinese trap before it was sprung and the only one to do anything about it, constructing logistics depots and airfields to support a fight. See also Sides, *On Desperate Ground*, 119–24.
7. Clausewitz, *On War* (2004), 167.
8. Vego, *Joint Operational Warfare*, III-3.
9. Jones, *Art of War in the Western World*, 666.
10. See Liddell Hart, *Strategy*.
11. Dupuy, *Understanding War*, 126.
12. Jomini, *Art of War*, 93.
13. Jones, *Art of War in the Western World*, 70–72.
14. On the culminating point of attack, see Clausewitz, *On War*, bk. 7, chap. 5.
15. Storr, *Hall of Mirrors*, 202.
16. See Friedman, *On Tactics*, chap. 10.
17. Naveh, *In Pursuit of Military Excellence*, 215–16.
18. Storr, *Hall of Mirrors*, 192.
19. Jones calls them strategies, but his definition of strategy is apolitical. Lacking the necessary political dimension, these concepts are more properly called campaigns than strategies. See *Art of War in the Western World*, 55.
20. Wylie, *Military Strategy*, 22–23.
21. Craig, "Delbrück," 341–42.
22. Liddell Hart, *Strategy*, 145.
23. See "Styles of Warfare," in Department of the Navy, MCDP 1, *Warfighting*, 36–40.
24. Brown, *New Conception of War*.
25. Garard, "Geopolitical Gerrymandering."

CHAPTER 10. FIRE SUPPORT

1. See Friedman, *On Tactics*, chap. 5.
2. Norris, *Artillery*, 2.
3. Norris, 2.
4. Norris, 7.
5. Norris, 19.
6. Norris, 163.
7. Norris, 159.
8. Grice, *On Gunnery*, 39.
9. Grice, 42.
10. Grice, 111.
11. Jones, *Art of War in the Western World*, 464.

12. Grice, *On Gunnery*, 151.
13. Garard, *Carl von Clausewitz's Guide to Tactics*.
14. Garard, "Targeting Clausewitzian Judgments."

CHAPTER 11. LOGISTICS

1. Van Creveld, *Command in War*, 35.
2. Van Creveld, *Supplying War*, 5–6.
3. Thorpe, *Pure Logistics*, 4.
4. Friedman, "Battle of Salamis."
5. Jones, *Art of War in the Western World*, 643.
6. Jones, 52–53.
7. Jones, 152–53.
8. Jones, 215–16.
9. Van Creveld, *Supplying War*, 21.
10. Van Creveld, 22.
11. Van Creveld, 233.
12. Jones, *Art of War in the Western World*, 439.
13. Jones, 487.
14. Jones, 563.
15. Jones, 557.
16. Van Creveld, *Supplying War*, 232–33.
17. Jones, *Art of War in the Western World*, 209–13.
18. Eccles, FMFRP 12-14, *Logistics in the National Defense*, 9.
19. Eccles, 10.
20. Eccles, 17.
21. Eccles, 16.
22. This was well over forty years before it actually appeared in doctrine.
23. Matheny, *Carrying the War to the Enemy*, 253.
24. Department of the Navy, MCDP 4, *Logistics*, 45.
25. Department of the Navy, 2-35.
26. See Friedman, *On Tactics*, chap. 11.
27. Garard and Schnappinger, "Beans, Bullets, Band-Aids . . . and Bytes?"

CHAPTER 12. COMMAND AND CONTROL

1. Taylor, *Munitions of the Mind*, 66.
2. Graff, *Medieval Chinese Warfare*, 68. It should be noted that the sources for this battle are extremely thin.
3. Jones, *Art of War in the Western World*, 100–101.
4. Jones, 222.
5. Citino, *Blitzkrieg to Desert Storm*, 282.
6. Armistead, *Information Operations*, 150.
7. Garard and Friedman, "Clarifying Command."

CHAPTER 13. CAMPAIGNS, BATTLES, AND DECISION

1. Nolan, *Allure of Battle*, 393–94.
2. Bungay, *Most Dangerous Enemy*, 135.
3. Arendt, *Origins of Totalitarianism*, 418.
4. To be fair, Nolan does not say this.
5. Biddle, *Military Power*.
6. See especially Clausewitz's note of 10 July 1827, describing the division, "The two kinds of war are, first, those in which the object is the *overthrow of the enemy*, whether it be that we aim at his destruction, politically, or merely disarming him and forcing him to conclude peace on our term[s]; and next, those in which our object is *merely to make some conquests on the frontiers of his country*, either for the purpose of retaining them permanently, or of turning them to account as matter of exchange in the settlement of peace." Clausewitz, *On War* (2004), xxxvii.
7. See Diniz and Proença, "A Criterion for Settling Inconsistencies in Clausewitz's *On War*."

CHAPTER 14. CAMPAIGN TAXONOMY I

1. Examples include "Effects-Based Operations," "Grey Zone Operations," "Asymmetric Warfare" (although all warfare is asymmetric), and many others. As of the time of this writing, the current flavor of the week is "Mosaic Warfare."

CHAPTER 15. CAMPAIGN TAXONOMY II

1. Jones, *Art of War in the Western World*, 166.
2. Jones, 355.
3. Jones, 544–48.
4. Jones, 417.
5. Jones, 546.
6. See Friedman, "Strategy of 'Small Wars,'" 165–77.
7. Armstrong, *Small Boats and Daring Men*, 41.
8. Just one example of this is the differing results of the Iraq surge in 2007–8 and the attempt to replicate it in Afghanistan in 2009.

CHAPTER 16. OPERATIONAL ART ACTUALIZED THROUGH A MODERN STAFF SYSTEM

1. Zegart, *Flawed by Design*, 121.
2. Zegart, 114.
3. McChrystal, *Team of Teams*, 18.
4. McChrystal, 20.
5. King, *Command*, 437–38.
6. King, 439.

7. Clausewitz, *On War* (1943), 488. "Now as the General Staff is usually that part of the army which writes and publishes most, it follows that these parts of campaigns [the topographical and movement details] are recorded more fully in history; and, furthermore, from this there arises a not unnatural tendency to systematize them, and out of the historical solution of one case to construct general solutions for all succeeding cases. But this is a futile, and, therefore, a mistaken endeavor. . . . However necessary and estimable the activity of the General Staff may be, which, following the common view, we have distinguished as most particularly its own, we must still raise a warning voice against the usurpations which often spring from it to the prejudice of the whole. The authority acquired by those leading members of it who are strongest in this branch of service often gives them a sort of general dominion over people's minds, beginning with the general himself, and from this arises a habit of thinking which leads to onesideness."
8. Rempfer, "Choose Your Job."

CHAPTER 17. A NOTE ON FORCE PROTECTION

1. Department of Defense, JP 1-02, *Department of Defense Dictionary of Military and Associated Terms*, 211.

CONCLUSION

1. Clausewitz, *On War* (2004), 71.
2. Gross, *Myth and Reality of German Warfare*, 12.
3. Freedman, *Strategy*, 203.
4. Strachan, "Strategy or Alibi," 157–82.
5. Kelly and Brennan, *Alien*.

CASE STUDY 1. THE AUSTERLITZ CAMPAIGN, 1805

1. Castle, *Austerlitz*, 11.
2. Castle, 22.
3. Roberts, *Napoleon*, 358.
4. Roberts, 364.
5. Castle, *Austerlitz*, 30.
6. Roberts, *Napoleon*, 365.
7. Castle, *Austerlitz*, 30.
8. Castle, 43. A mere forty-eight hours from the receipt of orders to actual mobilization is well beyond the capacity of many modern units of comparable size.
9. Castle, 45.
10. Castle, 47.
11. Roberts, *Napoleon*, 370–71.
12. Roberts, 372.
13. Castle, *Austerlitz*, 54.

14. Castle, 81.
15. Roberts, *Napoleon*, 373.
16. Castle, *Austerlitz*, 94.
17. Castle, 95.
18. Roberts, *Napoleon*, 375.
19. Castle, *Austerlitz*, 99.
20. Roberts, *Napoleon*, 376.
21. Castle, *Austerlitz*, 118.
22. Roberts, *Napoleon*, 376.
23. Castle, *Austerlitz*, 123.
24. Roberts, *Napoleon*, 377.
25. Castle, *Austerlitz*, 128–29.
26. Castle, 130.
27. Castle, 131.
28. Roberts, *Napoleon*, 382.
29. Castle, *Austerlitz*, 152–53.
30. Roberts, *Napoleon*, 384.
31. Roberts, 385.
32. Castle, *Austerlitz*, 169–71.
33. Castle, 187–89.
34. Castle, 197.
35. Quoted in Roberts, *Napoleon*, 358.
36. Roberts, 365.
37. Castle, *Austerlitz*, 70.
38. Castle, 72.
39. Castle, 85.
40. Castle, 114.
41. Rothenberg, *Art of Warfare in the Age of Napoleon*, 128.
42. Roberts, *Napoleon*, 355–56.
43. Castle, *Austerlitz*, 202.

CASE STUDY 2. THE KÖNIGGRÄTZ CAMPAIGN, 1866

1. Craig, *Battle of Königgrätz*, 11.
2. Craig, 30.
3. Goerlitz, *History of the German General Staff*, Location 2367.
4. Craig, *Königgrätz*, 39–40.
5. Craig, 37.
6. Goerlitz, *History of the German General Staff*, Location 2329.
7. Craig, *Königgrätz*, 45.
8. Goerlitz, *History of the German General Staff*, Location 2024.
9. Goerlitz, Location 2358.
10. Craig, *Königgrätz*, 57.

11. Craig, 49.
12. Craig, 50.
13. Craig, 61–64.
14. Craig, 68–70.
15. Craig, 72.
16. Craig, 76–77.
17. Craig, 82.
18. Craig, 83.
19. Craig, 84.
20. Craig, 84–85.
21. Craig, 88.
22. Craig, 91.
23. Craig, 95.
24. Craig, 100.
25. Craig, 101.
26. Craig, 98.
27. Craig, 104–10.
28. Craig, 111.
29. Craig, 120–21.
30. Craig, 124–28.
31. Craig, 114.
32. Craig, 137–38.
33. Craig, 123.
34. Craig, 154.
35. Craig, 141–42.
36. Craig, 151.
37. Craig, 161.
38. Craig, 160.
39. Craig, 6.
40. Craig, 7.
41. Craig, 7.
42. Craig, 17.
43. Craig, 19.
44. Craig, 50.
45. Craig, 54.
46. Craig, 46.
47. Craig, 8.
48. Craig, 131.
49. Craig, xi.
50. Craig, 49.
51. Craig, 10.
52. Craig, 13.

53. Craig, 15.
54. Craig, 17.
55. Craig, 27.
56. Wilkinson, *Brain of an Army*, 55.

CASE STUDY 3. THE ATLANTIC CAMPAIGN, 1914–18

1. Sondhaus, *Great War at Sea*, 12–14.
2. Keegan, *First World War*, 267.
3. See Herman, *To Rule the Waves*.
4. Sondhaus, *Great War at Sea*, 113–14.
5. Keegan, *First World War*, 212.
6. Sondhaus, *Great War at Sea*, 116–19.
7. Sondhaus, 75–76.
8. Sondhaus, 80–83.
9. Sondhaus, 91.
10. Keegan, *First World War*, 264.
11. Keegan, 138.
12. Keegan, 140.
13. Keegan, 265.
14. Sondhaus, *Great War at Sea*, 155.
15. Sondhaus, 157.
16. Sondhaus, 225.
17. Keegan, *First World War*, 268.
18. Liddell Hart, *Real War*, 209.
19. Keegan, *First World War*, 269–74.
20. Liddell Hart, *Real War*, 210.
21. Sondhaus, *Great War at Sea*, 234.
22. Sondhaus, 239.
23. Sondhaus, 234.
24. Liddell Hart, *Real War*, 212.
25. Sondhaus, *Great War at Sea*, 249.
26. Sondhaus, 253–55.
27. Sondhaus, 257.
28. Sondhaus, 260.
29. Sondhaus, 288.
30. Keegan, *First World War*, 274.
31. Keegan, 271.
32. Keegan, 262.
33. Keegan, 330.
34. Keegan, 263.
35. Keegan, 273.
36. Keegan, 337.

37. Keegan, 276.
38. For the Germans, see Sondhaus, *Great War at Sea*, 335. For the British, see Sondhaus, 259.
39. Sondhaus, 287–89.
40. Sondhaus, 336.
41. Keegan, *First World War*, 262.
42. Sondhaus, *Great War at Sea*, 38.
43. Keegan, *First World War*, 212.

CASE STUDY 4. THE BATTLE OF BRITAIN, 1940

1. Bungay, *Most Dangerous Enemy*, 10–11.
2. Bungay, 60, 171.
3. Murray and Millet, *War to Be Won*, 84.
4. Murray and Millet, 84.
5. Murray and Millet, 11.
6. Murray and Millet, 31.
7. Bungay, *Most Dangerous Enemy*, 42.
8. Murray and Millet, *War to be Won*, 85.
9. Bungay, *Most Dangerous Enemy*, 44.
10. Murray and Millet, *War to be Won*, 86.
11. Murray, *Strategy for Defeat*, 21.
12. Bungay, *Most Dangerous Enemy*, 40.
13. Bungay, 33.
14. Bungay, 119.
15. Bungay, 128.
16. Bungay, 134–37.
17. Murray and Millet, *War to be Won*, 87.
18. Bungay, *Most Dangerous Enemy*, 147–49.
19. Bungay, 149.
20. Bungay, 150.
21. Bungay, 152.
22. Bungay, 156–57.
23. Bungay, 193.
24. Bungay, 204–6.
25. Bungay, 184.
26. Bungay, 210.
27. Bungay, 211.
28. Bungay, 215–18.
29. Bungay, 233.
30. Bungay, 285–86.
31. Bungay, 274–75.
32. Bungay, 290.

33. Bungay, 305.
34. Bungay, 309–10.
35. Bungay, 325–27.
36. Bungay, 303.
37. Bungay, 336–37.
38. Bungay, 340.
39. Bungay, 64.
40. Bungay, 123, 162.
41. Bungay, 60–68.
42. Bungay, 187.
43. Bungay, 192.
44. Bungay, 218, 233, 236.
45. Bungay, 275–77.
46. Bungay, 87, 90–91.
47. Bungay, 203.
48. Bungay, 204.
49. Bungay, 181.
50. Bungay, 224.
51. Bungay, 40.
52. Bungay, 216.
53. Bungay, 60–67, 288.

CASE STUDY 5. OPERATION WATCHTOWER, 1942

1. Frank, *Guadalcanal*, 50–52.
2. Frank, 60–64.
3. Frank, 67–69.
4. Hornfischer, *Neptune's Inferno*, 65.
5. Frank, *Guadalcanal*, 121.
6. Hornfischer, *Neptune's Inferno*, 54.
7. Hornfischer, 88.
8. Frank, *Guadalcanal*, 141–43.
9. Frank, 146.
10. Frank, 148.
11. Frank, 151–53.
12. Frank, 156.
13. Hornfischer, *Neptune's Inferno*, 114–17.
14. Hornfischer, 118.
15. Frank, *Guadalcanal*, 193.
16. Frank, 199.
17. Frank, 202.
18. Frank, 204.
19. Frank, 218–19.

20. Frank, 222–25.
21. Frank, 237–45.
22. Hornfischer, *Neptune's Inferno*, 158–59.
23. Hornfischer, 160–65.
24. Hornfischer, 170.
25. Hornfischer, 175.
26. Frank, *Guadalcanal*, 309.
27. Frank, 293.
28. Frank, 322–24.
29. Frank, 327.
30. Frank, 339.
31. Frank, 339, 366.
32. Frank, 354–56.
33. Frank, 365.
34. Frank, 399.
35. Frank, 410.
36. Frank, 412.
37. Frank, 426.
38. Hornfischer, *Neptune's Inferno*, 252.
39. Frank, *Guadalcanal*, 460–61.
40. Hornfischer, *Neptune's Inferno*, 339.
41. Hornfischer, 350.
42. Frank, *Guadalcanal*, 483.
43. Frank, 490.
44. Hornfischer, *Neptune's Inferno*, 368.
45. Hornfischer, 376.
46. Frank, *Guadalcanal*, 503–6.
47. Frank, 518.
48. Frank, 499, 526–27.
49. Frank, 521.
50. Frank, 538–39.
51. Frank, 546.
52. Frank, 530–33.
53. Frank, 543–44.
54. Frank, 566.
55. Frank, 551.
56. Frank, 560.
57. Frank, 588.
58. Frank, 590–91.
59. Frank, 595.
60. Major General Patch has been criticized ever since for allowing so many Japanese troops to escape. This is entirely unfair. First, Patch did not and could not

know that the Japanese were even withdrawing. Second, even if he did know, his mission was not to kill as many enemy soldiers as he could but primarily to maintain possession of Henderson Field and prepare for the offensive that his chain of command believed to be imminent. Third, Patch also needed time to allow his men, many of whom had recently arrived in the South Pacific, to acclimate to the hot, humid environment before committing them to combat. The slow and steady advance during the final offensive and his retaining a division-sized reserve at Henderson Field was not a mistake but a reflection of his priorities based on a true understanding of his mission.

61. Frank, *Guadalcanal*, 597.
62. Frank, 612.
63. Frank, 142.
64. Frank, 210.
65. Frank, 264.

BIBLIOGRAPHY

Arendt, Hannah. *The Origins of Totalitarianism*. New York: Harcourt, 1968.

Armistead, Leigh, ed. *Information Operations: Warfare and the Hard Reality of Soft Power*. Washington, D.C.: Brasseys, 2004.

Armstrong, Benjamin F., ed. *21st Century Mahan: Sound Military Conclusions for the Modern Era*. Annapolis: Naval Institute Press, 2013.

———. *Small Boats and Daring Men: Maritime Raiding, Irregular Warfare, and the Early American Navy*. Norman: University of Oklahoma Press, 2019.

Army Doctrine Update #1. Fort Leavenworth, KS: Combined Arms Doctrine Directorate, US Army Combined Arms Center, 24 February 2007.

Arsht, Ethan. "Napoleon Was the Best General Ever, and the Math Proves It." Towards Data Science. 4 December 2017. https://towardsdatascience.com/napoleon-was-the-best-general-ever-and-the-math-proves-it-86efed303eeb.

Bell, David A. *The First Total War: Napoleon's Europe and the Birth of Warfare as We Know It*. Boston: Mariner Books, 2007.

Bellinger, Vanya Eftimova. "Introducing Scharnhorst: On the Nature of Leadership in War and the Role of Socio-Political Conditions." Strategy Bridge. 14 May 2019. https://thestrategybridge.org/the-bridge/2019/5/14/introducing-scharnhorst-on-the-nature-of-leadership-in-war-and-the-role-of-socio-political-conditions?rq=Introducing%20%23Scharnhorst.

Beyerchen, Alan. "Clausewitz, Nonlinearity, and the Unpredictability of War." *International Security* 17:3 (Winter 1993): 59–90.

Biddle, Stephen. *Military Power: Explaining Victory and Defeat in Modern Battle*. Princeton, NJ: Princeton University Press, 2010.

Blythe, Wilson C., Jr. "A History of Operational Art." *Military Review* 98:6 (November–December 2018): 37–49.

Bolt, Neville. *The Violent Image: Insurgent Propaganda and the New Revolutionaries*. Oxford: Oxford University Press, 2012.

Brooks, Risa. "Paradoxes of Professionalism: Rethinking Civil-Military Relations in the United States." *International Security* 44:4 (Spring 2020): 7–44.

Brown, Ian. *A New Conception of War: John Boyd, the U.S. Marines, and Maneuver Warfare*. Quantico, VA: Marine Corps University Press, 2018.

Bruscino, Thomas. "The Theory of Operational Art and Unified Land Operations." Unpublished School of Advanced Military Studies Theoretical Paper, Summer 2012.

Bungay, Stephen. *The Most Dangerous Enemy: A History of the Battle of Britain*. London: Aurum, 2015.

Camus, Albert. *The Rebel*. New York: Vintage International, 1991.

Castle, Ian. *Austerlitz: Napoleon and the Eagles of Europe*. Yorkshire, UK: Pen & Sword, 2018.

Citino, Robert M. *Blitzkrieg to Desert Storm: The Evolution of Operational Warfare*. Lawrence: University Press of Kansas, 2004.

———. *The German Way of War: From the Thirty Years War to the Third Reich*. Lawrence: University of Kansas Press, 2005.

Clausewitz, Carl von. *On War*. Translated by J. J. Graham. New York: Barnes and Noble, 2004.

———. *On War*. Translated by O. J. Matthijs Jolles. New York: Random House, 1943.

———. *Principles of War*. Translated by Hans Gatzke. Mineola, NY: Dover, 2003.

Cormier, Youri. *War as Paradox: Clausewitz and Hegel on Fighting Doctrines and Ethics*. Montreal: McGill-Queen's University Press, 2016.

Craig, Gordon A. *The Battle of Königgrätz: Prussia's Victory over Austria, 1866*. Philadelphia: University of Pennsylvania Press, 2003.

———. "Delbrück: The Military Historian." In *Makers of Modern Strategy from Machiavelli to the Nuclear Age*, edited by Peter Paret, 326–53. Princeton, NJ: Princeton University Press, 1986.

———. *The Politics of the Prussian Army, 1640–1945*. Oxford: Oxford University Press, 1955.

David, G. J., and T. R. McKeldin, eds. *Ideas as Weapons: Influence and Perception in Modern Warfare*. Washington, D.C.: Potomac Books, 2009.

Denning, Dorothy E. *Information Warfare and Security*. Boston: ACM, 1999.

Department of Defense. JP 1-02, *Department of Defense Dictionary of Military and Associated Terms*. Washington, D.C.: Department of Defense, 2007.

Department of the Air Force. Air Force Manual 1-1, *Basic Aerospace Doctrine of the United States Air Force*. Washington, D.C.: Department of Defense, 1984.

———. Air Force Manual 1-1, *Basic Aerospace Doctrine of the United States Air Force*. Washington, D.C.: Department of Defense, 1992.

Department of the Army. ADP 3-0, *Operations*. Washington, D.C.: Department of the Army, 2019.

———. ADP 3-0, *Unified Land Operations*. Washington, D.C.: Department of the Army, 2011.

———. FM 100-5, *Operations*. Washington, D.C.: Department of the Army, 1993.

Department of the Navy. MCDP 1, *Warfighting*. Washington, D.C.: Department of Defense, 1997.

———. MCDP 1-1, *Campaigning*. Washington, D.C.: Department of Defense, 1990.

———. MCDP 4, *Logistics*. Washington, D.C.: Department of the Navy, 1997.

———. NDP 1, *Naval Warfare*. Washington, D.C.: Department of Defense. 1994.

Diniz, Eugenio, and Domício Proença. "A Criterion for Settling Inconsistencies in Clausewitz's *On War*." *Journal of Strategic Studies* 37:6–7 (December 2012): 1–24.

Doane, Lawrence M. "It's Just Tactics: Why the Operational Level is an Unhelpful Fiction and Impedes the Operational Art." *Small Wars Journal*. 24 September 2015. https:

//smallwarsjournal.com/jrnl/art/it%E2%80%99s-just-tactics-why-the-operational-level-of-war-is-an-unhelpful-fiction-and-impedes-the-.

Dupuy, T. N. *A Genius for War: The German Army and General Staff, 1807–1945*. Englewood Cliffs, NJ: Prentice-Hall, 1977.

———. *Understanding War: History and Theory of Combat*. St. Paul, MN: Paragon House, 1987.

Eccles, Henry E. FMFRP 12-14, *Logistics in the National Defense*. Washington, D.C.: Department of the Navy, 1989.

Eikmeier, Dale C. "Operational Art and the Operational Level of War, Are They Synonymous? Well, It Depends." *Small Wars Journal*. 9 September 2015. https://smallwarsjournal.com/jrnl/art/operational-art-and-the-operational-level-of-war-are-they-synonymous-well-it-depends.

Elkus, Adam, "The Continuing Relevance of Military Denial and Deception." *Military Operations* 1:1 (Summer 2012): 21–24.

Engberg-Pederson, Anders. *Empire of Chance: The Napoleonic Wars and the Disorder of Things*. Cambridge, MA: Harvard University Press, 2015.

Epstein, Robert M. *Napoleon's Last Victory: 1809 and the Emergence of Modern War*. Lawrence: University Press of Kansas, 1994.

Frank, Richard B. *Guadalcanal: The Definitive Account of the Landmark Battle*. New York: Penguin, 1990.

Freedman, Lawrence. *Strategy: A History*. Oxford: Oxford University Press, 2013.

Friedman, B. A. "The Battle of Salamis: Themistocles and the Birth of Strategy." Strategy Bridge. 29 September 2015. https://thestrategybridge.org/the-bridge/2015/9/29/the-battle-of-salamis-themistocles-and-the-birth-of-strategy.

———. *On Tactics: A Theory of Victory in Battle*. Annapolis: Naval Institute Press, 2017.

———. "The Strategy of 'Small Wars.'" In *On Strategy: A Primer*. Edited by Nathan Finney, 165–77. Fort Leavenworth, KS: Army University Press, 2020.

Garard, Olivia, ed. *Carl von Clausewitz's Guide to Tactics*. Quantico, VA: Marine Corps University Press, forthcoming.

———. "Clausewitz on Alliances." N.p., forthcoming.

———. "Geopolitical Gerrymandering and the Importance of Key Maritime Terrain." War on the Rocks. 3 October 2018. https://warontherocks.com/2018/10/geopolitical-gerrymandering-and-the-importance-of-key-maritime-terrain/.

———. "The Interface: Reestablishing the Relationship between Politics and Tactics." *War Room*. U.S. Army War College. 20 August 2020. https://warroom.armywarcollege.edu/articles/the-interface/.

———. "Targeting Clausewitzian Judgments: Fusing Precision and Targeting to Strategy and Tactics." Strategy Bridge. 20 September 2016. https://thestrategybridge.org/the-bridge/2016/9/20/targeting-clausewitzian-judgments-fusing-precision-and-accuracy-to-strategy-and-tactics.

Garard, Olivia, and B. A. Friedman. "Clarifying Command: Keeping Up with the [John Paul] Joneses." War on the Rocks. 7 April 2020. https://warontherocks.com/2020/04/clarifying-command-keeping-up-with-the-john-paul-joneses/.

Garard, Olivia, and Craig M. Schnappinger. "Beans, Bullets, Band-Aids . . . and Bytes? Networking as Digital Logistics." *Marine Corps Gazette*. May 2019. https://mca-marines.org/wp-content/uploads/Beans-Bullets-Band-Aids . . . and-Bytes.pdf.

Gaudi, Robert. *African Kaiser: General Paul Von Lettow-Vorbeck and the Great War in Africa, 1914–1918*. New York: Dutton Caliber, 2017.

Glantz, David. *Soviet Military Operational Art: In Pursuit of Deep Battle*. Abingdon-on-Thames, UK: Routledge, 2012.

Goerlitz, Walter. *History of the German General Staff, 1657–1945*. Lucknow Books, 2015. Kindle Edition.

Golby, Jim. "The Danger of Military Partisanship." *Small Wars Journal*. 1 July 2018. https://smallwarsjournal.com/jrnl/art/danger-military-partisanship.

Graff, David A. *Medieval Chinese Warfare, 300–900*. London: Routledge, 2001.

Gray, Chris Hables. *Postmodern War*. New York: Guilford, 1997.

Gray, Colin S. *The Strategy Bridge: Theory for Practice*. Oxford: Oxford University Press, 2016.

Grice, Michael D. *On Gunnery: The Art and Science of Field Artillery from the American Civil War to the Dawn of the 21st Century*. Charleston, SC: Booksurge, 2009.

Gross, Gerhard P. *The Myth and Reality of German Warfare: Operational Thinking from Moltke the Elder to Heusinger*. Lexington: University Press of Kentucky, 2016.

Hastings, Max. *Vietnam: An Epic Tragedy, 1945–1975*. New York: Harper Perennial, 2018.

Herman, Arthur. *To Rule the Waves: How the British Navy Shaped the Modern World*. New York: HarperCollins, 2004.

Hone, Trent. *Learning War: The Evolution of Fighting Doctrine in the U.S. Navy, 1898–1945*. Annapolis: Naval Institute Press, 2018.

Hornfischer, James D. *Neptune's Inferno: The U.S. Navy at Guadalcanal*. New York: Bantam Books, 2011.

Howard, Michael. *War in European History*. Updated edition. Oxford: Oxford University Press, 2009.

Howarth, Stephen. *To Shining Sea: A History of the United States Navy, 1775–1998*. Norman: University of Oklahoma Press, 1999.

Hughes, Wayne R. "Naval Operations." *Naval War College Review* 65:3 (Summer 2012): 23–46.

Johnson, Thomas H. *Taliban Narratives: The Use and Power of Stories in the Afghanistan Conflict*. Oxford: Oxford University Press, 2018.

Jomini, Antoine-Henri. *The Art of War*. Translated by G. H. Mendell and W. P. Craighill. Westport, CT: Greenwood, 1971.

Jones, Archer. *The Art of War in the Western World*. Urbana: University of Illinois Press, 1987.

Jonsson, Oscar. *The Russian Understanding of War*. Washington, D.C.: Georgetown University Press, 2019.

Keegan, John. *The First World War*. New York: Vintage Books, 1998.

———. *Intelligence in War*. New York: Knopf, 2003.

Kelly, Justin, and Michael Brennan. *Alien: How Operational Art Devoured Strategy.* Carlisle, PA: Strategic Studies Institute, 2009.

King, Anthony. *Command: The Twenty-First Century General.* Cambridge: Cambridge University Press, 2019.

Kornberger, Martin, and Anders Engberg-Pederson. "Reading Clausewitz, Reimagining the Practice of Strategy." *Strategic Organization* (June 2019): 1–13. https://www.researchgate.net/publication/333879860_Reading_Clausewitz_reimagining_the_practice_of_strategy.

Kott, Alexander. "The Future of War Technology Whispers to Us from the Past, and We Must Listen Better." War on the Rocks. 3 December 2019. https://warontherocks.com/2019/12/the-future-of-war-technology-whispers-to-us-from-the-past-and-we-must-listen-better/.

Krepinevich, Andrew F. *The Army and Vietnam.* Baltimore: John Hopkins University Press, 1986.

Kuehn, John T. *America's First General Staff: A Short History of the Rise and Fall of the General Board of the Navy, 1900–1950.* Annapolis: Naval Institute Press, 2017.

Ledwidge, Frank. *Aerial Warfare: The Battle for the Skies.* Oxford: Oxford University Press, 2018.

Lenin, Vladimir. "War and Revolution." 27 May 1914 (lecture). Marxists Internet Archive. Uploaded 2005. https://www.marxists.org/archive/lenin/works/1917/may/14.htm.

Liddell Hart, B. H. *The Real War 1914–1918.* Boston: Back Bay Books, 1964.

———. *Strategy.* New York: Penguin, 1954.

Luttwak, Edward. "The Operational Level of War." *International Security* 5:3 (Winter 1980–81): 61–79.

———. *Strategy: The Logic of War and Peace.* Cambridge, MA: Belknap Press of Harvard University Press, 1987.

Lylall, Jason. "The Strongest Military Is an Inclusive One: Why Equality Wins Wars." *Foreign Affairs.* 14 February 2020. https://www.foreignaffairs.com/articles/2020-02-14/strongest-military-inclusive-one.

Maalouf, Amin. *The Crusades through Arab Eyes.* New York: Shocken Books, 1984.

Mahoney, Shane. *The Role of the Soviet General Staff in Military Management: Persistence and Change.* Final Report to the National Council for Soviet and East European Research, 1982.

Matheny, Michael R. *Carrying the War to the Enemy: American Operational Art to 1945.* Norman: University of Oklahoma Press, 2011.

Mayzel, Matitiahu. "The Formation of the Russian General Staff, 1880–1917." *Cahiers du Monde russe et soviétique.* 16:3–4 (July–December 1975): 297–321.

McChrystal, Stanley. *Team of Teams: New Rules of Engagement for a Complex World.* New York: Portfolio, 2015.

McReynolds, Joe, ed. *China's Evolving Military Strategy.* Washington, D.C.: Jamestown Foundation, 2016.

Murray, Williamson. *Strategy for Defeat: The Luftwaffe, 1933–1945.* Hertfortshire, UK: Quintent, 2003.

Murray, Williamson, and Allan R. Millet. *A War to Be Won: Fighting the Second World War*. Cambridge, MA: Belknap Press of Harvard University Press, 2000.

National Technical Information Service. *Dictionary of Basic Military Terms*. Springfield, VA: U.S. Department of Commerce, 1976.

Naveh, Shimon. *In Pursuit of Military Excellence: The Evolution of Operational Theory*. New York: Frank Cass, 2004.

Nolan, Cathal. *The Allure of Battle: A History of How Wars Have Been Won and Lost*. Oxford: Oxford University Press, 2017.

Norris, John. *Artillery: A History*. Gloucestershire, UK: History, 2011.

Oman, C. W. C. *The Art of War in the Middle Ages*. Ithaca, NY: Cornell University Press, 1968.

Owen, William. "The Operational Level of War Does Not Exist." *Military Operations* 1:1 (Summer 2012): 17–20.

Paret, Peter. *Clausewitz and the State*. Oxford: Clarendon, 1976.

Paret, Peter, and Daniel Moran, ed. and trans. *Carl von Clausewitz: Two Letters on Strategy*. Fort Leavenworth, KS: Combat Studies Institute, 1984.

Pichichero, Christy. *The Military Enlightenment: War and Culture in the French Empire from Louis XIV to Napoleon*. Ithaca, NY: Cornell University Press, 2017.

Potter, E. B. *Nimitz*. Annapolis: Naval Institute Press, 1976.

Quimby, Robert S. *The Background of Napoleonic Warfare: The Theory of Military Tactics in Eighteenth-Century France*. 1957. Reprint, Whitefish, MT: Literary Licensing, 2011.

Rempfer, Kyle. "Choose Your Job: Army Offers Soldiers Career Agency to Bolster Retention." *Army Times*. 27 February 2020. https://www.armytimes.com/news/your-army/2020/02/27/choose-your-job-army-offers-soldiers-career-agency-to-bolster-retention/.

Reznichenko, V. G., ed. *Tactics: A Soviet View*. Washington, D.C.: U.S. Air Force, 1987.

Rhodes, Andrew. "Thinking in Space: The Role of Geography in National Security Decision-Making." *Texas National Security Review* 2:4 (November 2019): 90–108.

Rice, Condolezza. "The Making of Soviet Strategy." In *Makers of Modern Strategy from Machiavelli to the Nuclear Age*. Edited by Peter Paret, 648–76. Princeton, NJ: Princeton University Press, 1994.

Ricks, Thomas E. *The Gamble: General David Petreaus and the American Military Adventure in Iraq, 2006–2008*. New York: Penguin, 2009.

Roberts, Andrew. *Napoleon: A Life*. New York: Penguin, 2014.

Roberts, Geoffrey. *Stalin's General: The Life of Georgy Zhukov*. London: Icon Books, 2013.

Rogers, Clifford J., ed. *The Military Revolution Debate: Readings on the Military Transformation of Early Modern Europe*. Boulder, CO: Westview, 1995.

Rothenberg, Gunther E. *The Art of Warfare in the Age of Napoleon*. Bloomington: Indiana University Press, 1980.

Schneider, James J. "The Loose Marble—and the Origins of Operational Art." *Parameters* 19:1 (1989): 85–99.

———. *The Structure of Strategic Revolution: Total War and the Soviet Warfare State*. Novato, CA: Presidio, 1994.

Schroden, Jonathan. *Why Special Operations? A Risk-Based Theory.* Arlington, VA: Center for Naval Analyses, 2020. https://www.cna.org/CNA_files/PDF/COP-2020-U-028160-Final.pdf.

Schulman, Loren Dejonge. "Washington Is Never Quite Sure Where It Is at War." *Atlantic.* 1 November 2017. https://www.theatlantic.com/international/archive/2017/11/niger-aumf-war-terrorism/544652/.

Sides, Hampton. *On Desperate Ground.* New York: Doubleday, 2018.

Sondhaus, Lawrence. *The Great War at Sea: A Naval History of the First World War.* Cambridge: Cambridge University Press, 2014.

Sorley, Lewis, ed. *Press On! Selected Works of General Donn A. Starry.* 2 vols. Fort Leavenworth, KS: Combat Studies Institute Press, US Army Combined Arms Center, 2009.

Spector, Ronald H. *Eagle against the Sun: The American War with Japan.* New York: Free Press, 1985.

Stern, Jessica, and J. M. Berger. *ISIS: State of Terror.* New York: Harper Collins, 2015.

Sterne, Brendan. Review of *One More Time: How Do You Motivate Employees,* by Frederick Herzberg. Blog. 25 November 2012. https://brendansterne.com/2012/11/25/a-review-of-one-more-time-how-do-you-motivate/.

Stoecker, Sally W. *Forging Stalin's Army: Marshal Tukhachevsky and the Politics of Military Innovation.* Boulder, CO: Westview, 1998.

Stoker, Donald. *Why America Loses Wars: Limited War and US Strategy from the Korean War to the Present.* Cambridge: Cambridge University Press, 2019.

Storr, Jim. *The Hall of Mirrors: War and Warfare in the Twentieth Century.* Warwick, UK: Helion, 2018.

Strachan, Hew. *Clausewitz's* On War: *A Biography.* New York: Grove, 2007.

———. "Strategy or Alibi: Obama, McChrystal, and the Operational Level of War." *Survival* 52:5 (September 2010): 157–82.

Svechin, Aleksandr A. *Strategy.* Edited by Kent D. Lee. Minneapolis: East View Information Services, 2004.

Taylor, Philip M. *Munitions of the Mind: A History of Propaganda from the Ancient World to the Nuclear Age.* Manchester: Manchester University Press, 1990.

Thorpe, George C. *Pure Logistics: The Science of War Preparation.* Kansas City, MO: Franklin Hudson, 1917.

Trauschweizer, Ingo. *The Cold War U.S. Army: Building Deterrence for Limited War.* Lawrence: University Press of Kansas, 2008.

Tuchman, Barbara. *Stilwell and the American Experience in China, 1911–45.* New York: Macmillan, 1971.

Van Creveld, Martin. *Command in War.* Cambridge, MA: Harvard University Press, 1987.

———. *Supplying War: Logistics from Wallenstein to Patton.* Cambridge: Cambridge University Press, 1980.

Vego, Milan N. *Joint Operational Warfare: Theory and Practice.* Washington, D.C.: Department of the Navy, 2009.

Venable, Heather. *How the Few Became the Proud: Crafting the Marine Corps Mystique, 1874–1918*. Annapolis: Naval Institute Press, 2019.

Viggers, Will. "Policy, Strategy, and Tactics: Rethinking the Levels of War." *Australian Army Journal* 16:1 (2020): 47–60.

Wass de Czege, Huba. "Thinking and Acting like an Early Explorer: Operational Art Is Not a Level of War." *Small Wars Journal*. 14 March 2011. https://smallwarsjournal.com/blog/journal/docs-temp/710-deczege.pdf.

White, Charles. *The Enlightened Soldier: Scharnhorst and the Militärische Gesellschaft in Berlin, 1801–1805*. Westport, CT: Praeger, 1989.

Whitman, James Q. *The Verdict of Battle: The Law of Victory and the Making of Modern War*. Cambridge, MA: Harvard University Press, 2012.

Wilkinson, Spenser. *The Brain of an Army: A Popular Account of the German General Staff*. Westminster, UK: Archibald Constable, 1890. Reproduced by Andesite Press.

Winton, Harold R. "An Imperfect Jewel: Military Theory and the Military Profession." *Journal of Strategic Studies* 34:6 (2011): 853–77.

Woodward, Bob. *Obama's Wars*. New York: Simon & Schuster, 2010.

Wylie, J. C. *Military Strategy: A General Theory of Power Control*. Annapolis: Naval Institute Press, 1976.

Zegart, Amy. *Flawed by Design: The Evolution of the CIA, JCS, and NSC*. Stanford, CA: Stanford University Press, 1999.

INDEX

Abe, Hiroaki, 195
Active Defense, U.S. Army's, 40
Adad-nirari I, King of Assyria, 70
adjutants, internal administration and, 63
administration: Atlantic Campaign (1914–18), 170–71; Austerlitz Campaign (1805) and, 148–49; Battle of Britain (1940), 181; combat operations and, 68; external, 64–65; in history, 61; internal, 63–64; Königgrätz Campaign (1866), 160–61; loss of prestige for, 62; Mahan on, 62–63; motivator-hygiene theory, 65; as operational art discipline, 57, 60–61; in Pacific theater of World War II, 65–68
Afghanistan: information warfare in, 82; Taliban's public-affairs campaign in, 80; U.S. civil military relationship and, 49–50
African theater, Soviets on operational level of war and, 8
Air Force, U.S., 42–43
air operations, 92–93. *See also* Cactus Air Force; Royal Air Force
AirLand Battle, 40–41, 45
AirLand Battle, U.S. Army, 41–42, 45
Alexander, Tsar, 146–47, 148
Alexander the Great, 21, 70, 85, 101, 123
Alien: How Operational Art Devoured Strategy (Kelly and Brennan), 6
Allies: Austerlitz Campaign (1805) and, 145–48; command and control by, 152; information issues for, 149–50; against Napoleon's Grand Armée, 144. *See also* Operation Watchtower
Alligator Creek, Guadalcanal, 189
Allure of Battle, The: A History of How Wars Have Been Won and Lost (Nolan), 113–15
Almond, Edward, 86
Americal Division (164th Infantry Regiment), 193, 197, 198
American. *See* United States

American Civil War: general-staff system and tactics during, 206n32; information warfare and, 72–73; railroads and, 102–3; Sherman's asymmetric maneuver in, 88; Siege of Petersburg, 89; U.S. operational art and, 43
American War for Independence or Revolution (AD 1775–83), 4, 72, 115, 122
amphibious operations: Atlantic Campaign and, 165, 167–68; British withdrawal at Dunkirk, 174; German, against England, 175, 176; Ichiki's regiment and Battle of Tenaru River, 188–89; by Japanese Seventeenth Army, 194; Japanese withdrawal from Guadalcanal, 197–98; against Kawaguchi's base area, 191; logistics, 106–7; Operation Albion against Russia, 170; Operation Watchtower, 185, 186–87
annihilation of forces, 91, 119–20
Aoba (Japanese cruiser), 192–93
Arab Conquests (AD 622–750), 4
d'Argenson, comte (Marc-Pierre de Voyer de Paulmy), 61
Army, U.S.: air forces of, 199; Americal Division (164th Infantry Regiment), 193, 197, 198; Assignment Interactive Module 2.0, 136; Bolshevization of the Red Army and, 31; doctrine, operational level of war and, 6; operational level of war and, 39–40, 43–44, 140; Raiders at Guadalcanal, 191, 201–2; staff system adopted by, 18; warfighting functions of, 57
Army of England, Napoleon's, 16, 143–44. *See also* Grande Armée, French
Army of Italy, 102
Army of Northern Virginia, 88, 89, 128
Army of the Elbe, Prussia's, 155, 156–57, 158–59, 163
Army of the Potomac, 128
Army of the Tennessee, 126

Art of War, The (Jomini), 100
Artemisium (480 BC), 115
Assurnasirpal II, King of Assyria, 70
asymmetric employment, weighting the main effort in, 87–88
Atlantic Campaign (1914–18): administration, 170–71; command and control, 173; fire support, 172; historical narrative, 165–70; information, 171; logistics, 172–73; operations, 171–72; overview, 165
attrition: aim of the war and, 115–16; maneuver versus, 92; winning wars and, 114–15
Austerlitz Campaign (1805): administration during, 148–49; command and control, 152–53; fire support, 151–52; historical narrative, 143–48; information and, 149–50; logistics, 144, 152; mobilization speed, 215n8; as an OPA campaign, 121; operations, 150–51; Third Coalition's DPA campaign at, 128
Austria and Austrian military: Napoleonic Revolution and, 19. *See also* Austerlitz Campaign; Königgrätz Campaign
Austro-Prussian War (1866), 25, 28, 154. *See also* Königgrätz Campaign

Bagration, Peter, 146, 148, 151
Banks, Nathaniel, 73
Barca, Hasdrubal, 71, 89
battles: as decisive or indecisive, 115; use of term, 113, 117
Beatty, David, 166, 168–69
Belgium, German invasion (1939) of, 174
Benedek, Ludwig von: command and control under, 163; Königgrätz Campaign and, 156, 157, 158, 159, 160, 161
Berthier, Alexandre, 18
Berthier, Louis-Alexandre, 143, 149, 153
Bewegungskrieg (war of movement), 28
Bismarck, Otto von, 26, 47, 139
Bistritz River, Königgrätz Campaign and, 157
Blitz of London, 179–80
Blücher, Gebhardt von, 89
Bohemia, Austria, Königgrätz Campaign and, 155, 156
Bolshevik revolution (1917), 30

Bomber Command, Britain's, 176, 179
Bourcet, Pierre-Joseph, 14, 17
Boyd, John, 69, 76–79
breech-loading artillery, 95
Brennan, Mike, 6, 10, 38, 54–55
Britain: Napoleon's plan of war with, 143–44. *See also* Allies; Royal Air Force; Royal Navy
Britain, Battle of (1940): administration, 181; command and control, 183–84; decision in, 114; fire support, 183; historical narrative, 174–81; information, 181–82; operations, 182–83; overview, 174
British army: Enlightenment and military innovations by, 14; general-staff system and tactics during World War I, 206n32; staff system adopted by, 18
Brüchmuller, Georg, 95
Bruhl, Friedrich Wilhelm von, 47
Bruscino, Thomas, 55
Buckner, Simon Bolivar, Jr., 68

Cactus Air Force, 186, 193, 194, 195, 196, 199
Caldiero, Italy, Austerlitz Campaign and, 146
Callaghan, Daniel J., 195
campaign level, operational level of war and, 9–10
Campaigning (Marine Corps, 1990), 42
campaigns: categorization of, 118–20; copying from one context to another, 129, 214n8; decisiveness and, 117; defensive-persisting-annihilation, 120, 122, 124, 143; defensive-persisting-cumulative, 120, 121, 125; defensive-raiding-annihilation, 120, 126–27; defensive-raiding-cumulative, 120, 122, 128, 184; historical analysis using taxonomy, 121; hybrids and interactions, 128–29; offensive-persisting-annihilation, 120, 121, 123, 143; offensive-persisting-cumulative, 120, 124; offensive-raiding-annihilation, 120, 125–26; offensive-raiding-cumulative (ORC) campaigns, 120, 127–28, 184; taxonomy overview, 118, 214n1; type selection, to buy time, 122–23; use of term, 113

Camus, Albert, 15
Cannae, Battle of (216 BC), 114
cannons, fire support using, 95
Cape Esperance, Battle of (1942), 192–93
Carlson, Evan, 201–2
Carnot, Lazare, 15
Carter, Nick, 82
centralized command and control, 111
chaplains, 63–64
chevauchée, development of, 127
chief of staff, Napoleon's use of, 18
China: medieval, military bureaucracy in, 61. *See also* People's Liberation Army
Chlum, Königgrätz Campaign and, 159–60
Churchill, Winston, 199
Citino, Robert, 23, 25, 27–28
civil bureaucracies, national armies and, 15
civil-military relationship: in Germany, 46–47; operational level and, 50–51; in Russia, 47–48; in the United States (2021), 49–50; in the United States during Vietnam War, 48–49
Clausewitz, Carl von: on doctrinal straitjackets of General Staff, 134, 215n7; on intelligence and information, 74–75, 211n32; lampooned in *War and Peace*, 47; Lenin's interpretation of, 2; Military Enlightenment and, 19; Paret and Howard translation of *On War* by, 40; on plan of battle, 83; on preparations for War, 5; Prussian army reforms and, 20; Scharnhorst general-staff system and, 22; tactical-decision game and, 46; tactical-strategic dialectic and, 53–54, 209n6; on testing a theory, 8, 139
close combat, fire combat versus, 96
coalition warfare: liaison officers and, 64–65. *See also* Allies
Coast Watchers, Operation Watchtower and, 200–201
combined arms: Napoleon's corps system as, 151; weapons systems and, 85–86
Combined Army-Marine Division (CAM Division), 67
command and control: ancient history of, 108–9; Atlantic Campaign, 173; Austerlitz Campaign, 152–53; centralized versus decentralized, 111–12; discipline of, 110–12; Königgrätz Campaign, 163–64; medieval to modern history of, 109–10; as operational art discipline, 58; overview, 108
Command: The Twenty-First-Century General (King), 132–33
communication, lines of, 106
communications: Luftwaffe and, 183–84; modern, command and control and, 110–11; secure, 137. *See also* information
coordination, as operational art discipline, 58
Corbett, Julian, 116
Coronel, Battle of, 167
corps system: French Grande Armée, 16–17, 151; Königgrätz Campaign and, 163; Napoleonic Revolution and, 19
councils of war, Napoleon Bonaparte and, 17–18
counterreconnaissance, 79
Cradock, Christopher, 73–74, 167
cumulative strategies, 91
cyberwarfare, 80, 98, 110

Danish War (1864), Germany and, 47
Danube Valley. *See* Austerlitz Campaign
Davout, Louis, 147
DeCarre, Alphonse, 67
decentralized command and control, 111–12
deception, military, 81, 179
decisiveness: draw of, 115; Nolan on outcome of a war and, 113–14; operational art and, 113; use of term, 117
deep operations, Soviet (*glubokaia operatsiia*), 35, 36, 38
defense: campaign taxonomy on, 118–20; force protection and, 138
defensive information warfare, 76, 79
defensive-persisting-annihilation (DPA) campaigns, 120, 122, 124, 143
defensive-persisting-cumulative (DPC) campaigns, 120, 121, 125
defensive-raiding-annihilation (DRA) campaigns, 120, 126–27
defensive-raiding-cumulative (DRC) campaigns, 120, 122, 128, 184
Delbrück, Hans, 91, 119
Department of Defense Dictionary of Military and Associated Terms (JP 1-02), 36
dialectic theory of war, 54

Dictionary of Basic Military Terms (Soviet, 1965), 36–37
divisions, French army and, 14
doctrine, for general-staff system, 134–35
Dowding, Hugh, 176, 177
Dowding System, British: command and control and, 184; radar, 176, 177–78, 179
Dunkirk, British withdrawal at, 174
Dupuy, Trevor, 23
Dupuy, William E., 40

Eagle Day, in Battle of Britain, 178–79
Eastern Solomons, Battle of the (1942), 189–90
Eccles, Henry E., 105, 107
Edson, Merritt "Red Mike," 191–92, 201
Edson's Ridge, Battle of (1942), 191–92
education, for general staff, 135
Elbe River, Königgrätz Campaign and, 158
electronic warfare, 80–81, 110, 211n35
encirclement. *See* Mack, Karl
Engberg-Pederson, Anders, 16, 55
English Channel, Battle of Britain and, 175, 176, 177–78
English Civil War (1642– 46), 72
Enlightenment: French military administration and, 61; militaries during, 13–15, 18; military staffs and, 137; nonmilitary aspects of, 12–13; rationality, war and, 19. *See also* Military Enlightenment; Napoleon Bonaparte
Enterprise, 189–90, 194
enveloping, as asymmetric maneuver, 87–88
Epstein, Robert M., 3–4
Erprobungsgruppe 210, Battle of Britain and, 178
Europe, political changes, Napoleonic Revolution and, 12
exhaustion of forces, 91, 119–20
external administration, 64–65

Fabius Maximus Verrucosus, Quintus, 122
facilities, general-staff system, 137
Farenholt, 193
Fei River, Battle of the (383 in China), 109, 213n2
feudalism, 101–2
Fighter Command, Britain's, 176, 177, 178, 179–80

fighter-bombers, Battle of Britain and, 178, 179, 183
fire support: Atlantic Campaign, 172; Austerlitz Campaign, 151–52; Battle of Britain, 183; discipline of, 96–98; effects, 98; emergent capabilities, 98; fire combat versus close combat, 96; historical survey of, 94–96; importance, 99; Königgrätz Campaign, 162; McChrystal's Team of Teams and, 132; observation, processing, and delivery of, 97; as operational art discipline, 58; overview, 94
First Army, Prussia's, 155, 156–57, 158–59, 160, 163
flanking, as asymmetric maneuver, 87–88
Fletcher, Frank, 186, 188, 189–90
FM 100-5, U.S. Army, 40–42
food, daily, internal administration and, 63
forces: annihilation versus exhaustion of, 91; campaign taxonomy and, 118–21; force protection, 138; indirect approach to, 91–92; maneuver versus attrition of, 92
force-to-space ratios, 87
France: military administration in (seventeenth century), 61; Napoleon's reforms of army, 16–17
Franco-Prussian War (1870–71), 25, 28, 47, 164
Frank, Richard, 201
Franklin, Benjamin, 72
Franz Ferdinand, Archduke, 165
Franz Joseph I, Emperor, 156
Frederick Charles, Prince of Prussia, 157, 163
Frederick the Great, 14, 21
French and Indian War (AD 1756–63), 4. *See also* Seven Years' War
French Historical and Topographical Bureau, 17
French Revolution, Scharnhorst general-staff model and, 22
French Royal Army, 14

Gallic Wars (58–50 BC), 4, 71
Gavutu, Operation Watchtower and, 186
Geiger, Roy, 68
general-staff system: Austerlitz Campaign and, 153; doctrine, 134–35; expanding complexity of war, 1; facilities, 137;

Germans and operational level of war and, 27–28; King's collaborative-command, 132–33; leadership, 136; matériel, 135–36; McChrystal's Team of Teams, 132; Moltke the Elder and, 24–25; Navy's General Board and, 45; operational art actualized through, 130; operational art discipline management and, 58–59; as operational artists, 140–41; organization, 135; origins, 21; personnel, 136; Prussian, 20–21; Scharnhorst Model, 21–24; strengths and weaknesses, 133–34; training and education, 135; world at war and, 25–27. See also staff officers; *specific country general staffs*

German General Staff, 25, 26–27, 117, 131–32, 139, 156. See also Prussian General Staff

German Way of War, The (Citino), 27–28

Germans: American AirLand Battle adopted from, 45; chief of military personnel for, 62; civil-military relationship for, 46–47; decision in World War II and, 114; operational art of war and, 20–29, 203n8; staff system adopted by, 18. See also Imperial German Navy

Ghormley, Robert L., 66

Gifu (Japanese position on Guadalcanal), 198

Girondins, war of worldwide liberation and, 13

Gitschin, Königgrätz Campaign and, 157

Goldwater-Nichols Department of Defense Reorganization Act (1986), 131

Göring, Herman, 176, 179, 182

Goto, Aritomo, 192–93

Grande Armée, French: Austerlitz Campaign (1805) and, 121, 144, 145–47; corps system, 16–17, 151; Enlightenment and, 19

Grant, Ulysses S., 88, 89, 113

Gray, Alfred M., 42

Gray, Chris Hables, 11

Gray, Colin S., 7, 9, 56, 115

Grossgörchen, Battle of (1813), 22

Guadalcanal: the landing, 186–87; Naval Battle of, 194–96. See also Operation Watchtower

Guibert, comte de, 15, 19

Gustavus Adolphus, 72

Hahlweg, Werner, 47

Halsey, William, Jr. "Bull," 66, 195, 196

Hannekan, Herman H., 194

Hannibal, 71, 89, 114, 125–26

heavy infantry and cavalry, 84–85

Hegel, Georg Wilhelm Friedrich, 54

Heligoland Bight, First Battle of, 167

helmets, command and control and, 108–9

Henderson Field: Battle of (1942), 193–94; landing on Guadalcanal near, 186–87

Herzberg, Frederick, 65

Hirohito, Emperor, 197

History of the Art of War (Delbrück), 91

Hitler, Adolf: attrition and decisions of, 114; Battle of Britain and, 176, 180; experience and strengths of, 175–76; German General Staff and, 21, 25, 27, 131–32

Holcomb, Thomas, 67

Holder, L. Don, 41

Hornet, 194

Hotchkiss, Jedediah, 72–73

Howard, Michael, 1, 13–14, 15, 40, 140

human resources. See administration

Hundred Years' War (1337–1457), 71

Huntington, Samuel, 48–49

Hussein, Saddam, 116

Ia, Prussian general-staff system and, 23

Ichiki, Kiyoano, 188–89

Imperial German Army, 20–21, 47

Imperial German Navy: Atlantic Campaign and, 165–66, 170, 172, 173; cruiser forces, 167–68; High Seas Fleet, 167–69, 170; World War I administration, 171

Imperial Japanese Army, 67, 186, 188, 199, 200

Imperial Japanese Navy: Allies landing on Guadalcanal and, 186; Battle of Savo Island and, 188; Battle of Tassafaronga and, 197; Battle of the Eastern Solomons and, 189; Coast Watchers and, 200–201; Naval Battle of Guadalcanal and, 194–95, 196; Tokyo Express and, 190–91

Imperial Russian Army, 30. See also Red Army

indirect approach in warfare, 91–92
Industrial Revolution, 2, 8, 29, 130, 137
infantry squads, first use, at Guadalcanal, 201
information: analysis and intelligence, 75–76; ancient history of, 70–71; Atlantic Campaign, 171; Austerlitz Campaign and, 149–50; Battle of Britain, 181–82; fire support overlap with, 94; Königgrätz Campaign, 161; means of information warfare, 79–81; medieval history of, 71–73; modern history of, 73–74; Napoleon's use of, 143, 144; Operation Watchtower, 200–201; as operational art discipline, 58, 69–70, 74–79; processing, staff systems and, 133; warfare using, 76–79. *See also* intelligence
information warfare: Clausewitz on, 75; cyberwarfare, 80; electronic warfare, 80–81; as emergent capability, 98; historical examples, 72–74; military deception, 81; Napoleon Bonaparte and, 17, 145; OODA Loop for conceptualizing, 76–79; public affairs, 80; reconnaissance and counterreconnaissance, 79; subcomponents, 211n35
institutional cohesion, motivator-hygiene theory and, 65
intelligence: Battle of Britain and, 182; electronic and signals, World War I and, 165, 171; as information warfare subcomponent, 211n35; interaction with information, 81–82; Japanese, Operation Watchtower and, 188; Napoleon's use of, 150; on Operation KE, 198; as separate from information, 75–76; Sun Tzu on, 69. *See also* information warfare
interior and exterior lines, 88–89, 161–62
Iraq: unlimited war against, 116; U.S. civil military relationship and, 49–50
Iron Bottom Sound, Guadalcanal, 195
Israel, electronic warfare by, 81
Italy. *See* Allies

Jackson, Thomas J. "Stonewall," 72–73
Japan. *See* Imperial Japanese Army; Imperial Japanese Navy
Jellicoe, John, 166, 168–69

Jena-Auerstedt disaster (1806), 20, 21, 24
Jews of Masada (AD 73–74), 116
joint, or multidomain, campaigns. *See* Operation Watchtower
Joint Staff, U.S., design characteristics, 131–32
Jomini, Antoine-Henri, 89, 100
Jones, Archer, 84, 90–91, 119, 212n19
judge advocates, 64
Julius Caesar, 70–71
Jun'yō (Japanese carrier), 194

Kawaguchi, Kiyotake, 191, 192
Kelly, Justin, 6, 10, 38, 54–55
Kesselring, Albert, 179, 182–83
Khalkhin Gol, Battle of (1939), Soviet deep operations and, 35
King, Anthony, 130, 132–33
Kirishima, 196
Kondo, Nobutake, 196
Königgrätz Campaign (1866): administration, 160–61; command and control, 163–64; fire support, 162; historical narrative, 154–60; information, 161; logistics, 162–63; as Moltke test, 25; operations, 161–62; overview, 154
Korean War, Chinese combined arms and, 86, 212n6
Kornberger, Martin, 55
Krulak, Charles, 42
Kutuzov, Mikhail, 128–29, 145–46, 148, 151, 152

Le Tellier, François Michel, 63, 102
leadership: egalitarian, Napoleon Bonaparte and, 16; general-staff system, 136
Lee, Robert E., 88, 89
Lee, Willis, 196
legislative oversight, Scharnhorst general-staff model and, 25, 26
Lenin, Vladimir, 2, 30, 34
Lepanto, Battle of (1571), 104
Liddell Hart, Basil, 87, 91
light infantry and cavalry, Jones on, 84–85
limited wars, 116
logistics: Atlantic Campaign, 172–73; Austerlitz Campaign, 144, 152; Battle of Britain, 183; command and control,

183–84; functions of, 106–7; historical survey of, 101–5; Königgrätz Campaign, 156, 162–63; lines of communication, 106; Operation Watchtower and, 185, 190, 200–201; as operational art discipline, 58; as the operational level, 105; overview, 100; systems, Napoleon's reforms, 17; systems, Scharnhorst Model inheritors and, 28
Louis XIV, king of France, 12
Luftwaffe: Battle of Britain and, 174, 175, 176–79, 182–83; Blitz of London, 179–80
Luttwak, Edward, 41, 69
Luxembourg, German invasion (1939) of, 174

MacArthur, Douglas, 186
Mack, Karl, 121, 144, 145, 149–50, 151
Madison, James, 46
magazines, logistics and, 102
Mahan, Alfred Thayer, 62–63, 108
maneuver: asymmetry and, 87–88; attrition versus, 92; coordination of, 83–85. See also operations
Mansfeld, count von (Ernst), of Bohemia, 102
Manzikert, Battle of (1071), 109
Mao Tse-Tung, 128
Marine Air Wing, First, 199
Marine Corps: Scout-Snipers, 201–2. See also *Warfighting*
Marine Division, 1st: Battle of Edson's Ridge and, 191–92; Battle of Henderson Field and, 194; landing on Guadalcanal, 186–87; Operation Watchtower and, 185, 188, 199; planning Operation Watchtower, 186, 189; Tokyo Express and, 190–91. See also amphibious operations; Operation Watchtower; Vandegrift, Alexander
Marine Division, 2nd, 194, 198
Marston, John, IV, 67
Marxism-Leninism on War and Army, 31, 206n4
Massena, Andre, 146
matériel, general-staff system and, 135–36
Matheny, Michael R., 43, 105
Maurice, comte de Saxe, 15, 19
Maurice of Nassau, 109
McChrystal, Stanley, 130, 132, 133

Meade, George, 88, 89
medical staff, 63–64
mental-health professionals, 63–64
Middle Ages, weapons systems during, 85
Middle East theater, Soviets on operational level of war and, 8
Midway, Japanese defeat at, 186
Mikawa, Gunichi, 187–88
Military Enlightenment, 11, 15–18, 19
Military Reorganization Commission, Prussian, 21–23, 205n14
Military Revolution, Napoleonic Revolution and, 204n27
military rewards, administration of, 65
Miliutin, Dmitry Alekseyevich, 48, 209n9
mission command, 111. See also command and control
Moltke the Elder, Helmuth Karl Bernhard von: civilian policymakers and, 47; command and control under, 163–64; as general-staff officer, 24–25; Königgrätz Campaign and, 155, 156, 157, 158, 159, 160, 161–62; logistics for Königgrätz Campaign, 162–63; logistics systems and, 28–29; railroads for logistics and, 103; on Scharnhorst general-staff model, 23
Mongols and Mongol Conquests (AD 1237–91), 4, 94, 123, 127
morale, motivator-hygiene theory and, 65
mortuary affairs, 63–64
motivator-hygiene theory, 65
Münchengrätz, Königgrätz Campaign and, 157
Murat, Joachim, 145

Náchod, Königgrätz Campaign and, 156
Napoleon Bonaparte: campaigns of, 121; Continental System, 13; external administration under, 64; as great general, 11, 12; information warfare and, 72; interior and exterior lines and, 88–89; as model for modern warfare, 153; ORA campaigns by, 126; on revolution (epigram), 1; staff functions under, 21; Third Coalition's DPA campaign and, 128. See also Austerlitz Campaign
Napoleonic Code, in Europe, 15

Napoleonic Revolution: developments sparking, 11; information requirements of, 69–70; Military Enlightenment and Scientific Revolution and, 15–18; Military Revolution and, 204n27; operational art and, 130; operational level of war and, 139; Russian military and, 48; Scharnhorst general-staff model and, 22; use of term, 19

Napoleonic Wars: operational level of war and, 3–4; Russian experience during, 30

nationalism, Napoleonic Revolution and, 19

Nationalist Socialism, 31

naval operations: combined arms and, 93; logistics, 101, 104–5; Soviets on operational level of war and, 8

Naval War College, 44

Naval Warfare, 43

Naveh, Shimon, 5, 28

Navy, U.S.: air forces of, 199; Atlantic Campaign and, 169, 170; Battle of the Eastern Solomons and, 189–90; Naval Battle of Guadalcanal and, 196; Navy Board, 44; on operational level of war, 43; supply chain at Guadalcanal and, 199–200. *See also* Operation Watchtower

Nazis. *See* Hitler, Adolf; Luftwaffe; Wehrmacht

Nero, Gaius Claudius, 89

Netherlands, German invasion (1939) of, 174

network/cyberwarfare, 211n35

Nimitz, Chester, 66, 74, 198

Nolan, Cathal, 113–15, 214n4

North American military conflicts, Soviets on, 8

North Sea, Royal Navy blockade of, 166

Noyes, Leigh, 186

Oberkommando der Wehrmacht (OKW). *See* Wehrmacht

Oberkommando des Heeres (OKH), 27

offense: campaign taxonomy on, 118–20; force protection and, 138

offensive information warfare, 76, 79

offensive-persisting-annihilation (OPA) campaigns, 120, 121, 123, 143

offensive-persisting-cumulative (OPC) campaigns, 120, 124

offensive-raiding-annihilation (ORA) campaigns, 120, 125–26

offensive-raiding-cumulative (ORC) campaigns, 120, 127–28, 184

Office of the Chief of Naval Operations, 44

Ogarkov, Nikolai, 36

Olmutz, Germany, Königgrätz Campaign and, 155

On War (Clausewitz): on assembly of forces, 86; coordination of maneuver in, 83; Howard and Paret mistranslation, 40, 140; information warfare and, 75; on political aim of war, 116, 214n6; posthumous publication, 47; on tactical-strategic dialectic, 209n6

OODA Loop (Observe-Orient-Decide-Act Loop), 69, 76–79

Operation Albion (1917), 170

Operation Desert Storm (1991), 110

Operation Desert Storm, *AirLand Battle* and, 45

Operation Eagle, Germany's, 176, 178–79

Operation Enduring Freedom, 110

Operation Iraqi Freedom (2003), 110

Operation KA, 191, 201

Operation KE, 197–99

Operation Overlord, 180

Operation Sealion, Germany's, 176, 180

Operation Watchtower (1942): Battle of Cape Esperance, 192–93; Battle of Edson's Ridge, 191–92; Battle of Henderson Field, 193–94; Battle of Savo Island, 187–88; Battle of Tassafaronga, 196–97; Battle of the Eastern Solomons, 189–90; Battle of the Tenaru River, 188–89; historical narrative, 185–99; Japanese withdrawal and, 197–99; the landing, 186–87; Naval Battle of Guadalcanal, 194–96; operational disciplines, 199–202; overview, 185; plans, 185–86; Tokyo Express, 190–91, 192, 193, 195, 196–97, 198–99

operational art: as actualization of tactics, 56; Clausewitz's test for theory and, 8; definition of, 5; disciplines of, 56–59; Germans and, 20–29; logistics and, 105, 213n22; operational artists and, 140–41; physical forces and, 10; Red Army textbook *Tactics* on, 37; Soviet doctrine, 34–35; Soviet innovations, 30–31; Soviet theorists on, 31–34, 38; staff officers and, 12; strategy and, 116–17; Svechin's definition, 32; theory of, 52–59; U.S. conflation with operational level of war and, 41–42, 45; use of term, 113; Vego on operational level of war and, 9. *See also* battles; campaigns; general-staff system; Königgrätz Campaign; Scharnhorst Model

operational level of war: civil-military relationship and, 46–51; Clausewitz's test for theory and, 8, 139; emergence of, 3–4; pushback against, 5–7; Red Army and, 1–2, 30; Soviet ideas transmitted to American doctrine and, 31, 38, 39, 140; Soviets on, 34–35, 37–38; strategy and tactics and, 2–3; U.S. conflation with operational art and, 41–42, 45. *See also* deep operations, Soviet

"Operational Level of War, The" (Luttwak), 41

operational-maneuver-group (*operativnaia maneuverennaia gruppa*) units, Soviet, 36

operations: air operations, 92–93; Atlantic Campaign, 171–72; Austerlitz Campaign, 150–51; Battle of Britain, 182–83; Bolshevization of the Red Army and, 31; forces and, 91–92; historical survey of, 84–86; Königgrätz Campaign, 161–62; naval operations, 93; as operational art discipline, 58; overview, 83–84; Red Army definition, 34; resurgence in Soviet thought on, 36–37; space and, 86–89; Svechin's definition, 32; theory of, 86–93; time and, 89–91; Triandafillov's definition, 33; Tukhachevsky on tactics vs., 33–34

Operations, U.S. Army, 40–41, 43–44
orders, operations staff and, 83–84
Otis, Glenn K., 41, 208n10
outlooping an opponent, 79
Owen, William F., 6, 10, 55

Pacific theater of World War II: Buckner, Geiger, and Stilwell, 67–68; Ghormley versus Halsey in, 66; information warfare in, 74; Vandegrift versus Patch in, 66–67. *See also* Operation Watchtower

Paine, Thomas, 72
Paret, Peter, 40, 140
Park, Keith, 177, 182
Patch, Alexander M., 67, 197, 198
pay, military, internal administration and, 63
Peloponnesian Wars (431–405 BC), 4
Pentomic Army, U.S., 40
People's Liberation Army, 76
Persia: invasion of Greece (480–479 BC), 101, 123; military bureaucracy in, 61
persisting campaigns: Archer on, 90–91, 119, 212n19; in campaign taxonomy, 119–20
personnel: general-staff system, 136; tracking, 63
Peter the Great, tsar of Russia, 47
Phony War (1939), 174
Pichichero, Christy, 11
Pitt, William, 144
Pohl, Hugo von, 168
political power, unlimited war against, 116
political/psychological warfare, 211n35
politics: campaign-type decisions and, 129; Clausewitz on strategy in war and, 53–54; Clausewitz on war as continuation of, 46; Russian military thought and, 30, 37; strategy as, Marxist-Leninist beliefs and, 31
Princip, Gavrilo, 165
"Principles of Naval Administration, The" (Mahan), 62–63
Principles of War (Clausewitz), 75
propaganda. *See* information
Prussian General Staff, 22–23, 65, 155, 164. *See also* German General Staff
Prussian military: Napoleonic Revolution and, 19; severing war from politics by, 46
public affairs, 80
Puller, Lewis "Chesty," 194
Punic Wars, 114. *See also* Second Punic War; Third Punic War

quartermaster, role of, 21
Quimby, Robert S., 15

Rabaul, Japanese stronghold at, 187, 190–91
radar: British Dowding System, 176, 177–78, 179; British versus German, 181–82
raiding campaigns, 90–91, 119–20, 212n19
railroads, 102–3, 155, 156, 163
"reach back" capability loop, 137
reconnaissance, 79
Red Army: Bolshevization of, 31; operational level of war and, 1–2, 4, 8–9; Provisional Field Service Regulations (1936), 34; Stalin's purges and staff officers for, 48; transition from Imperial Russian Army, 30. *See also* Svechin, Aleksandr A.; Triandafillov, Vladimir K.; Tukhachevsky, Mikhail N.
Reorganization Objective Army Division, U.S., 40
revolution, Camus' definition, 15
Richelieu, Cardinal, 100
rocket artillery, 95–96
Rogers, Clifford J., 15
Roman Civil War (49–45 BC), 4
Roman military, 21, 61, 71, 101
Roon, Albrecht von, 47
Roosevelt, Theodore, 45
Royal Air Force (RAF): administration, 181; Battle of Britain and, 174, 177–81; Fighter Command against German bombers, 176–77
Royal Australian Navy, 200
Royal Navy: Atlantic Campaign and, 165–66, 173; Battle Cruiser Fleet, 166; global network of stations, 172; Grand Fleet, 166; World War I administration, 170–71
Royal Observer Corps, 182
Royal Prussian Army, 20–21, 154, 160, 161. *See also* Königgrätz Campaign
Russia. *See* Allies
Russian Civil War (1918–21), 8, 30, 33, 34, 48
Russian military, 19, 47–48, 203n8
Russian Revolution, 30, 48
Ryūjō (Japanese carrier), 189–90

Sadowa, Königgrätz Campaign and, 157
Saladin, information gathering by, 71
Saratoga, 189–90
Saratoga, Battle of (1777), 115
Savo Island, Battle of (1942), 187–88

Saxe. *See* Maurice, comte de Saxe
Scharnhorst, Gerhard Johann von, 20
Scharnhorst Model: Clausewitz and creation of, 47; development of military staffs and, 52, 139; German advantage and, 130; Königgrätz Campaign and, 154, 163; legislative oversight and, 25, 26; Napoleonic Revolution and, 22; operational art of war and, 21–24, 29, 205n14; strengths and weaknesses, 133
Scheer, Reinhard, 168, 172
Scheer Program, Germany's, 171
Schlieffen Plan, 26, 29
Schneider, James J., 31, 43, 203n10
Schroden, Jonathan, 7
Schulmeister, Charles, 150
Scientific Revolution, 13, 15–18
Scott, Norman, 192, 195
Second Army, Prussia's, 155, 156–57, 159, 160, 163–64
Second Punic War (218–202 BC), 4, 71, 89, 122, 128
Second Schleswig War (1864), 25, 154–55
Secretary of the Navy, staff modernization, 44
security, force protection and, 138
Seeckt, Hans von, 26
sequencing attacks, 90
sequential strategies, 91
Seven Years' War (AD 1756–63), 4, 17
Seventeenth Army, Japanese, 188–89, 193–94, 195, 198
Sherman, William T., 88, 94, 103, 126
Shōkaku (Japanese carrier), 189–90, 194
Sims, William S., 169
simultaneity in attacks, 90
Skalitz, Königgrätz Campaign and, 156
Smith, O. P., 86, 212n6
Smith, Sydney, 72
sniper units, American, 201
Solomons, Eastern, Battle of, 189–90
Soor, Königgrätz Campaign and, 156
South American military conflicts, Soviets on, 8
Soviet Union: American operational doctrine borrowed from, 31, 38, 39, 140; operation doctrine, 34–35; operational level of war and, 1–2, 139; operational theorists, 31–34; on operations and

operational art, 30. *See also* Red Army; Russian military
space: asymmetric employment in, 87–88; campaign taxonomy and, 118–21; force-to-space ratios, 87; interior and exterior lines, 88–89; operations and, 86–89
Spanish Civil War (1936–39), 175, 181
Spanish Succession, War of (1701–14), 61
special forces, at Guadalcanal, 201
Special Operations Command, U.S., 21
Spee, Maximillian von, 73–74, 167–68, 171
spying, 150. *See also* information; intelligence
staff officers, 1, 12, 17–18, 22, 202, 203n2. *See also* general-staff system
Stalin, Josef, 2, 30, 34, 35, 38, 48
Starry, Donn A., 40–41, 208n12
Stavka (Russian General Staff), 35, 38
Stellungskrieg (war of position), 28
Stilwell, Joseph W., 68
Stoecker, Sally W., 33
Stoker, Donald, 116
Storr, Jim, 3, 90
Strachan, Hew, 6
strategic effect: decisiveness and, 115; operational art and, 5, 10, 56; tactical action and, 7; tactical-strategic dialectic and, 4
strategy: Clausewitz vs. Soviets on, 38; Clausewitz's definition of, 9; Marxist-Leninist beliefs and, 31; operational art and, 116–17; operational level of war and, 2–3, 4, 7; Red Army textbook *Tactics* on, 37; restoring dialectic of tactics with, 52–55; Svechin on operations and, 32
Strategy (Liddel Hart), 91
Strategy (Svechin), 31–32
Sturdee, Doveton, 171
submarines: Atlantic Campaign and, 168, 169; Japanese supplies for Guadalcanal and, 197
Sun Tzu, 69
Sunni leadership, in Iraq, 49–50
supply. *See* logistics
Svechin, Aleksandr A., 30, 31–32, 34, 37, 38
Sweden. *See* Allies
Swiepwald (forest), Königgrätz Campaign and, 158–59

tactical fire direction, 98
tactics: Clausewitz vs. Soviets on, 38; Clausewitz's definition of, 9; German General Staff and, 26; operational art as actualization of, 56; operational level of war and, 2–3, 4, 7; restoring dialectic of strategy with, 52–55; Svechin on strategy and, 32; Tukhachevsky on operations vs., 33–34
Tactics (Red Army textbook, 1984), 37
Taliban, 80, 82
Tanaka, Raizo, 197
targeting, of fire support, 97
Task Force (TF) 61, U.S., 186
Task Force (TF) 64, U.S., 192, 193
Task Force (TF) 67, U.S., 196–97
Task Group (TG) 62.6, U.S., 187–88
Task Group (TG) 67.4, U.S., 195, 196
Tassafaronga, Battle of (1942), 196–97
technical fire direction, 98
technologies of war: missile weapons and, 85; Napoleonic Revolution and, 11–12, 18
Tenaru River, Battle of the (1942), 188–89
Texel Island, Battle of, 167
Thermopylae (480 BC), 115
Third Coalition: concentrating at Olmutz, 156; DPA campaign at Austerlitz, 128; War of, 143
Third Punic War (149–146 BC), 123
Thirty Years' War (1618–48), 61, 71–72, 102, 104
Thorpe, George, 100, 105
time: campaign taxonomy and, 118–21; operations and, 89–91; sequencing, 90; simultaneity, 90
Tirpitz, Alfred von, 166
Tokyo Express, 190–91, 192, 193, 195, 196–97, 198–99
Tolstoy, Leo, 11, 47, 209n7
Toulon, Siege of (1793), 16
training, for general staff, 135
Training and Doctrine Command (TRADOC), U.S. Army, 39–40
Trautenau, Königgrätz Campaign and, 156
Triandafillov, Vladimir K., 30, 32–33, 35, 38
Truppenführung (German military manual, HD-300), 28

Tukhachevsky, Mikhail N., 30, 33–34, 35, 37, 38
Tulagi, Operation Watchtower and, 186
Turner, Richmond Kelly, 186, 187, 188, 193, 196, 201

udar (hit), Tukhachevsky rebranding German infiltration as, 34
Ulm (Germany), Austerlitz Campaign and, 145
Unified Land Operations, U.S. Army, 43
unit cohesion, motivator-hygiene theory and, 65
United States: civil-military relationship (2021), 49–50; Joint Staff of, 131–32; military doctrine, Soviet ideas transmitted to, 31, 38, 39, 140; staff system, 130; Vietnam War and civil-military relationship, 48–49. *See also* American Civil War; American War for Independence or Revolution; Army, U.S.; Navy, U.S.
unlimited wars, 116
Upton, Emory, 206n32

Van Creveld, Martin, 104
Vandegrift, Alexander: administration by Patch versus, 66–67; Battle of Henderson Field and, 193; Battle of Tenaru River and, 189; Japanese logistics failures and, 201; Naval Battle of Guadalcanal and, 195, 196; Operation Watchtower landing force and, 186, 187; Tokyo Express and, 190; turns over command to Patch, 197
Vego, Milan, 5, 9, 56, 84, 86, 105
Vienna, Austria, Austerlitz Campaign and, 145–47
Vietnam War, 48–49, 81
Viggers, Will, 7
Voroshilov, Kliment, 34–35

war: Clausewitz on strategy and politics in, 53–54; political aim of, 115–16; as problem of knowledge, 16; technologies of war and, 12, 204n4
Warfighting (Marine Corps, 1989), 42, 92
warfighting functions, operational art and, 57
Washington, George, 39, 122
Wass de Czege, Huba, 41, 45
Wavell, A. C. P., 60
weaponeering, science and art of, 97–98
weapons: Enlightenment developments in, 14; Jones' historical survey of, 84–86
Wehrmacht, 26–27, 28, 31, 47
Wendt, Hauptmann, 150
Wilhelm II, Kaiser, 166
Wilkinson, Spenser, 23–24
William I, King of Prussia, 155, 157
Wilson, Woodrow, 168
Winton, Harold R., 4, 52
World War I: artillery advances during, 95; decision in, 114; German General Staff and, 25, 26–27; German logistics systems and, 28; information warfare during, 73–74; logistics during, 103; operational level of war and, 8; Soviet army and industrial warfare of, 34. *See also* Atlantic Campaign
World War II: artillery advances during, 95–96; electronic warfare during, 80–81; German logistics during, 103–4; German logistics systems and, 28; information warfare during, 74; OPA campaigns during, 123; operational level of war and, 3; Soviet operations and, 35–36. *See also* Britain, Battle of
Wright, Carleton H., 196–97
Wylie, J. C., 91

Xerxes, 101

Yamamoto, Isoroku, 191, 192, 195, 196, 200
Yom Kippur War (1973), 40

Zhukov, Georgy, 34–35, 48
Zuikaku (Japanese carrier), 189–90, 194

ABOUT THE AUTHOR

B. A. FRIEDMAN retired from the U.S. Marine Corps in 2022. He grew up in Cleveland, Ohio, and entered the Marine Corps after graduating from high school in 2000. He earned a BA in history from The Ohio State University, as well as an MA in national security and strategic studies from the U.S. Naval War College. He works as a strategy analyst in the Washington, D.C., area.

THE NAVAL INSTITUTE PRESS is the book-publishing arm of the U.S. Naval Institute, a private, nonprofit, membership society for sea service professionals and others who share an interest in naval and maritime affairs. Established in 1873 at the U.S. Naval Academy in Annapolis, Maryland, where its offices remain today, the Naval Institute has members worldwide.

Members of the Naval Institute support the education programs of the society and receive the influential monthly magazine *Proceedings* or the colorful bimonthly magazine *Naval History* and discounts on fine nautical prints and on ship and aircraft photos. They also have access to the transcripts of the Institute's Oral History Program and get discounted admission to any of the Institute-sponsored seminars offered around the country.

The Naval Institute's book-publishing program, begun in 1898 with basic guides to naval practices, has broadened its scope to include books of more general interest. Now the Naval Institute Press publishes about seventy titles each year, ranging from how-to books on boating and navigation to battle histories, biographies, ship and aircraft guides, and novels. Institute members receive significant discounts on the Press' more than eight hundred books in print.

Full-time students are eligible for special half-price membership rates. Life memberships are also available.

For more information about Naval Institute Press books that are currently available, visit www.usni.org/press/books. To learn about joining the U.S. Naval Institute, please write to:

Member Services
U.S. NAVAL INSTITUTE
291 Wood Road
Annapolis, MD 21402-5034

Telephone: (800) 233-8764
Fax: (410) 571-1703
Web address: www.usni.org

www.ingramcontent.com/pod-product-compliance
Ingram Content Group UK Ltd.
Pitfield, Milton Keynes, MK11 3LW, UK
UKHW041917140426
5217IPUK00013B/196